THE PROBLEMS OF U.S. MARINE CORPS PRISONERS OF WAR IN KOREA

by
James Angus MacDonald, Jr.

Occasional Paper

HISTORY AND MUSEUMS DIVISION
HEADQUARTERS, U.S. MARINE CORPS
WASHINGTON, D.C.

1988

Published by Books Express Publishing
Copyright © Books Express, 2010
ISBN 978-1-780391-09-0
To purchase copies at discounted prices please contact
info@books-express.com

Foreword

The History and Museums Division has undertaken the publication for limited distribution of various studies, theses, compilations, bibliographies, and monographs, as well as proceedings at selected workshops, seminars, symposia, and similar colloquia, which it considers to be of significant value for audiences interested in Marine Corps history. These "Occasional Papers," which are chosen for their intrinsic worth, must reflect structured research, present a contribution to historical knowledge not readily available in published sources, and reflect original content on the part of the author, compiler, or editor. It is the intent of the division that these occasional papers be distributed to selected institutions, such as service schools, official Department of Defense historical agencies, and directly concerned Marine Corps organizations, so the information contained therein will be available for study and exploitation.

At the time he wrote this thesis for his master of arts degree in American history at the University of Maryland, J. Angus MacDonald, Jr., was a major serving in the Policy Analysis Division at Headquarters Marine Corps. He had been an enlisted Marine in World War II serving in the 2d Marines in 1943, before going to Pennsylvania State College as a part of the V-12 program, and being commissioned in 1945. In the initial stages of the Korean War, he served as a instructor with the Troop Training Unit, Pacific, an assignment which evolved into a stint as platoon commander with 41 Independent Commando, Royal Marines, in Korea.

Throughout a series of stateside and overseas assignments in the 1950s and 60s, he pursued and obtained his bachelor's (1959) and master's (1961) degrees through the University of Maryland's off-campus programs. He was a student of the Marine Corps Junior School in 1956, an instructor at the Command and Staff College from 1963-66, and a student at the Army War College in 1968. He was an infantry battalion commander in the 2d Marine Division in 1966-67 and served on the plans staff at MACV in Vietnam in 1968-69. After a tour as head of the Personnel Assignment and Classification Branch at Headquarters, he served as the Marine member of the Chairman of the Joint Chiefs of Staff staff group until his retirement as a colonel in 1973.

Post retirement, Colonel MacDonald was staff director of a House of Representatives Select Committee of Missing Persons in Southeast Asia, and then project manager for a number of studies for BDM Corporation on strategic lessons learned in Vietnam. Since 1982 he has made his home in the Phoenix area of Arizona.

The thesis which Colonel MacDonald authored has had a remarkable and continuing influence on the many Department of Defense studies of prisoners of war since it was written. We are reprinting it, just as it appeared in 1961 including some minor errata changes, for the use of the serious student of the POW experience and as a reference source for interested libraries. The opinions and facts represented in this publication are those of the author and do not necessarily represent those of the Marine Corps or the Department of the Navy. In pursuit of accuracy and objectivity, the History and Museums Division welcomes comments on this publication from interested individuals and activities.

E. H. SIMMONS
Brigadier General, U.S. Marine Corps (Retired)
Director of Marine Corps History and Museums

TABLE OF CONTENTS

	Page
LIST OF MAPS	vii
LIST OF PHOTOGRAPHS	viii

Chapter

I.	TO A SHORT WAR AND A MERRY ONE	1
II.	HORDES FROM THE ROOF OF KOREA	16
III.	BREAKOUT	45
IV.	THE LENIENT POLICY	60
V.	A PUNCHBOWL AND A PALACE	93
VI.	A TUG OF WAR	139
VII.	STIGMA AND ASTIGMATISM	197
APPENDIX A.	GLOSSARY OF TERMS AND ABBREVIATIONS	240
APPENDIX B.	TABLE OF MARINES CAPTURED BY MONTH	245
APPENDIX C.	ALPHABETICAL ROSTER OF OFFICER POW'S RETURNED TO MILITARY CONTROL	249
APPENDIX D.	ALPHABETICAL ROSTER OF ENLISTED POW'S RETURNED TO MILITARY CONTROL	251
APPENDIX E.	ALPHABETICAL ROSTER OF OFFICER POW'S WHO DIED OR ARE PRESUMED DEAD	257
APPENDIX F.	ALPHABETICAL ROSTER OF ENLISTED POW'S WHO DIED OR ARE PRESUMED DEAD	258
APPENDIX G.	ROSTER OF MARINES CAPTURED BY DATE	260
APPENDIX H.	ROSTER OF MARINES RETURNED TO MILITARY CONTROL MAY 25, 1951	270

APPENDIX I. ROSTER OF MARINES RETURNED TO MILITARY
           CONTROL DURING OPERATION LITTLE
           SWITCH - APRIL AND MAY, 1953. 271

APPENDIX J. MARINE POW'S BY RANK 272

SELECTED BIBLIOGRAPHY 274

LIST OF MAPS

Map		Page
1.	Pusan Perimeter	7
2.	Inchon - Amphibious Assault	12
3.	North Korea - November, 1950	20
4.	Yudam-ni - 27-28 November, 1950	28
5.	Task Force Drysdale Ambush	36
6.	Breakout from Yudam-ni	47
7.	North Korea - May, 1951	81
8.	The Hook	148
9.	POW Camps in which Marines Were Held	215

LIST OF PHOTOGRAPHS

Photos   Page

1. "Christ in Barbed Wire" carved by
    Captain Gerald Fink, USMC 172

2. POW Olympics - Pyoktong, November, 1952.
    Soccer and Tug of War 192

3. POW Olympics - Pyoktong, November, 1952.
    Basketball and unidentified photo 193

CHAPTER I

TO A SHORT WAR AND A MERRY ONE

As the Marine F4U-5 Corsair made its low-altitude photo run, an antiaircraft shell arced through the air and exploded in the port wing of the plane. The pilot, Captain Jesse V. Booker, saw oil dripping from his wing and knew immediately that the port oil cooler was severely damaged. He turned toward the Yellow Sea and radioed his two wingmates that he was returning to their carrier, the USS Valley Forge.[1]

Within about a minute and a half the Corsair lost all of its oil supply making it impossible to continue the flight to the sea. Captain Booker was faced with the choice of parachuting or attempting to land his crippled plane deep inside enemy territory. He elected to ride the plane down. His wingmates observed him land safely and run towards a wooded area. It was 5:30 P.M., August 7, 1950.[2]

Hidden from above by the foliage, North Korean soldiers closed in on the downed pilot. Their presence was unobserved by the two Marine aviators still flying cover over the area.

---

[1] USS Valley Forge message dated August 8, 1950.

[2] Personal interview with Major Jesse V. Booker, USMC. July 26, 1960.

Had the pilots been able to peer through the trees, they might have witnessed the capture of the first of 221 Marines known to have been taken prisoner of war by the enemy during hostilities in Korea.[1]

The purpose of this thesis is fivefold: (1) to record the combat actions in which Marines were captured by the enemy in Korea; (2) to discuss the method by which the enemy processed Marine captives; (3) to examine both North Korean and Chinese Communist interrogation and indoctrination techniques; (4) to describe individual and group experiences of Marine Corps prisoners of war in Korea; and (5) to present a phase of the Korean War which is nowhere else to be found in English except in classified security dossiers and other Marine Corps and Navy documents.

Historical and command diaries and official histories furnish the basis for describing most combat actions. Experiences of POW's are derived mainly from personal interviews and correspondence, official reports of captivity, sworn statements, official correspondence, and books and articles written by former POW's. In addition all books and documents listed in the card file of the Library of Congress were screened for any mention of U. S. Marines or any general information which might have been of value to this study including many propaganda documents published in English by

---

[1] U. S. Marine Corps, "Korean Casualties, 25 June 1950-27 July 1953", Personnel Accounting Section, Code DGB, September 22, 1956. (Typewritten). On file in the Casualty Branch, Division of Personnel, HQMC. Cited hereafter as "USMC Casualties".

the Chinese Communists or other Communist sources. Hearings before Congressional committees which are pertinent to this thesis are also referenced.

A shadow fell over American POW's in the aftermath of the Korean War. Courts-martial and other official inquiries revealed that a small segment of the Americans captured by the Communists had been guilty of behavior ranging from questionable to treasonable. Both the Secretary of Defense's Advisory Committee on Prisoners of War and the Congress of the United States were commendatory of Marine Corps POW's. Behind these general statements, however, lies the untold story of the Marines. They played a small but significant role.

Each of the 221 Marines captured faced critical problems which, to him at least, were unique. The problems ranged from such basic drives as survival to complicated and abstract questions involving honor, duty, compassion and understanding.

The first problem faced by most POW's was that of capture itself. Is capture unavoidable or is there in some cases a reasonable alternative? If capture is his unwitting fate, how should a Marine comport himself after capture? Is it his duty overtly to resist the enemy at all cost and at every turn, or should he attempt to outwit him, perhaps by giving useless or false information? What are his responsibilities of leadership or subordination? What impact did the Communist germ warfare campaign have on Marines? Did treatment of Marines vary depending on rank, specialty, or date and circumstances of capture? And finally, how did Marines measure up?

The Marine Corps POW story began on August 7, 1950, the eighth anniversary of the amphibious attack on Guadalcanal and the date the first Marine was captured in a new war. A Department of Defense press release of that date listed 873 American soldiers and airmen missing in action.[1] A few of that number were alive and in enemy hands, and Captain Booker met some of them shortly after his capture.

Captain Booker's introduction to captivity was painful and abrupt. He barely cleared his aircraft and reached the concealment of nearby trees when a group of North Korean soldiers surrounded him. The only alternative to surrender was to fight a hopeless battle using his service revolver against the more powerful and numerous rifles of his enemies. Had he done so he would inevitably have been killed or wounded. The Koreans denied him any freedom of choice by rushing in and overwhelming him.

There had been no chance for escape. He was some 200 miles from the nearest friendly ground troops, and helicopter rescue operations were not highly developed at that stage in hostilities, so rescue by that means was virtually impossible.

During World War II, in which he destroyed three Japanese aircraft, Captain Booker had received numerous briefings on escape and evasion. Such briefings have long been a routine part of combat aviators' daily lives, tacit recognition of the possibility of capture in the event of misfortune while over enemy territory. Similar briefings were conducted

---

[1] The Evening Star (Washington), August 7, 1950, p. A4.

during the Korean War, and at no time was it suggested that death was preferable to capture.

As soon as he was disarmed, the North Koreans beat him mercilessly. They struck him repeatedly across the chest and body with their rifles until they beat him senseless. He was then dragged and pushed to a temporary cell in a nearby village. Eventually he reached the vicinity of Pyongyang where he joined a group of American officer prisoners. They were as pitiful a sight as Booker himself---beaten, half starved, and filthy. Many had foul-smelling, septic wounds. The Marine became the 39th member of the group.[1]

By the end of August the Communist propaganda mill showed that it had been at work. The Russian delegate to the United Nations, Jacob A. Malik, claimed to have received a cable in the form of a protest by 39 captured American officers "against further senseless bloodshed in Korea." The supposed petitioners included the name of Jesse V. Booker.[2]

On several occasions the North Koreans took one or two captured American officers from their cell and placed them before a firing squad. Sometimes they went through all the motions of an execution without actually firing the fatal shots. At other times the tableau ended with the sharp crack of rifles and one or two American officers fell dead. Some, like Major John Joseph Dunn of the Army and Captain Booker of the Marine Corps, faced the firing squads several times. Others were less fortunate. The original group of 39 officers

---

[1] Booker interview.

[2] The Evening Star, August 31, 1950, p. B14.

dwindled to eight. Major Dunn and Captain Booker were among the eight.[1]

In September the Communists released a photograph of several prisoners of war. Eastfoto, a New York agency distributing official Russian pictures in the United States, obtained the picture from the China Photo Service in Peking, China. Two prisoners in the foreground were easily identifiable as Major Dunn and Captain Booker.[2] Shortly after the photograph was taken the small group of prisoners began a long tortuous march north to the Yalu River.[3]

The 1st Provisional Marine Brigade (Reinforced) debarked at Pusan on August 2, 1950 and received its baptism of fire on August 7th, the same day that Booker was shot down. During the 67 days of its existence, the Brigade spent 41 days in the Pusan Perimeter fighting three significant offensive engagements with the North Korean enemy. Their aggressiveness, discipline and esprit were noted by a British observer, among others, and the Brigade was later awarded the Korean Presidential Unit Citation.[4]

Marines traditionally take care of their dead and wounded and the thought of Marines missing in action is repugnant. Yet on August 13, 1950 within the Pusan Perimeter

---

[1] Booker interview.

[2] The Evening Star, September 22, 1950, p. A6.

[3] Booker interview.

[4] Louis Heren, "The Korean Scene", Brassey's Annual, The Armed Forces Yearbook, (New York: The MacMillan Co., 1951), p. 102.

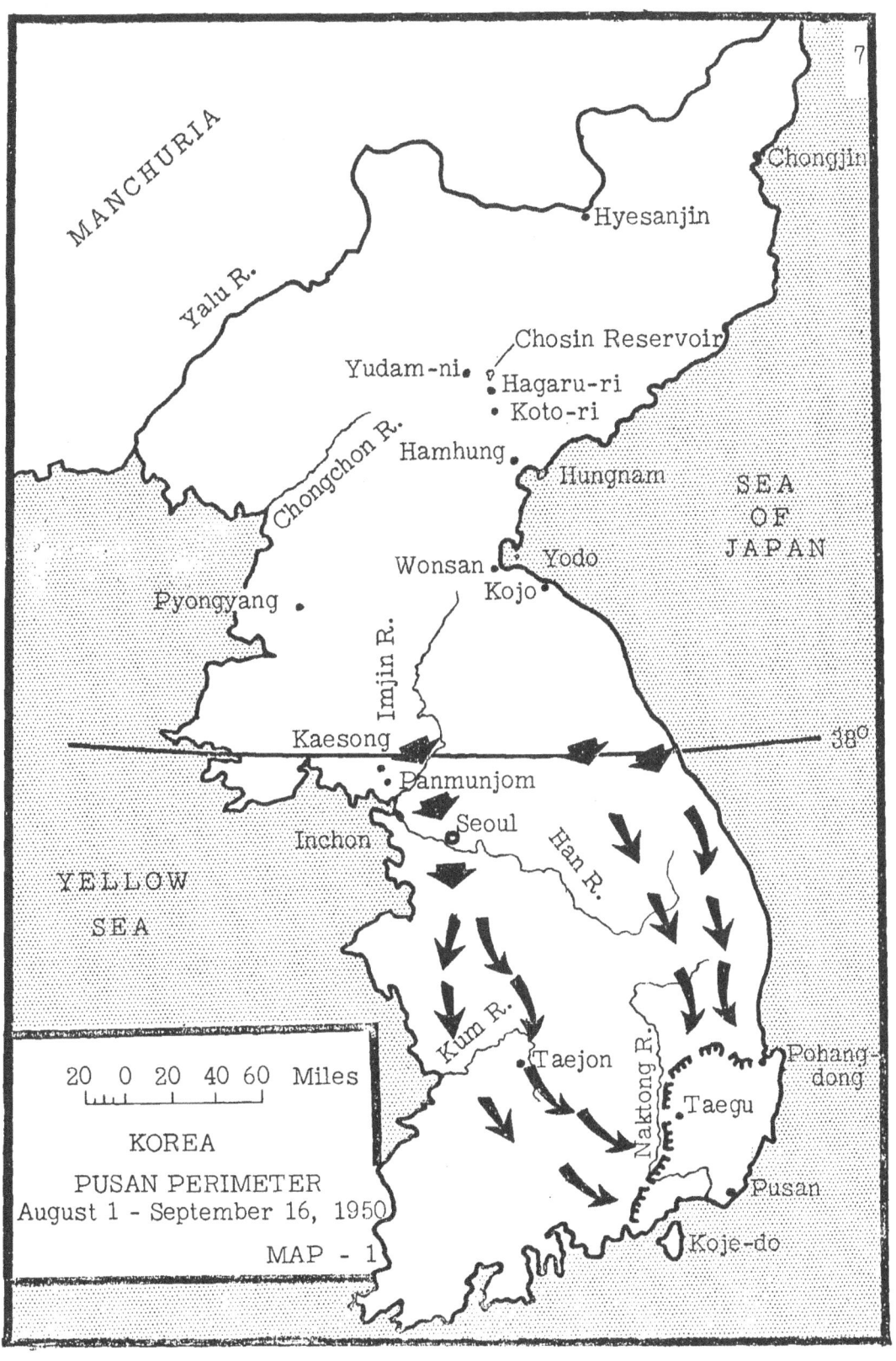

eight Marines were left to the enemy.[1] Company B, 5th Marines, on Hill 202[2] received the brunt of a North Korean attack beginning at 4:55 A.M. that morning. The initial onslaught overran a machine gun section wiping out all but two men. The company commander was directed to disengage at 6:30 A.M. Although it appeared certain that the eight Marines of the machine-gun section had been killed, the company commander requested a delay of one hour before withdrawing in order to counterattack and recover the bodies. The urgency of their redeployment ruled out any delay, however, and the Marines reluctantly left Hill 202. Seven of the missing Marines were transferred to the killed in action list the following month when their bodies were recovered.

One ground Marine captured during the hectic days of August, 1950, made good his escape shortly after capture. Private First Class Richard E. Barnett, a radio-jeep driver, was returning to his own unit when he made a wrong turn and blundered into a group of North Koreans. The enemy opened fire with automatic weapons and disabled his motor. The

---

[1] Derived from the following sources:
1st Provisional Marine Brigade (Reinforced), Fleet Marine Force, Special Action Report, 2 August to 6 September, 1950. A Report of Operations with Eighth U. S. Army in Korea. Appendix 8 to Annex A, p. 1; and
Lynn Montross and Captain Nicholas A. Canzona, U. S. Marine Operations in Korea, Vol. 1: The Pusan Perimeter (Washington: U. S. Government Printing Office, 1957), pp. 152-56; and
Andrew Geer, The New Breed (New York: Harper & Brothers, 1952), pp. 53-55.

[2] 202 meters high. Hills are generally designated by their height above sea level, and often descriptive names will be used as well.

windshield was shattered. Barnett started to return the fire, but he was successful in getting off only one shot. The magazine of his carbine had fallen out of the receiver, and after the round in the chamber fired he was unable to fire again.

The Koreans closed in and took him prisoner. He was beaten, searched, and then interrogated. His personal belongings were taken from him, including his wedding ring. His captors refused to feed him, and he was placed in a root cellar of a Korean house. Four North Koreans were posted as guards in the area to prevent his escape. During two days and nights of captivity, he was given no food other than a few crackers. On the third night, for some unaccountable reason, the Koreans took him along on what presumably was an attack against UN positions.

As they moved towards the objective Barnett noticed that of the several Koreans with him all but one had gotten considerably ahead. As he crossed a dry stream bed he stumbled deliberately and grabbed a rock as he fell. Then he struck the nearby guard in the face with the rock and ran for safety. Although the other guards fired at him, the distance between them gave him some measure of protection and he safely eluded the guards. Later he hid in another root cellar and shortly thereafter rejoined his own forces.[1]

Barnett was one of the early Marine captives and one of the few to escape. While there is nothing unusual about

---

[1] Headquarters, U. S. Marine Corps, Public Information Release 81, September, 1950.

his experience, the treatment he received at the hands of the North Koreans was similar to the pattern that developed throughout the war in that he was isolated, refused food and water, and kept under a strong guard. Had it not been for the fortuitous laxity of his guards and his own ingenuity under pressure, Barnett might well have been another statistic on the missing in action lists. As it was, he returned to his parent unit before his name ever appeared on the casualty lists, and, therefore, he is not one of the cases with which we will deal later.

On the evening of September 5th, the 1st Marine Brigade was relieved by elements of the 2d Division of Eighth Army. The Marines commenced moving to Pusan in the icy rain preparatory to embarkation for the Inchon landing ten days later. The score for 42 days of violent combat was 148 killed, 15 died of wounds, nine missing (of whom seven were reclassified "killed in action" when their bodies were found in September), and 730 wounded in action.[1] An estimated 9,900 casualties were inflicted on the enemy. The two missing Marines were never found, and screening of all repatriated prisoners of war failed to disclose any information concerning their fate. It is reasonable to presume that they were killed in the action and their bodies lost.

Considering the intensity of action and the losses suffered by other units during the same period, the Brigade casualties were remarkably light.

---

[1] Montross and Canzona, I, 239.

The 1st Marine Brigade was deactivated on September 13th, and its units reverted to their normal parent organizations within the framework of the newly arrived 1st Marine Division. General MacArthur's master thrust, the amphibious assault on Inchon, took place on September 15, 1950, and the operation was spearheaded by the 1st Marine Division.

D-Day was dark and cloudy. Skies were overcast and rain fell intermittently during the late afternoon and into the night. Visibility was obscured by the rain and by clouds of dust and dirt thrown into the air by naval gunfire bombardment and air strikes. The Marines landed against moderate opposition and casualties were light. The assault on Wolmi-do, an island lying off the port of Inchon and guarding its approaches, took place on September 15th, and the attack was successful. The simultaneous landing at Inchon resulted in the successful seizure of that city by the 16th. Kimpo Airfield fell on the 18th, and at dawn on the 20th the Han River crossing began.[1] By the night of the 20th, the 5th Marines were well established beyond the north bank of the river. Amphibious vehicles and tractors rumbled back and forth across the river carrying wiremen who laid telephone wire and attempted to repair breaks in submerged lines already laid. The services of about 50 wiremen were required to keep wire communications in between the command posts of the division commander and the 5th Marines.

---

[1]Lynn Montross and Captain Nicholas A. Canzona, U. S. Marine Operations in Korea, Vol. II: The Inchon-Seoul Operation (Washington: U. S. Government Printing Office, 1957), p. 194.

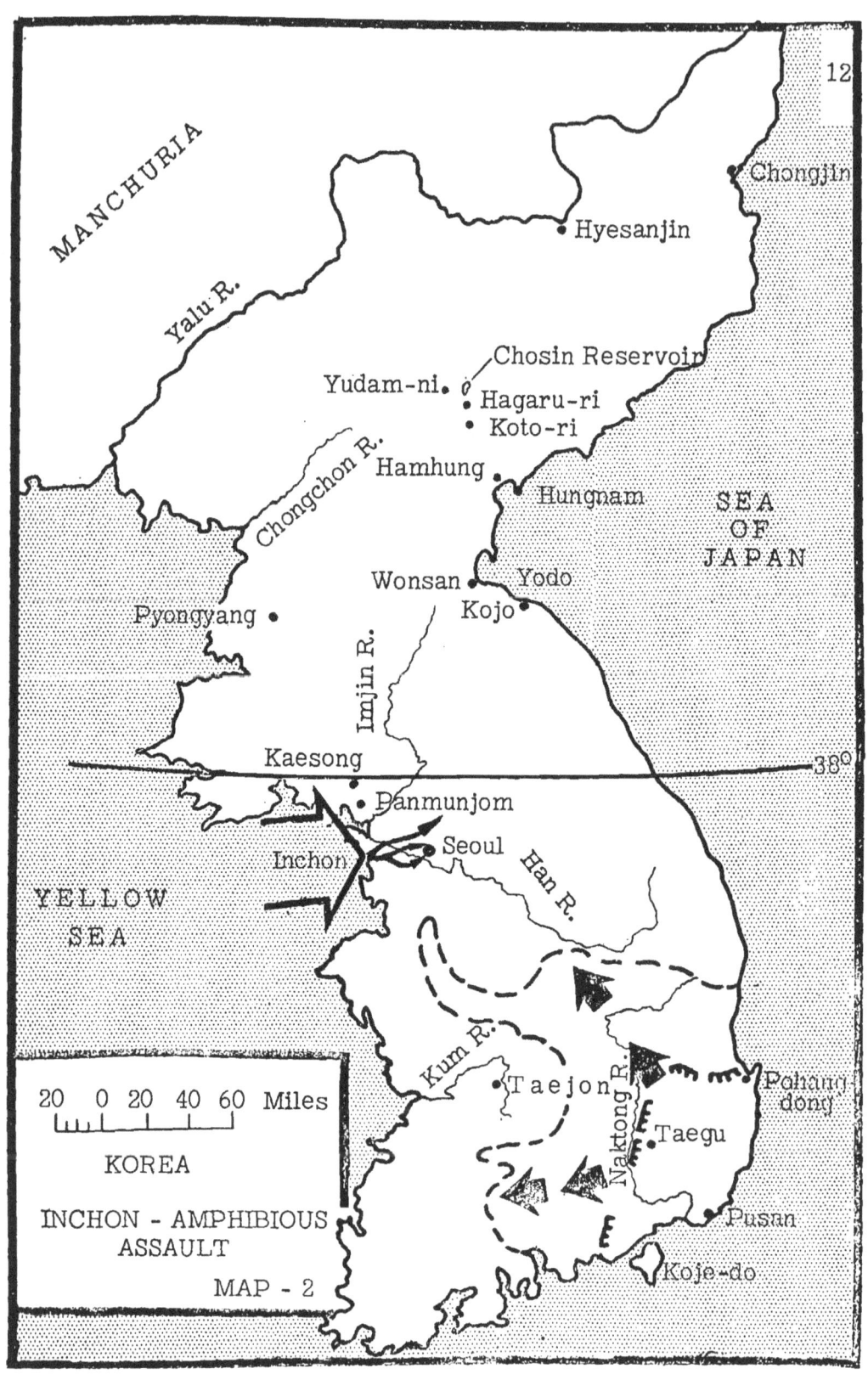

One party of five wiremen from the Division Signal Battalion was assigned to the 5th Marine Regiment to aid in keeping the wire in.[1] The wire laying party did not report back to their parent unit on the 21st. At first little concern was felt over their absence. It was assumed that they were still with the regiment. When reports received at the 1st Signal Battalion command post indicated that a second party of wiremen had been ambushed, suffering three killed and two wounded an inquiry was made to the communications officer of the 5th Regiment. He reported that the wire party assigned to him on the previous day was not with the 5th Marines at that time. The following day, September 21st, it was learned that the five men had been ambushed much like the second group. Two of the group were killed and their bodies recovered. The remaining three Marines were missing.[2] North Korean prisoners captured on September 21st stated they believed other North Korean soldiers in the locality had taken three or four Marines back to Yong Dong Po as prisoners.[3]

---

[1] 1st Signal Battalion, 1st Marine Division, Special Action Report on Inchon-Kimpo-Seoul Operation, Annex GG to 1st Marine Division Special Action Report, 15 September- 8 October, 1950, Vol. II of III. (Mimeographed).

[2] 1st Marine Division Casualty Bulletin 6-50, September 26, 1950.

[3] Letter from the Commanding Officer, 1st Signal Battalion, 1st Marine Division, dated September 25, 1950 cited by Casualty Reviewing Officer, Headquarters, U. S. Marine Corps, letter DNA-1702-mjl of September 17, 1951 to Head, Personnel Affairs Branch, Personnel Department, Headquarters U. S. Marine Corps. Cited hereafter as Casualty Section letter.

When all returning American prisoners of war had been debriefed after the end of hostilities, only one of the three missing Marines could positively be listed as having been a prisoner of war. He was Corporal Gilbert A. Vannosdall.[1] The twenty-two year old corporal died from malnutrition, exposure and frostbite on November 12, 1950 less than two months after his capture along the Han River.[2]

After successfully fighting its way across the Han, the Marine division continued the attack for Kalchong Creek, Yong Dung Po, and finally Seoul itself.

The final attack on Seoul began on September 25, 1950. In two weeks the 1st Marine Division had taken that city and plunged on to seize Suyuhyon, 15 miles northwest of Seoul, and Uijongbu, 10 miles due north from the capital city. Marine casualties for the entire period of the Inchon-Seoul operation, September 15 to October 7, were 366 killed in action, 49 died of wounds, 2,029 wounded in action, and six missing in action. The six included Corporal Vannosdall, the only ground Marine known to have been captured alive by North Koreans up to that time. The 1st Marine Division was responsible for adding some 6,492 enemy prisoners to our stockades. This figure represents the final tally after

---

[1] USMC Casualties.

[2] Based on information furnished by recovered prisoners of war after the Armistice. Casualty Section letter DNA-2305-mmt, November 17, 1953.

intelligence screening of captives weeded out innocent civilians who, through the fortunes of war, were unavoidably seized and detained by the Marines. In addition to the prisoners captured, the Marine Division inflicted an estimated 13,666 killed and wounded on the reeling Korean forces.[1]

After the Inchon and Seoul operations, the war appeared to be entering its final stages. North Korean forces facing Army and Marine units in west central Korea had been thoroughly beaten. The bulk of the Communists, who only weeks earlier had been hammering at the shrinking Pusan perimeter, now fell backward under pressure from the U. S. Eighth Army, U. S. Tenth Corps, and the rejuvenated Republic of Korea forces.

Royal Marines of the 41st Independent Commando, then assigned to the Commander of U. S. Naval Forces, Far East, were impatient to carry out demolition raids against lines of communication of the east coast. They feared there would be no tunnels or bridges left to destroy. As they readied themselves for combat raids in the waning days of September, they drank to a short war and a merry one.[2]

---

[1] Montross and Canzona, II, Appendix J, 333.

[2] The author commanded a platoon of D Troop, 41st Independent Commando, Royal Marines, on two combat raids in October, 1950, and joined in the toast.

CHAPTER II

HORDES FROM THE ROOF OF KOREA

After completing the Inchon-Seoul campaign, the 1st Marine Division returned to the ships of Amphibious Group One and prepared to move around to the opposite coast of Korea. The Marines were scheduled to land in amphibious assault at Wonsan, the strategic eastern terminus of the transpeninsula communication system. D-Day, initially set for 15 October, was pushed back repeatedly because of two factors: the Republic of Korea I Corps advanced up the east coast of Korea and seized the Marine objective of Wonsan by October 11, and the North Koreans, under Soviet tutelage, laid an estimated 2,000 mines in and around the approaches to Wonsan Harbor and Kalma Peninsula, thus making an early landing impossible.[1] The Marines were delayed until October 25, the day after Bob Hope, Marilyn Maxwell, and their entertainment group flew in to the Wonsan airstrip and put on their show.[2]

---

[1] Geer, p. 18.

[2] Lynn Montross and Captain Nicholas A. Canzona, U. S. Marine Operations in Korea, Vol. III: The Chosin Reservoir Campaign (Washington: U. S. Government Printing Office, 1957), p. 31.

Unhampered by Communist mines, Marine aviation units had flown in to Wonsan airfield beginning on October 14.[1] Marine Fighter Squadron 312 and All-Weather Fighter Squadron 513 operated from the Wonsan strip. Two additional Marine Fighter Squadrons, VMF's-214 and 323, operated from the decks of the Escort Carriers <u>Sicily</u> and <u>Badoeng Strait</u>.

Optimism was growing over the possibility of an early end to the fighting. Even General MacArthur, then Commander in Chief, Far East, predicted that the war would end shortly.[2] In this aura of confidence and enthusiasm United Nations aircraft ranged unopposed through Korean skies. The Marines flew sorties to provide cover for administrative landings of their own troops, to evacuate casualties, to reconnoiter lines of communications, and to attack retreating bodies of North Koreans.[3]

Meanwhile, after seemingly endless delays, elements of the 1st Marine Division landed on Kalma Peninsula and proceeded to move out in accordance with 1st Marine Division Operation Order 18-50. The 1st Marine Regiment deployed in the Wonsan area with battalions at Kojo, 35

---

[1] 1st Marine Aircraft Wing, Historical Diary, October 1950. Cited hereafter as 1st MAW HistD, and
Marine Aircraft Group - 12, Special Action Report, Annex K to 1st Marine Aircraft Wing, Special Action Report, 10 October 1950 to 15 December 1950. pp. 1-2. Cited hereafter as MAG-12 SAR and 1st MAW SAR.

[2] James F. Schnabel, <u>The Korean Conflict: Policy, Planning, Direction</u>. (Washington: Office of the Chief of Military History). Cited by Montross and Canzona, III, 35.

[3] 1st MAW HistD, October 1950.

miles to the south, and at Majon-ni, 28 miles to the west.[1] The 1st Battalion, 1st Marines, entrained to Kojo on October 26 to set up defensive positions surrounding a Republic of Korea Army supply dump which, ironically, the Korean garrison stripped bare when they departed the same date. The following night well disciplined North Korean troops struck the 1st Battalion perimeter. According to subsequent prisoner interrogation, the enemy numbered over 1,000.[2] Twenty-three Marines were killed and 47 were wounded in the action. The missing in action figure, the dread of all Marine commanders, was initially reported as 34.[3] When stragglers returned and bodies were recovered and identified, only four Marines were unaccounted for. Presumably they were killed in the action. Their bodies were never recovered and none of the four was ever reported alive in any of the prisoner of war camps.

As November dawned crisp and cold in North Korea, only one Marine, Captain Jesse V. Booker, was in the hands of the enemy. November, however, was to prove one of the most costly of all months for Marines.

North Korean resistance was no longer organized, but ominous reports of contact with Chinese troops began

---

[1] Montross and Canzona, III, 56.

[2] Commander in Chief, Far East, message of October 29, 1950.

[3] Commanding Officer, 1st Marines, message of October 28, 1950.

cropping up. One Chinese soldier was captured on October 28 at Unsan and two more were taken at Onjong the following day.[1] During the first week of November, 1950, the 7th Marines fought several spirited engagements against Chinese and North Korean forces. Total Marine division casualties for the week were 93 killed in action or died of wounds, 434 wounded in action, and one missing in action.[2] The latter was never heard of again.

Ground activity fell off for most of the remainder of the month. Sporadic contacts were made until the final week of November when the Chinese intervened in force.

Eighth Army launched a general assault at 10:00 A.M. on November 24th.[3] The operation was heralded by a MacArthur communique of the same date:

> The United Nations massive compression envelopment in North Korea against the new Red Armies operating there is now approaching its decisive effort. . . . If successful, this should for all practical purposes end the war, restore peace and unity to Korea, enable the prompt withdrawal of United Nations military forces and permit the complete assumption by the Korean people and nation of full sovereignty and international equality.[4]

---

[1] Commander in Chief, Far East, Situation Report for the period 6:00 A.M. October 29, 1950 to 6:00 A.M. October 30, 1950. Cited hereafter as CinCFE Sit Rep.

[2] Montross and Canzona, III, Appendix E, 381, and "USMC Casualties."

[3] CinCFE Sit Rep November 24, 1950.

[4] Commander in Chief, United Nations Command, Communique 12, November 12, 1950. Cited by Montross and Canzona, III, 144.

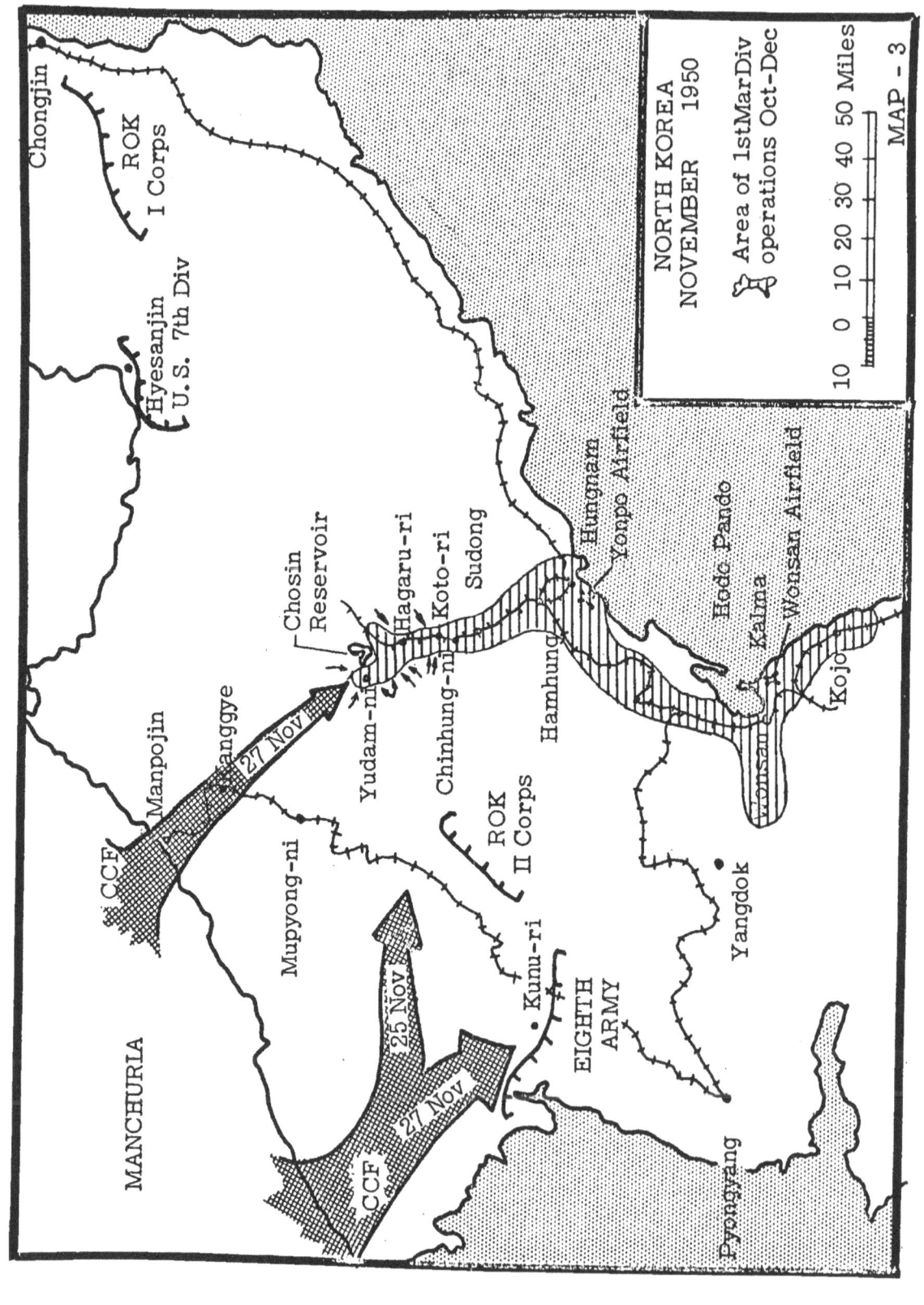

The 1st Marine Division was to be the right jaw of the "massive compression" pincers. Previous orders to attack north along the east side of the Chosin Reservoir were changed and the Marines were directed to seize Mupyong-ni, 55 miles to the west and on the Pyongyang-Manpojin railroad line. Seizure of Mupyong-ni would destroy the final assembly area of the NKPA remnants, close the jaws on the enemy, and permit the Marines to turn right and drive to the Yalu.

At this point, the 1st Marine Division was disposed as follows. The 5th Marines were east of Chosin Reservoir preparing to turn over that area to Army units from the 7th Division. These army units suffered a tragic fate within a week. The 7th Marines were enroute to Yudam-ni where they later occupied four of the five major ridges surrounding the town. These two Marine regiments were the first to meet the opening Chinese offensive in northeast Korea. The 1st Marines were in the act of displacing north to the Chinhung-ni, Koto-ri, Hagaru-ri area. The 11th Marine Regiment, the organic division artillery, was also about to displace most of its battalions to the Yudam-ni perimeter from which it could support the planned attack to the west. The division commander directed that the attack west begin at 8:00 A.M. on November 27th.[1]

The 1st Marine Aircraft Wing, now under operational control of 5th Air Force, was to provide tactical air

---

[1] 1st Marine Division, Operation Order 24-50, November 26, 1950. Cited hereafter as 1st MarDiv OpnO.

support for the Tenth Corps. The Wing was deployed principally at Wonsan, Korea, but with two squadrons aboard carriers and other elements at Itami, Japan.[1] Although Wing units played a vital role in supporting the division during the crucial period in northeast Korea, no aviation personnel were captured by the enemy during these operations, and therefore the aviation half of the Marine team will not come in for more than brief mention. Marine aviation casualties were light throughout the Chosin Reservoir campaign; two officers were killed and one was wounded, and six enlisted personnel were killed and five were wounded during the two months of combat in far North Korea.[2]

The first inkling of disaster came on the 25th. The II ROK Corps operating in northwestern Korea as part of Eighth Army, was suddenly hurled back by Chinese forces. The situation seemed stable elsewhere, but the status of the ROK Corps was referred to by Eighth Army's intelligence officer as "...the relatively vague situation on the east flank..."[3]

A Marine unit made contact with Chinese on the 26th. Three prisoners captured by the 7th Marines asserted that the 20th CCF Army had arrived in the Yudam-ni area a week

---

[1] 1st MAW SAR, October-December, 1950, pp. 1-2.

[2] Ibid., Annex A, p. 3.

[3] Eighth U. S. Army in Korea, Periodic Intelligence Report 137, p. 4. Cited by Montross and Canzona, III, 146-47.

earlier. The prisoners reported that the Chinese planned to move south and cut the main supply route after two Marine regiments passed.[1] Six Chinese divisions had now been identified in the vicinity of X Corps, but what course of action they might pursue was problematical.

The enemy demonstrated his intent to fight in northwestern Korea when, on the 26th, the second day of his attack caused the II ROK Corps virtually to disintegrate.[2] That night the temperature dropped abruptly to zero degrees Fahrenheit.

November 27th was clear and cold. The Marine attack began as planned and almost immediately encountered resistance. By nightfall the main attack, by the 2d Battalion, 5th Marines, had netted less than a mile. Ancillary attacks by the 3d Battalion, 7th Marines, on adjacent ridges gained from 1,200 to 2,000 yards.[3] Resistance had been heavy throughout the day.

A jeep from the 4th Battalion, 11th Marines, left the artillery regiment message center in Hagaru bound for Battery H to the north. The driver turned south by mistake, and, after proceeding for about two miles, the jeep and its driver were captured by an enemy roadblock and apparently the driver was killed. Until that time no

---

[1] Commanding Officer, 7th Marines, message of November 26, 1950.

[2] Montross and Canzona, III, 163-72.

[3] Ibid., p. 157.

enemy activity had been observed in the area.[1]

First Lieutenant Robert C. Messman and his Battery K, 4/11, equipped with 155mm howitzers, had been attached to the 1st Battalion, a 105mm howitzer unit. The larger guns were used principally to provide illuminating fires. Having recently displaced from the east side of Chosin Reservoir to the Yudam-ni area, Lieutenant Messman was concerned about the arrival of his ammunition supply. As darkness approached he talked to the 1/11 operations officer, Captain Philip N. Pierce, and informed the Captain of his intention to drive south to Hagaru in order to speed up the delivery of his 155mm ammunition. Messman and his driver, PFC George H. Vann, climbed into their jeep and embarked on the lonely trip along the solitary mountain road. The two Marines never arrived at Hagaru. Chinese had already infiltrated the mountains between Yudam-ni and Hagaru-ri and even then were preparing a major attack scheduled to begin within minutes.

From the standpoint of the artillery regiment, the Battery K Commander and his driver simply vanished. Their jeep, abandoned alongside the road, gave inconclusive evidence of the fate that had overtaken the two Marines.[2]

---

[1] 11th Marines, Special Action Report, Annex SS to 1st MarDiv SAR, October-December, 1950, p. 6. Cited hereafter as 11th Mar. SAR.

[2] Personal interview with LtCol Philip N. Pierce, USMC, December 7, 1960. 1st MarDiv Casualty Bulletin 73-50 dated December 12, 1950, reported 1stLt Messman and PFC Vann missing in action.

At dusk the temperature dropped abruptly for the second day in a row, this time to a numbing 20 degrees below zero Fahrenheit. With the coming of darkness and intense cold, thousands of Chinese began to move over the crusted snow. Three divisions of the enemy closed in on two regiments of Marines. Two of the Communist divisions struck Yudam-ni. The third slipped south to cut the 14 mile-long supply route which led southeast to Hagaru.[1]

At 8:45 P.M., November 27, 1950, a platoon outpost north of Yudam-ni repulsed a minor probe. Fifteen minutes later and two and a half miles west, elements of Company D, 5th Marines, likewise repulsed a minor probe. Within minutes a sustained mortar bombardment struck the Marine positions to the west. Machine-gun fire raked the same positions. By midnight Northwest Ridge and North Ridge were under heavy attack.[2] The Chinese took full advantage of the terrain and sneaked up on Companies E and F, 5th Marines. Their initial attack was repulsed, but at daybreak whistles and bugles signalled another effort and the determined Asiatics launched a battalion strength attack in a second attempt to overwhelm the Marines by sheer numbers.[3] Two Company F Marines were captured

---

[1] Montross and Canzona, III, 163-72.

[2] Except as noted the actions in the Chosin Reservoir area are based upon 1st MarDiv HistD's, November and December, 1950; 1st MarDiv SAR, October-December, 1950; and Montross and Canzona, III.

[3] 2d Battalion, 5th Marines, SAR, Annex B to 5th Mar. SAR., Annex QQ to 1st MarDiv SAR, October-December, 1950, pp. 33-34. Cited hereafter as 2/5 SAR.

during the confusion and close-in action. They were Privates First Class Kyle Reasor, who died in captivity, and Troy Williford who survived to return home during the POW exchange after the armistice.

In the predawn hours Company H, 7th Marines, was forced to pull back, opening a portion of Northwest Ridge to the enemy. A platoon outpost of Company I, 5th Marines, on North Ridge was overrun exposing the battalion commander's command post to direct enemy attack. Elsewhere on North Ridge the Chinese paid some 250 casualties in their attempt to dislodge Company E, 7th Marines, from Hill 1282. Marines suffered about 150 casualties on that same hill including Corporal Robert Arias who was captured. He lived to return during Operation Big Switch.

On the adjacent hill, 1240, Captain Milton Hull's Company D, 7th Marines, was cut to ribbons and overrun. The rugged company commander, though wounded, led a fierce counterattack and restored the position. He had only 16 men left capable of fighting. The Chinese had managed to capture one Company D Marine, Private First Class Mickey K. Scott. Counting one Marine captured earlier on Southwest Ridge, Corporal Clifford R. Hawkins, and the two artillerists, the enemy bagged five prisoners of war for their night's activities. They killed 38 and wounded 186 Marines. Their own cost was fearful. A reasonable estimate places their casualties at 600 to 700 killed in the action.[1]

---

[1] Ibid.

To the southeast, Companies C and F of the 7th Marines each maintained lonely vigils at widely separated points along the sole route of egress from Yudam-ni south. The 59th CCF Division, which had slipped past Yudam-ni, hurled attacks in strength against both company perimeters. Company C was hard hit and was withdrawn the following day.

Company F held Toktong Pass, the most vital terrain along the entire 14-mile route.[1] The pass was located six miles southeast of Yudam-ni as the crow flies, at extreme range for supporting artillery. They were to hold at all cost. Captain William E. Barber, commanding Company F, had required his men to dig in before erecting any warming tents. They had completed their task as darkness fell on the 27th. The perimeter remained quiet past midnight. But at 2:30 A.M. on the 28th, the Chinese struck from three directions. In his first assault from the high ground to the north the enemy swarmed over the forward positions of Lieutenant Robert C. McCarthy's platoon.[2] The lieutenant had deployed his men with two

---

[1] Except as noted the action at Toktong Pass is derived from the following sources:
  Interview of First Sergeant Charles C. Dana and Staff Sergeant Richard E. Danford, Company F, 7th Marines, by Captain A. Z. Freeman, in Korea on April 7, 1951. Filed with 1st Provisional Historical Platoon Interviews, April 17, 1951, No. 1, in G-3 Historical Branch Archives, Headquarters, U. S. Marine Corps; and,
  Lynn Montross, "Ridgerunners of Toktong Pass", Marine Corps Gazette, May 1953, pp. 16-23; and
    Montross and Canzona, III, pp. 177-96; and
    Geer, pp. 288-90.

[2] Robert C. McCarthy, "Fox Hill," Marine Corps Gazette, March 1953, pp. 16-23.

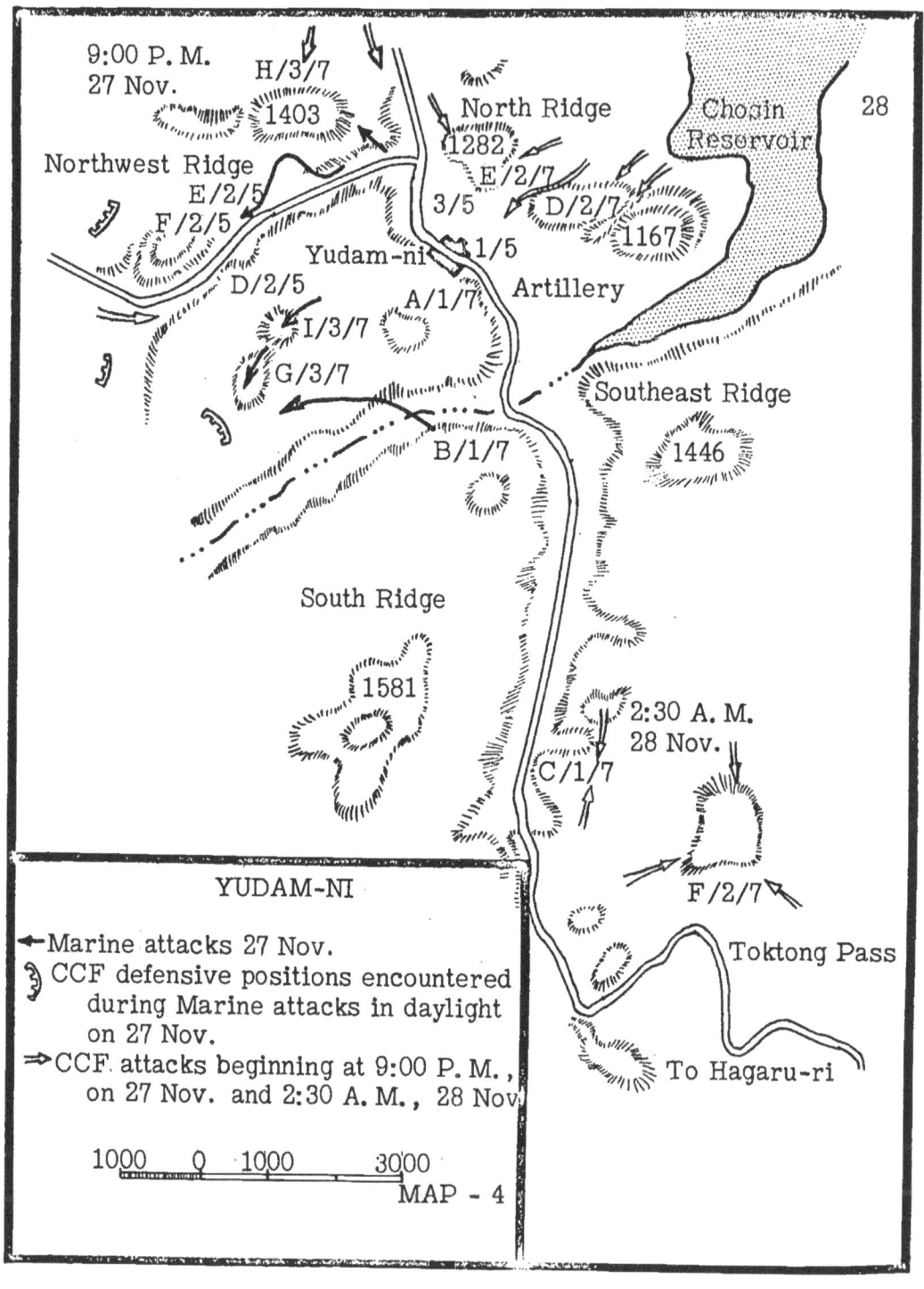

squads forward and one slightly to the rear in supporting positions. Fifteen Marines were killed and nine wounded in the initial onslaught. The eight remaining Marines fell back slightly. A head count later revealed that three Marines were missing. They were Corporal Wayne A. Pickett and Privates First Class Robert L. Batdorff and Daniel D. Yesko.[1] Search of the area after the position was restored failed to locate the three missing Marines and for very good reason. The Chinese had captured them in the first rush, and had immediately taken them back into the hills. All three were returned in the prisoner exchange at the end of hostilities.

The Chinese persisted for four more days in their attacks against Fox Hill as it came to be known. Casualties mounted inside the perimeter, but with supply by air drop, occasional artillery support from Yudam-ni, and close air support at critical times in the battle, Company F was able to exact an exhorbitant price from the attackers.

At 2:00 A.M. on November 30th, Marines at their fighting positions heard a voice yelling in English, "Fox Company, you are surrounded. I am a Lieutenant from the 11th Marines. The Chinese will give you warm clothing and good treatment. Surrender now!"[2] The Chinese did, in

---

[1] 1st MarDiv, Casualty Bulletin 89-50, December 27 1950.

[2] McCarthy, Marine Corps Gazette, May 1953, p. 21.

fact, hold Marine First Lieutenant Messman from the 11th Marines. He had been captured two days earlier within a few miles of Toktong Pass. Was it he? Or was it really an Oriental voice?

When finally relieved after five gruelling days of incessant battle, the gallant Fox Company had suffered 26 killed, 89 wounded, and three captured. This was almost exactly half of the 240 Marines who made up the reinforced company. By their efforts, the Marines of Company F assured the use of the road and facilitated the return of the two regiments to Hagaru later. They also helped win for Captain Barber, their commander, the Medal of Honor for their heroic stand under his brilliant leadership.

To recapitulate, Yudam-ni was attacked on the night of November 27th. After midnight, Company F at Toktong Pass came under assault. Before noon on the 28th the Marine Division was cut into four distinct segments; Yudam-ni, Toktong Pass, Hagaru-ri and Koto-ri. Each segment was isolated from the others by defended Chinese roadblocks.

In response to a directive from his division commander, the much decorated commanding officer of the 1st Marines, Colonel Lewis B. Puller, prepared to send a force north from Koto-ri to clear the main supply route. This was the only land route leading to Hagaru and Yudam-ni. The troops which cleared the route of Chinese roadblocks would also serve to reinforce the beleagured garrison at Hagaru.

Attempts to clear the Hagaru-ri-Koto-ri main supply route proved fruitless on the 28th. Company D, 1st

Marines, moved north out of the Koto perimeter in the early afternoon. Within three hours Company F, 1st Marines, was ordered out to assist the first company which was hotly engaged only a mile from the perimeter. By dusk both companies were recalled; their withdrawal was covered by Marine close air support.

There was no through traffic on the Koto-Hagaru road on the 28th. Most attempts to traverse the road were turned back. One truck, driven by Corporal Frederick G. Holcomb of the 11th Marine Artillery Regiment, did not make it back. The truck's passenger, PFC Charles M. Kaylor, was a Marine reservist hitch-hiking a ride to Hungnam from whence he could embark for the United States and a dependency discharge which had just then been approved. When the two left Yudam-ni on the night of the 27th, they were part of the last convoy out of that perimeter before the general withdrawal in December. Their convoy negotiated Toktong Pass and arrived in Hagaru-ri without incident late the 27th. In an attempt to continue the trip south from Hagaru to Koto-ri on the 28th, the luckless Marines were captured by Chinese. These same Chinese were part of the force which even then was setting a trap for the next convoy.[1]

First Lieutenant Felix L. Ferranto, Radio Relay Platoon Commander of the Division Signal Battalion, departed Koto-ri at 7:30 A.M. on the 28th enroute to

---

[1] Geer, pp. 269, 325.

Hagaru-ri. He drove alone and was captured after leaving the Koto-ri perimeter.[1]

While Holcomb, Kaylor, and Ferranto were being taken prisoner by the enemy, other Chinese were massing for an assault on the Hagaru perimeter. The Hagaru defenders anticipated their forthcoming ordeal, even to the time and place of the main attack. Intelligence agents and interrogator reports proved to be extremely accurate.[2] A Chinese division struck Hagaru beginning at about 10:30 P.M. November 28, 1950. They were beaten off after a night of vicious fighting and near success. They took no Marine prisoners; at least no Marines missing in that action were reported in any of the POW camps.

Colonel Puller's 1st Marines still had the job of opening the road and reinforcing Hagaru. At the same time they had their hands full defending the vital Koto-ri perimeter. Colonel Puller could spare only one rifle company of his own organic units to reinforce the Marines to the north. Clearly this was insufficient, particularly in light of the action fought by D and F Companies that same day. Therefore a composite unit was formed on November 28th consisting of personnel from ten different organizations.

The 41st Independent Commando, Royal Marines, had just arrived at Koto-ri enroute to Hagaru-ri, so its

---

[1] 1st SigBn., Unit Report No. 12, December 3, 1950, p. 3.

[2] Montross and Canzona, III, 203-04.

commander, Lieutenant Colonel Douglas B. Drysdale, was assigned to lead the composite force which bore his name. Included in the make-shift unit were the 41st Commando of some 235 officers and men; about 205 U. S. Marines of Company G, 3d Battalion, 1st Marines; some 190 soldiers of Company B, 31st Infantry, 7th Infantry Division, of the Army; and about 82 additional U. S. Marines in the persons of postal clerks, truck drivers, military policemen, and communicators, plus several U. S. Navy hospital corpsmen attached to the 1st Marine Division. After commencing the move north, the task force was reinforced with 29 tanks, 76 vehicles and trailers, and 210 Marines from four different Marine units. Their arrival swelled the task force virtually to battalion size. The official Marine Corps history of the operation accounts for approximately 922 men, 141 vehicles and trailers, and the 29 tanks.[1] In spite of its impressive numerical total, the heterogeneous make-up of the unit rendered much of it ineffective as a fighting organization. This fact soon became evident.[2]

---

[1] Ibid., p. 228.

[2] Except as noted the actions of Task Force Drysdale are derived from the following sources:
    Letter from Capt Charles L. Harrison, USMC (Retired), July 24, 1960, captured with Task Force Drysdale while serving as a SSgt with an MP Detachment; and
    Interview with Sgt Charles W. Dickerson, SSgt James B. Nash, TSgt Charles L. Harrison, Sgt Morris L. Estess, and Cpl Calvin W. Williams, by Historical Division, HQMC July 25-31, 1951, (filed as Dickerson interview, Interview File, G-3 Historical Branch Archives, HQMC); and
    1st Mar Div, HistD, November, 1950, pp. 63-4; and
    Montross and Canzona, III, 225-35; and
    Geer, pp. 316-25.

Mist lay over the snow covered countryside when the point of Task Force Drysdale cleared Koto-ri perimeter at 9:45 A.M. on November 29. The commandos and the Marine rifle company were to fight their way in leapfrog-fashion through the Chinese positions while the remainder of the column followed in trucks on the road.

Slight resistance was encountered at the first objective a few hundred yards beyond Koto-ri. Resistance increased steadily thereafter, and progress was slow. The column inched its way northward, the constant halts and starts causing it to expand and contract like some giant human concertina. Chinese small-arms fire and mortar concentrations exacted a steady toll of casualties. To the men in trucks enemy action appeared to be minor harassing attacks of no particular consequence. Aside from the inconvenience of disembarking from their vehicles at each stop, which seemed to occur every 100 yards, the troops on the road experienced no great difficulty during the day. Jeeps shuttling the wounded back to the Koto-ri perimeter passed the rear elements of the convoy still moving out of Koto-ri.

Marine aviation provided close support attacks and helped fend off the Chinese along the route during daylight. At dusk the head of the column, which included most of the commandos, all of the Marine rifle company, and several tanks, pushed on to the village of Hagaru. Continuation of the move had been directed by division headquarters.[1]

---

[1] 1st MarDiv SAR, October-December, 1950, Annex C. p.64.

The positions at Hagaru were considered to be sufficiently in danger to warrant taking the calculated risk.

Progress of the center of the column was barred by a damaged truck, and Chinese small-arms and mortar fire prevented its removal. While the troops waited for the road to be cleared, the enemy severed that portion of the convoy stalled south of the roadblock. The rear elements of the task force spent the night fighting their way back into the perimeter they had left that afternoon. Communications had been lost because of weather, distance, terrain, and other circumstances, so neither the front nor the rear of the convoy realized that the center was isolated. The Chinese had succeeded in fractionalizing the column. Now began the final mastication. The gauntlet of fire, the vulnerability of the thin-skinned vehicles, and the actions of the troops were, in microcosm, almost identical with the misfortunes of the 2d Infantry Division on the road between Kunu-ri and Sunchon three days later.[1]

The center portion of the convoy was truly the most cosmopolitan of the three segments. Included were some commandos, most of the Army company, a Marine military police detachment, and Marines from several service and support units. To make matters even more complicated,

---

[1] S. L. A. Marshall, CCF in the Attack (Part II), A Study Based on the Operations of 1st Marine Division in the Koto-ri, Hagaru-ri, Yudam-ni Area 20 November-10 December, 1950. Prepared by the Operations Research Office, the Johns Hopkins University, Far East Command, 1951, p. 4; and
S. L. A. Marshall, The River and the Gauntlet (New York: William Morrow & Company, 1953), pp. 261-360.

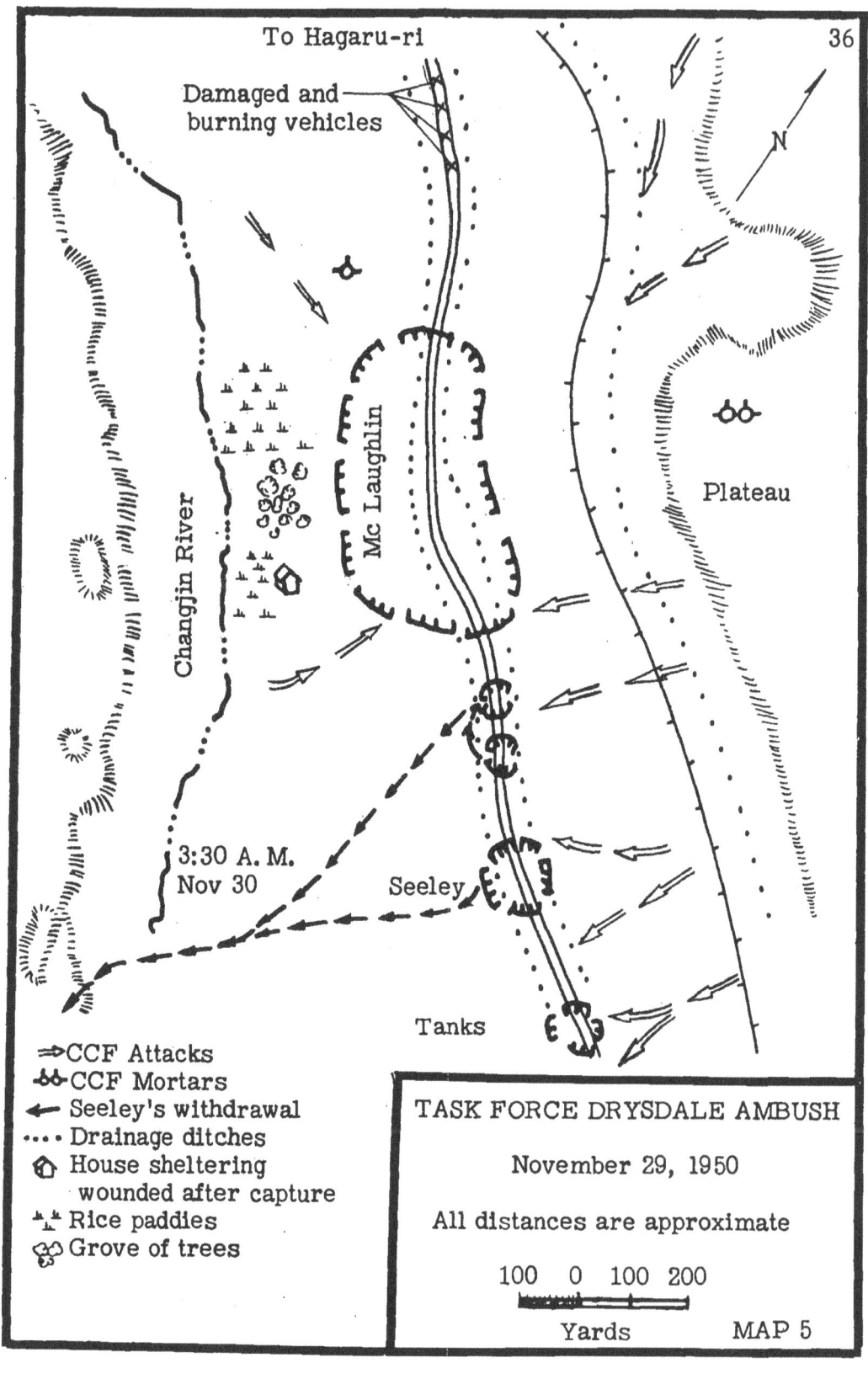

two U. S. Marines were attached to the 41st Commando to provide transportation. The drivers, Corporal Joseph B. Harbin and Private First Class Uda G. Flanery, were from the 4.5" Rocket Battery, a Fleet Marine Force unit attached to the artillery regiment of the Marine division for operations in Korea. Harbin's truck was set on fire by the Chinese, and he found himself afoot with the isolated portion of the task force. Flanery returned to his parent unit on December 11th, having been with the advance elements of the task force, and he reported having seen the burning truck.[1] Harbin was captured in the ensuing action and spent almost three years as a prisoner of war.

The center portion of the task force came under increasingly heavy fire. The Chinese succeeded in splintering the group even further, reducing it to one large perimeter and three smaller positions. The northernmost and largest group contained about 130 to 140 men. Lieutenant Colonel Arthur A. Chidester, assistant Division G-4, was the senior officer with this group. He attempted to turn the stalled convoy around and return to Koto-ri, but the Chinese cut the column to his rear before the vehicles could be turned. Major James K. Eagan began to organize the southern part of Chidesters' group but was wounded in the legs and captured during a limited attack by the enemy. Lieutenant Colonel Chidester also received disabling wounds. Casualties mounted and bodies were

---

[1] C Battery, 1st 4.5" Rocket Battalion, Fleet Marine Force, SAR, Appendix 5 to 11th Marines SAR, Annex SS to 1st MarDiv SAR, October-December, 1950, pp. 5-6.

stacked around the hastily formed perimeter. Freezing temperatures threatened to take an even greater toll. Army medical personnel travelling with the column tended the wounded even after their meager supplies gave out.

Reports of the action are garbled and often contradictory, particularly with respect to distances, personalities, and time factors. But in some matters there is virtually complete agreement. Major John N. McLaughlin assumed command of the ill-fated segment of Task Force Drysdale, and his courage and leadership are the central theme of its brief history.

Major McLaughlin's own case illustrates the diverse make-up of the group he organized. Like the author, he was an instructor with Mobile Training Team "A" from the Marine Troop Training Unit, Pacific, with headquarters at Coronado, California. The team was on temporary duty in Japan to provide amphibious instruction to units of the Eighth Army when the Korean War began. Together with other members of Team "Able", Major McLaughlin was ordered to the staff of the U. S. Tenth Corps. On November 29, 1950 it was his ill fortune to be travelling to Hagaru-ri in the capacity of liaison officer to the 1st Marine Division. He accompanied the only convoy scheduled to make the trip at that time. Initially his role was simply that of a passenger with the column. As November 29th faded into a new day, he assumed command of the battered center portion of the task force. Before November 30th was five hours old, he and his command were prisoners of the so-called Chinese Communist People's Volunteers.

Major McLaughlin, Warrant Officers Lloyd V. Dirst and Felix L. McCool, and several Marine noncommissioned officers organized the tattered elements of the convoy. They set personal examples of courage and leadership. The officers moved about in the open directing the defenders' fire. Royal Marine Commandos who remained with that portion of the column were as impressed with Major McLaughlin's leadership under fire as were the United States Marines.[1]

Casualties mounted. Ammunition dwindled and by 3:00 A.M. only about two clips or about sixteen cartridges remained per man. The temperature fell to 20 degrees below zero Fahrenheit. Shortly before dawn the Chinese demanded the surrender of the perimeter. By this time Warrant Officer Dirst had been seriously wounded as he strode about the perimeter. Staff Sergeant James B. Nash braved the intense enemy fire to drag the wounded officer to safety. For his act of gallantry the sergeant was later awarded the Silver Star medal. With about 40 dead, 40 able bodied and 40 wounded in dire need of shelter and medical care, and with ammunition now down to less than eight rounds per man, Major McLaughlin had no choice but to consider Chinese demands for the surrender of his hodgepodge agglomeration of soldiers, commandos, and Marines.

Through the medium of sign language and pidgeon English, the Chinese had arranged for a cease fire and

---

[1] Letter from Warrant Officer Day, then a Quarter Master Sergeant, Instructor, Royal Marines (Retired), April, 14, 1960. Warrant Officer Day was captured in 1951 and eventually was confined in the same camp with Major McLaughlin.

consultation with the Marine leader to discuss possible surrender. During the parley between Major McLaughlin and the Chinese, most of the able-bodied men in the ditches stood on the road and walked up and down to restore their circulation. Army medical personnel continued ministering the wounded as best they could. Throughout the cease fire, the Chinese remained quiet and did not fire on the task force remnants even though some of the Americans, not knowing a cease fire had been arranged, fired occasional shots at the Chinese.

The three splinter-groups of Marines, commandos, and soldiers lying south of the main group took advantage of the lull in fighting by joining forces. Under the capable leadership of Major Henry J. Seeley, Division Motor Transport Officer, they gathered their wounded and slipped away to the west of the road. They ascended a steep mountain and wormed their way back to Koto-ri shortly after dawn.

When it became obvious that further resistance by the main party would be fruitless, and when the word was passed that surrender was imminent, most of the men remaining with Major McLaughlin rendered their weapons useless by throwing vital parts into the snow or by breaking the stocks of their rifles and carbines.

The Chinese had continued slipping in closer during the conversations, and when the surrender was agreed upon many CCF soldiers sprang to their feet from positions all around the perimeter and at distances as close as forty feet.[1] The first Communist soldiers to enter the task force positions ignored their captives and immediately began to loot the vehicles. The troops who followed them surprised the Americans and British by their friendly attitude. They smiled, shook hands, and clapped their captives on the back. The only case of rough treatment reported was observed by one of the Marines, Corporal Calvin W. Williams. Williams, a headquarters postal clerk, was among a group of Marines freed six months later. He stated that one prisoner was sitting on a rock when a wounded Chinese soldier walked up and kicked him. Another Chinese intervened and prevented any further rough treatment.

Once the soldiers, commandos, and Marines were disarmed the Chinese permitted movement of some of the seriously wounded into the shelter of a nearby Korean house. They reneged on their promise to permit evacuation of the wounded to Koto-ri, but by allowing some to be sheltered in the house a few lives were saved. Warrant Officer Dirst was among those placed in the hut. He survived the ordeal although he remained unconscious for several days even after his eventual evacuation to a hospital ship. The wounded were picked up about eight days later when division elements fought their way south from Yudam-ni and Hagaru-ri to rejoin the Marines holding the Koto-ri

---

[1] Commander, Naval Forces, Far East, Chinese Communist Treatment and Attempted Political Indoctrination of U. S. Marine Prisoners of War. (Mimeographed). July 11, 1951. Cited hereafter as ComNavFE Report of Chicom Indoctrination.

perimeter.

Shortly, the Chinese formed the prisoners into groups and marched them across the railroad tracks, onto the plateau east of the scene of carnage, and thence off into the mountainous countryside. The wounded received no medical treatment from the Chinese then or later.

The captured Army medical personnel provided what treatment they could. All day long on the 30th of November Chinese and United Nations' wounded straggled up into the hills. The Communists removed their own dead, carrying the bodies into the hills for burial.

Most of the prisoners were taken to a hidden depression in the mountains and ushered into one of two log huts. Some of the men had taken the precaution to slip a can or two of C rations into their parka pocket before capture. Consequently, most of them had some food during their first day of captivity.

The prisoners were searched but were permitted to keep most of their possessions except for knives, cigarette lighters, and matches. On the night of the 30th, they were allowed to have fires.

During interrogations, apparently conducted on the spot, the Marines were told that their division had been wiped out.[1] The enemy seemed intent on lowering their

---

[1] It is doubtful that even the Chinese believed this lie because even then they were throwing wave after wave of soldiers against the 1st Marine Division in a futile attempt to destroy it. By early December the Communists spent almost three armies without achieving their goal

morale. Questions generally concerned the organization and weapons of the 1st Marine Division. At least two of their interrogators had been raised near the International Settlement in Shanghai, long the pre-World War II home of the 4th Marine Regiment. As a consequence, the interrogators were familiar with American customs and slang.

The prisoners were again formed up in column and marched off to the west towards the Pyongyang-Manpojin railroad. They numbered some 30 enlisted Marines, Major McLaughlin and three other Marine officers, 22 Royal Marines,[1] and roughly 70 American soldiers. From all appearances the Communist guards were provided by the sector through which the column was passing. When Koreans provided the guard, the treatment was noticeably rough. On several occasions Chinese guards intervened to protect the prisoners from the North Koreans.

There was virtually no opportunity for escape. Freezing weather, lack of food, and numerous Communist troop units in the vicinity in addition to the adequate guard discouraged any attempts to break away.

The prisoners made their way under guard along winding foot trails through the rugged terrain. They moved

---

and without seriously hurting the Marine division, though it must be admitted that that the weather and their bullets did exact a higher than usual number of casualties in the ranks of the division.

[1] Marine Andrew M. Condron, a young Scot, was one of the 22 Royal Marines. He was the only Englishman and the only Marine of any nationality to refuse repatriation after the armistice. See Virginia Pasley Schmitz, <u>22 Stayed</u> (London: W. H. Allen & Co., Ltd.), pp. 184-206.

either at night or during heavy snow storms, apparently to avoid detection by United Nations aircraft. The troops were on the verge of freezing and all were suffering from malnutrition.

A brief respite was provided when the column halted for several days. The officers were held in a Korean farm house from the 11th to the 22d of December. By this time Lieutenant Messman and Army Lieutenant George Shedd had joined the group.[1] A four day march brought the officers to Kanggye on December 26th. Other groups of prisoners filtered into Kanggye at about the same time.

Marine Sergeant R. J. Darden never completed the trip. Exhausted, stricken with pneumonia, he died en route. A second Marine Sergeant, R. P. Frazure, and Private First Class Edwin P. Ogrodnik succumbed to the dual complications of dysentery and pneumonia shortly after arrival at Kanggye.[2] Proper care and diet could have prevented all three deaths. They were not the sole casualties of the march. Several of the soldiers died as well.

Kanggye offered some shelter from icy winds, and it meant also the end of the terrible trek northward. Food, such as it was, appeared more regularly than it had on the march. And something else appeared, too. The prisoners encountered the "Lenient Policy" of the Chinese.

---

[1] Letter from CWO 3 Felix J. McCool, USMC (Retired), February 3, 1961.

[2] Letter from Master Sergeant William Pettit, FMCR, February 3, 1961; and
Letter from First Sergeant Chester A. Mathis, FMCR, January 3, 1961.

CHAPTER III

BREAKOUT

As Task Force Drysdale was beginning its ordeal, the Marine Division Commander, Major General Oliver P. Smith, took action to regroup his widely separated forces. He ordered a redeployment which would assure him greater cohesion. At 3:45 P.M., November 29, 1950, General Smith directed the 5th Marines to protect the Yudam-ni area and the 7th Marines, in its entirety, to clear the main supply route to Hagaru. The two regiments and their supporting units regrouped on the 30th. On December 1st the 1st Battalion, 7th Marines, struck out across country to fight through to relieve Company F at Toktong Pass. Artillerymen of the 4th Battalion, 11th Marines, were formed into provisional infantry platoons. The dead were given a field burial at Yudam-ni; truck spaces were needed for casualties expected during the fight southward.[1]

Three battalions remained in position overlooking Yudam-ni. They were to hold that crucial terrain until all other elements cleared the area and were safely en

---

[1] Montross and Canzona, III, fn p. 255 relates that the remains of those buried at Yudam-ni were returned to the United States for burial after the armistice.

route to Hagaru. The 3d Battalion, 5th Marines, led the attack south along the road generally parallel to 1/7 which moved across country.¹ The two leading battalions were masked from each other by the precipitous terrain.

The 3d Battalion, 5th Marines, which had been attacking south with two companies in the van, held up shortly after dark. As midnight approached, the Marine attack was pressed again with Companies H on the right and I on the left. Company I, 3/5 met severe resistance from Chinese dug in on hill 1520 and was forced to fall back to its original positions from which it could protect the supply route better. The Chinese followed up their advantage by pressing home repeated attacks in estimated battalion strength and by concentrating heavy mortar fires on the company positions. PFC Edward G. Wilkins, Jr. was captured by the enemy during the hotly contested battle. By morning's light on the 2d only about 20 of the Marines from I/3/5 were able to continue fighting. They were combined into one platoon and attached to Company G, 5th Marines.² The Chinese left 342 bodies of their "Volunteers"

---

[1] For the sake of brevity and variety unit designations may hereafter be shown in abbreviated form. For example A/1/7 indicates Company A, 1st Battalion, 7th Marines; 2/1 refers to the 2d Battalion, 1st Marines. During the Korean War, Marine infantry battalions included three lettered rifle companies and one weapons company. Companies A, B, and C were always in the 1st Battalion, Companies D, E, and F were in the 2d Battalion, and Companies G, H, and I were in the 3d Battalion. Weapons companies (W/3/5 for example) provided mortar, machine gun and rocket support in each battalion.

[2] 3d Battalion, 5th Marines, SAR, Annex C to 5th Marines SAR, Annex QQ to 1st MarDiv SAR, October-December, 1950, pp. 15-16.

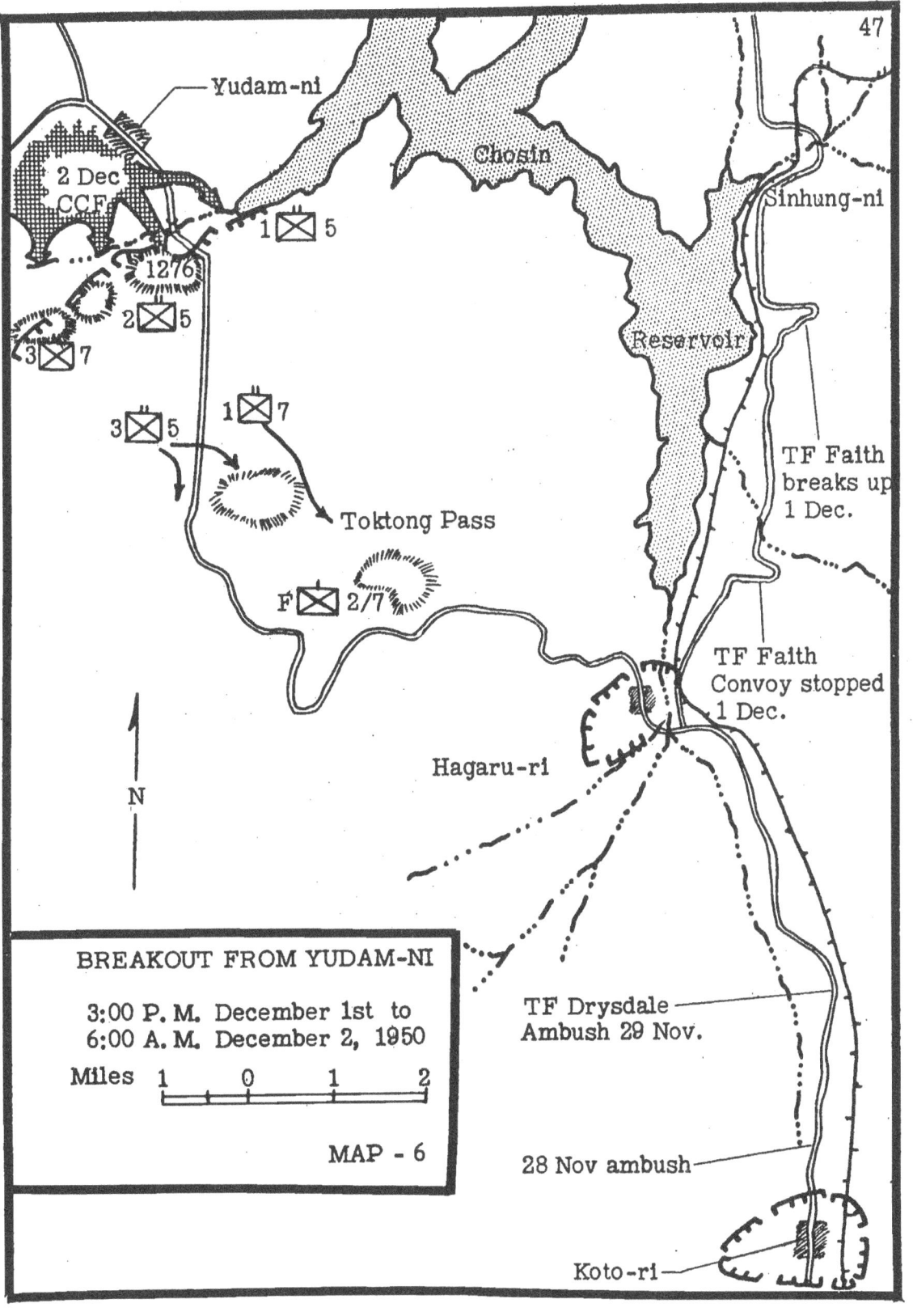

stacked around the Company I perimeter. How many additional Chinese were wounded is pure conjecture.

The covering force of three battalions which had remained at Yudam-ni faced the difficult task of fending off the enemy, trying to break contact, and then defending the rear of the entire division as it moved south. Company F, 2d Battalion, 5th Marines, in particular came under heavy attack on hill 1276.[1] The Chinese began closing in on F/2/5 in the early morning hours of December 2d. Leading elements crawled close to the Marine foxholes. A sudden fusillade of grenades signalled the assault, and the Communist troops rose to their feet to charge the Company F defenders. The attackers struck in an inverted "V".

The rifle squad led by Sergeant Donald M. Griffith was deployed well forward and received the initial brunt of the enemy attack. A grenade exploded directly in front of Sergeant Griffith's foxhole. The fragments tore a deep wound in his nose, blinded his right eye, and punctured one of his legs. The sergeant was unconscious for a short while. When he regained his senses, he found his squad had been overrun and the other two squads of his platoon had been forced to pull back within effective supporting distance of the remainder of the company.

Aided by illuminating shells fired by F Company's organic mortars, Marine night-fighter aircraft strafed

---

[1] Ibid., and Montross and Canzona, III, 265-66.

the attacking Chinese. The welcome air support helped stop the onslaught, but it was too late to be of assistance to Sergeant Griffith. He had been bypassed when the first waves of Chinese swept by his hole. The Marine sergeant found his M-1 rifle useless because the firing pin had snapped in the extreme cold. His sole weapons then consisted of two hand grenades, and he succeeded in throwing both of them before he was detected.[1]

An enemy soldier jumped into the foxhole, and Sergeant Griffith leaped to his feet. The Chinaman screamed and several of his comrades joined him in taking the wounded Marine prisoner. While being led down the hill north of his original position, Sergeant Griffith was joined by two other members of his squad who had also been taken prisoner. They were Privates First Class Paul E. and Donald F. Dowling. Neither of the young brothers was wounded.

The three captives were taken north along precipitous mountain trails and through icy streams. Their march continued unabated for three days and nights. Approximately every eight hours their guards were changed for a fresh group, but the prisoners were forced to continue marching without rest. They were given neither food nor water for three days. Occasionally the Marines scooped up chunks of snow in an effort to quench their thirsts.

---

[1] Except where otherwise noted, this section is derived from a letter from Staff Sergeant Donald M. Griffith, U. S. Marine Corps (Retired), November 8, 1960.

At one point during the march, Sergeant Griffith suffered so intensely from hunger, thirst, cold, fatigue and pain from his several wounds that he almost lost the will to go on. He fell to the ground and motioned to one of the Chinese guards to shoot. The Dowling brothers intervened and somehow convinced the Chinese that the three prisoners required some rest before continuing the march. Next they offered to carry their squad leader in spite of their own fatigue. Their selfless concern provided the spark Griffith needed. After a few minutes rest when the Chinese guards ordered them to press on, Sergeant Griffith was able to continue.

At the end of three days of continuous marching they entered a small Korean village located in a deep valley. The mud huts of the village housed large numbers of wounded prisoners of war. Those who were able to travel were taken on to other camps without delay. The sick and wounded were placed in already overcrowded huts, ostensibly to recuperate. If they were lucky, they recovered and were transferred to a regular camp. Sergeant Griffith stayed at the separation center for about four months. The Dowling brothers were transferred from the valley almost immediately. Griffith never saw them again although he heard later that one brother died of pneumonia and the other died shortly thereafter of unknown causes.[1]

---

[1] Evidence from recovered POWs established the deaths of the two brothers while in enemy hands.

Meanwhile the 5th and 7th Marine Regiments continued their fight southward towards Hagaru-ri. The two regiments began entering the Hagaru perimeter late on December 3d. By 2:00 P.M. on the 4th, the rearmost elements arrived in the town. The severity of the action is indicated by the casualties; roughly 1,000 Marines were wounded and some 500 suffered frostbite from the 16-degrees-below-zero weather.[1]

As division units closed on Hagaru, the first requirement was to consolidate forces. Casualties had to be evacuated from the small hastily constructed airstrip. Replacements were needed, and they had to be integrated into combat units without delay for the fight south to Koto-ri and eventually to the port of Hungnam.

During the first five days of December approximately 3150 U. S. Marine, 1137 Army and 25 Royal Marine casualties were evacuated from Hagaru by Marine and Air Force transport planes, and some 537 Marine replacements were flown in on the return trips of many of the aircraft.[2] The replacements were drawn from hospitals in Japan where they had been recuperating from wounds received previously. The troops were given a one day respite before continuing the attack southward.

Hagaru perimeter had received only minor attention from the Chinese after the initial onslaught on November

---

[1] Montross and Canzona, III, 259, 275.

[2] Ibid., p. 279.

29th. The fortunate lull in fighting had enabled Marine engineers within the perimeter to hack out the 3,200 foot airstrip which made casualty evacuation possible.

The Chosin Reservoir Campaign furnished one episode which illustrates the unfathomable nature of the Chinese.[1] Task Force Faith, an Army unit composed of two infantry battalions and an artillery battalion, was isolated at Sinhung-ni on the east shore of the Chosin Reservoir. These were the units which had relieved the 5th Marines in that same area a week earlier. The Task Force numbered some 2,500 troops including a large proportion of Korean soldiers. On December 1st the Task Force commander, Lieutenant Colonel Don C. Faith, U. S. Army, decided to fight south to Hagaru. His 500 wounded were placed on trucks and the force began the slow, painful trek in face of mounting opposition. At dusk, when the unit was only four and a half miles from its destination, Lieutenant Colonel Faith received fatal wounds. With his death the Task Force lost all cohesion. By darkness on the following day, an estimated 1050 survivors of the original 2,500 troops had either wandered into Marine lines or had been rescued by troops under the direction of Lieutenant Colonel Olin C. Beall, U. S. Marine Corps. Marine patrols found

---

[1] Except where otherwise noted, this section is derived from the following sources:
    1st Motor Transport Battalion, 1st Marine Division, Historical Diary, December, 1950. Cited hereafter as 1st MT Bn HistD; and
    Montross and Canzona, III, 244; and
    Geer, pp. 345-46.

more than 300 bodies in the abandoned trucks of the Task Force. Many of the soldiers had been killed by Chinese grenades as they lay helpless in the trucks. Hundreds others were missing in action, and many were held by the enemy as prisoners.

In direct contrast to the slaughter of the seriously wounded, the Chinese did not materially hinder rescue operations of most of the stragglers and walking wounded. In some instances they even assisted the Marines in evacuating the Army survivors. Conversely one group of four soldiers which had been held captive by the Chinese for several days received more brutal treatment. Two enemy soldiers took them from the hut where they had been kept and led them onto the ice of the reservoir, ostensibly to release them. As the Americans began to walk away, the Chinese opened fire and shot their legs from under them. All four were badly wounded. They were rescued later by Lieutenant Colonel Beall.[1]

The Marine breakout from Hagaru to Koto-ri took place on the 6th and 7th of December, 1950. Approximately 10,000 troops and more than 1,000 vehicles made the 11-mile trip in 38 hours.[2] As had been anticipated, enemy resistance was light during daylight hours when Marine air support provided a protective umbrella over the mass of foot troops. At night the Chinese closed in and resistance

---

[1] 1st MT Bn., HistD, December, 1950, p. 3; and Geer, p. 345.

[2] Montross and Canzona, III, 303.

increased markedly. Division Headquarters Company formed "Charlie" Serial of the Division Train, and when the scene of the November 28th ambush was reached, Headquarters personnel were able to identify several of their comrades who had been slain at that site.[1]

In contrast to Communist treatment of prisoners, the Marines left their seriously wounded Chinese prisoners behind at Hagaru. The Communist sick and wounded were provided with shelter, food, and fuel before the Marines departed and only about 160 able-bodied POW's were taken southward to Koto-ri. During a fight, the Chinese attackers poured a heavy volume of fire into the prisoner group huddled in the middle of a road. When some of the POW's tried to escape, the Marines also fired on them. Only 13 of the original 160 survived.[2]

The two-day movement from Hagaru to Koto-ri cost the 1st Marine Division 103 killed, 506 wounded, and 7 missing in action. Of the latter, four were captured by the enemy while on a northbound convoy en route from Hamhung to Chinhung-ni on December 6th. Their 15-truck convoy was returning to Chinhung-ni through what was presumed to be fairly safe territory. Instead the Chinese sprang an am-

---

[1] Interview of Major Frederick Simpson, U. S. Marine Corps, by Captain Kenneth A. Shutts, U. S. Marine Corps Reserve, at the 1st Marine Division Command Post (Forward), Chunchon, Korea, April 11, 1951. Filed with 1st Provisional Historical Platoon Interviews - April 17, 1951 #1, in G-3 Historical Branch Archives, HQMC.

[2] Montross and Canzona, III, 299.

bush and destroyed four trucks. The convoy leader and six enlisted Marines were killed, three enlisted were wounded, and four reported missing in action, were captured.[1] Of those captured, Corporal James P. McInerney, PFC Charles A. Boulduc, and PFC Lloyd E. Osborne were returned to military control by the communists in 1953. PFC Billy W. Baker is presumed to have died while a POW.[2] The following day the parent unit, Company A, 1st Motor Transport Battalion, sent a patrol out which successfully recovered the 11 trucks that had escaped destruction.

Regroupment of division elements at Koto-ri had not been physically completed before orders were issued to continue the attack south.[3] But now the bulk of the 1st Marine Division was joined together. The records indicate that the division numbered approximately 11,686 U. S. Marines, 2,353 U. S. Army personnel, 150 Royal Marines, and 40 ROK Police. Again, all seriously wounded were evacuated by air.

The 1st Marine Regiment held Koto-ri while the balance of the division departed that perimeter en route to Chinhung-ni and thence Hungnam. On the afternoon of the 10th a 17-truck detachment from Company A, 7th Motor Transport Battalion, Fleet Marine Force, departed Koto-ri for Hamhung. An hour before midnight the trucks reached

---

[1] 1st MT Bn, HistD, December, 1950, p. 4.
[2] USMC Casualties.
[3] 1st MarDiv OpnO 26-50.

Sudong. In spite of daytime reconnaissance by an Army patrol, the enemy slipped into Sudong and prepared an ambush. When the A/7 MT Bn trucks approached, the Chinese sprang their trap. Seven trucks were destroyed and the convoy was unable to proceed. One Marine was killed in the exchange of fire and three were wounded. Three more were captured by the enemy. They were Sergeant Paul M. Manor and PFC Paul Phillips, Jr., both of whom gained their freedom five months later, and Corporal Billy G. Fields who died in captivity.[1]

The Division Commander, Major General Oliver P. Smith, had directed that the division tanks were to come out after the last regimental train.[2] Obviously the tragic lessons of Task Force Drysdale and of the 2d Division, Eighth U. S. Army, had been learned. Thin-skinned, wheeled vehicles cannot bypass stalled tanks on single-lane mountain roads nor can they withstand intense small-arms fire. Hence the trucks and jeeps were to precede the iron monsters. There can be little doubt that the decision was wise. At about 1:00 A.M. December 11, one of the tanks suffered a frozen brake.[3] Thirty-one tanks preceding the cripple trundled on south. Eight tanks of the 2d Platoon in the rear were forced to halt. The stalled tanks and

---

[1] 7th Motor Transport Battalion, Fleet Marine Force SAR, Annex VV to 1st MarDiv SAR, October-December, 1950; and
"USMC Casualties".

[2] Commanding General, 1st Marine Division, letter dated December 9, 1950, cited by Montross and Canzona, III, 328.

[3] Geer, p. 371.

their security, a 28-man platoon from the Division Reconnaissance Company, formed the tail end of the Marine column though an alien column followed them. Korean refugees were close behind the rear point and Chinese soldiers sneaked into the refugee column. They kept approaching the last tank.[1]

Radio communications were impeded by the rugged terrain, and the last tank in the column was unable to communicate with other elements of the platoon by radio. The commander of the last tank, Sergeant Robert J. Dolby, left his four crewmen and moved forward on foot to report that he was under attack and needed help. In the meantime, the platoon commander of the 1st Platoon who was in the van of Company B, 1st Tank Battalion, raised the last tank on his radio and after learning of their problem he advised them to abandon their tank.[2] Whether they ignored the instructions or were unable to carry them out is not clear. Shortly thereafter Sergeant Dolby reached his platoon commander and advised him of the situation. The platoon commander, First Lieutenant Philip H. Ronzone, then issued orders similar to what Lerond had already sent by radio, "Abandon tank!" Again the crew inside hull

---

[1] Except where noted otherwise, this section is derived from the following sources:
    Montross and Canzona, III, 328-31; and
    Geer, p. 371.

[2] Statement of First Lieutenant Jack M. Lerond, 047793, USMC, enclosure to letter from the Commanding Officer, 1st Tk Bn, 1st MarDiv, to CMC, serial 1123 of December 27, 1950.

number 22 did not comply.[1] Dolby tried to return to his tank but the Chinese were even then closing in on the rear point.

The Chinese finally attacked the rear of the column and after a sharp fight they drove the foot Marines back beyond the rearmost tank.[2] Two wounded Marines from the Reconnaissance Platoon had been placed under that tank when the fight first started. The Reconnaissance Platoon commander, four Marines and a Navy Hospital Corpsman attempted to rescue the two wounded Marines and the tank crewmen who were still inside the buttoned-up tank. The rescue attempt failed because of intense small-arms fire and grenades. Two of the would-be rescuers were wounded. By this time most of the tank crews had abandoned their tanks and continued south on foot. The enemy climbed onto the rear tank and set fire to it. The second last tank had already been abandoned. The crew inside number 22 kept their hatches closed and ignored the Reconnaissance Company Marines who repeatedly beat on the hull in an effort to communicate and coax them out to safety.

When the action was completed and noses were counted, the crewmen of the last tank were declared missing and presumed dead. The tankers were Corporals Andrew Aguirre, Joe E. Saxon and J. E. Glasgow and Private First Class

---

[1] Ibid., Statement of First Lieutenant Philip H. Ronzone, 048019, USMC.

[2] 1st Marines, SAR, Annex PP to 1st MarDiv SAR, October-December, 1950, p. 26.

Nick Antonis. As it turned out all four were captured by the enemy and only Glasgow failed to survive the two and three quarter years of captivity.

The following morning Marine planes destroyed the abandoned tanks.[1]

Tenth Corps Operation Order 10-50 directed the 1st Marine Division to begin embarkation in Hungnam immediately. The U. S. Army 3d and 7th Divisions defended the Hungnam perimeter against minor enemy patrol activities while the Marines loaded their ships and prepared to redeploy to South Korea where they were to fight for two and a half years longer. Marine Aircraft Groups joined with Navy and Air Force units to fend off hostile units near the port city.

On December 14, 1950, the 1st Marine Aircraft Wing shut down operations and departed for Japan. The next day the last of the major Marine ground units set sail. The first half year of the war closed.

The severe combat had proved costly. Since landing at Wonsan in October approximately 728 Marines had been killed in action or died of wounds, 3508 were wounded in action, and 192 were missing. Later events showed that roughly one third of the missing had been captured. They included Captain Booker, ten ground officers of whom two, Lieutenant Colonel Chidester and Major Eagan, are presumed to have died shortly after capture, and 68 enlisted ground Marines of whom 50 survived.[2]

---

[1] Montross and Canzona, III, 351.

[2] USMC Casualties.

CHAPTER IV

THE LENIENT POLICY

The North Koreans treated their prisoners cruelly, but their brutality was physical. The Chinese introduced a more insidious form of cruelty. With them physical violence was less general but more purposeful, and it was liberally spiced with mental pressure. The North Koreans made token efforts to extract military information from their prisoners taking more pleasure in maltreating than in exploiting them. The Chinese Communists were more effective in their intelligence activities. In addition they made an intensive effort to indoctrinate their prisoners of war or to gain a propaganda advantage. The prisoner of war camp system was designed to support Chinese aims for control and use of POW's, and they called it the "Lenient Policy".

The Communist prisoner of war camps developed under Chinese direction beginning in late December, 1950. In the first three months of 1951 a network of camps was created along the southern shores of the Yalu River. For this purpose Korean residents of selected villages were evacuated, and the POW's were moved in. Personnel captured in the Chosin Reservoir campaign and those taken in northwestern Korea were the first to encounter the lenient policy. Simply stated, this meant calculated leniency in return for co-operation, harassment in return for neutrality, and brutality in return for resistance.

To trace the movements of all the individual prisoners would be hopelessly confusing, yet not all of the Marines captured during the Chosin Reservoir campaign shared the same problems or experiences. Nor did all of the Marines face their problems or attempt to solve them in exactly the same manner. This period in the Korean War furnishes a pattern surprisingly different from all later periods in many respects. Thus it becomes necessary to recount the activities at Kanggye and the ultimate destination of the three major groups formed when that camp was abandoned. Of equal importance to this paper is the role that The Valley served in the Chinese scheme of things.[1] The evolution of the Chinese POW Camp system had its origin in Kanggye and The Valley, and Chinese indoctrination techniques inherited from the Soviets began to undergo subtle refinements as the Chinese gained experience with American prisoners of war. The Americans and other United Nations prisoners of war gained experience, too.

---

[1] Great Britain, Ministry of Defence, *Treatment of British Prisoners of War in Korea* (London: H. M. Stationery Office, 1955), Cited hereafter as British POW Report.
    The Valley was a temporary collection point and medical processing center located near Kanggye. This report refers to The Valley. Sergeant Griffith refers to the same camp as Death Valley, but the latter term is more often applied to a valley near Pukchon.

Between the 20th and 26th of December, 1950, small groups of exhausted United Nations POW's trickled in to Kanggye until the total swelled to 290. This number included 235 soldiers, mainly from the U. S. 7th Division's Task Force Faith, 36 U. S. Marines, 18 Royal Marine Commandos, and one sailor,[1] a U. S. Navy hospital corpsman who had been attached to the 1st Marine Division. The camp, generally referred to as Kanggye, was located about eight miles north of the village of Kanggye.[2]

The camp commander had a small staff of Chinese who worked directly for him and assisted in administering the two POW companies. The staff included about 15 interpreters and 15 administrative aides in addition to half a dozen medical personnel, several cooks, and over 100 guards. It is apparent from interviews with returnees that the administrative aides were charged with political instruction and indoctrination of the prisoners.

The Chinese made no attempt to segregate the officers from the enlisted personnel. Although the officers were grouped into one squad, they were interned in the same

---

[1] Hospitalman 3d Class Herman Castle.

[2] Except as otherwise noted the information concerning Kanggye is derived from the following sources:
    ComNavFE Report of Chicom Indoctrination; and
    Letter from Lieutenant Colonel William G. Thrash, USMC to the Commandant, U. S. Marine Corps, dated December 9, 1953; subject, Exemplary conduct, case of Major John N. McLaughlin, 08423 USMC, Report of and Recommendations of award for. Cited hereafter as Thrash letter to CMC.; and
    Harold H. Martin, "They Tried To Make Our Marines Love Stalin", The Saturday Evening Post, August 25, 1951, pp. 25, 107-109; and
    Harrison, McCool, and Mathis letters.

area and had occasional contact with the enlisted prisoners. The squads contained from eight to twelve men each depending on the size of the room to which they were assigned. The squad leaders were appointed by the Chinese who selected prisoners appearing to be more co-operative or "progressive" as they termed it. By Communist definition a "progressive" was one who co-operated with them and at least appeared to accept the Communist viewpoint. A "reactionary" was a prisoner who resisted indoctrination efforts.

Major McLaughlin was the senior officer among the prisoners, and in direct opposition to his captors he began the task of establishing communications between the small scattered groups. By so doing, he sought to maintain effective control of the POW's and to present a united front against the enemy. Because the 290 United Nations personnel were scattered throughout several farmhouses, it was extremely difficult to create any really effective organization. Every few days, however, the prisoners were brought together in a large barn where they were required to listen to a Chinese indoctrinator. It was at the mass meetings that the major was able to issue instructions, advice and encouragement to the enlisted prisoners. The cold, smoke-filled barn was the locale for widespread exchange of information between the many little groups.

McLaughlin issued instructions to the enlisted personnel through five Marine noncommissioned officers,

Technical Sergeants Albert J. Roberts and Robert J. Pettit, Staff Sergeant Charles L. Harrison, and Corporals Theodore R. Wheeler and Leonard J. Maffioli. The Marines made a conscious effort to stick together, and they achieved some measure of success.

As part of their lenient policy, the Chinese informed the POW's that they were not angry with them for being in Korea, that they realized the Americans and others had been duped by warmongers and Wall Street imperialists. They assured the prisoners that treatment would be fair and lenient, but that wrongdoers would be publicly criticized and made to stand at attention for long periods. On Christmas Eve the Chinese decorated the barn with wreaths, candles, two Christmas trees, red paper bells, and a sign bearing the cheerful inscription, "Merry Christmas." Two huge placards also decorated the barn; they read:

> If it were not for the Wall Street Imperialists you would be home with your wives and families on this Christmas night.
>
> Who is responsible for your being away from your wives and families at this Christmas time? We too want to be with our families.

Within a week after arrival at Kanggye, the lenient policy manifested itself in still another way. Several of the prisoners managed to write letters home. The Chinese mailed at least some of them, and several letters were received by the prisoners' families within two months of mailing. In one case PFC Charles M. Kaylor wrote to his wife in January, 1951, and she received the letter in

Minneapolis, Minnesota, in March, 1951.[1]

The daily routine was boring though not particularly arduous. Prisoners arose at 7:00 A.M. and either took a short walk or performed light calisthenics. They washed their faces and hands, and at 8:00 A.M. representatives from each squad drew the appropriate number of rations from the kitchen. Food was cooked by the Chinese, and the diet was essentially the same as that provided the Communist soldiers consisting of singular items such as sorghum seed, bean curd, soya bean flour, dikons, or cracked corn and on certain special occasions such as Christmas and Lunar New Year the prisoners received small portions of rice, boiled fatty pork, candy and peanuts. The prisoners were told that they were being fed because the Chinese were good; no reference was made to international agreements or the responsibilities of captors for their captives; they were fed simply because the Chinese were good.

After breakfast the prisoners were either marched to the barn which served as a communal lecture hall or they were required to conduct informal political discussions within their own huts. Squad leaders were held responsible for proper discussions by their squads of assigned topics in Marxian dialectical materialism. There seems to have been little or no direct organized opposition to the indoctrination; indeed there seems to have been little

---

[1] The Minneapolis Star, May 26, 1951, p. 1.

opportunity for it since study periods were mandatory; the POW's did not have the option of refusing to attend or to participate in lectures and discussions.

On rare days a noon meal was served, although frequently only two meals were prepared and the noon meal was omitted. After an hour set aside for resting, the afternoon lecture or discussion began and lasted for two hours. The supper meal was generally served at 5:00 P.M. when camp housekeeping details were completed. The prisoners retired at about 7:00 P.M. Holiday routine prevailed only on Christmas, New Years, and Lunar New Year so that Saturdays and Sundays passed like any other day. It is evident from the carefully established routine that the Chinese wanted the POW's to concentrate on their enforced studies. The curriculum was more intensive than most college courses. From the reports of other camps the treatment of most POW's at Kanggye was less brutal than that accorded any group of prisoners during this period. Yet this leniency was coldly calculated to neutralize possible resisters and to convert those who could be bent to the Communists' will. At the same time, when viewed objectively, many of the United Nations personnel at Kanggye were comparatively well treated and were fed as well as their captors, although all of the prisoners were suffering varying degrees of malnutrition from lack of a properly balanced diet.

Chinese doctors provided medications of a far lower standard than would be found in a normal field-first-aid station. Aspirin or APC pills were a common remedy; the next most common service seems to have been removing black, frozen toes without sedation. Some of the sickest personnel disappeared from camp; those who remained were told the others were en route to a hospital.[1]

In January Sergeant Robert J. Coffee and Corporal R. L. Wegner were among those taken away from Kanggye to the so-called Chinese hospital. Wegner had been wounded, and Coffee was suffering, among other ailments, from frozen feet.[2] Two others, Technical Sergeant Donald M. Duncan and Corporal Billy G. Fields were removed from Kanggye at about the same time. Duncan was suffering from wounds and Fields had acute dysentery.[3] Sergeant Coffee was the only one of the four who survived.[4] The Chinese hospital seems to have been a primitive collection of mud and wattle huts in a nearby valley, possibly the same valley in which Sergeant Griffith was being held.

Later, probably in February, several sick POW's were loaded on ox-carts ostensibly for movement to a hospital. One of the prisoners, Technical Sergeant Pettit, related that the sick Americans were told they were being taken to a place where there was a large hospital with beds, doctors and nurses. The small caravan of ox-carts departed

---

[1] Pettit letter.

[2] Letter from CG, 1st MarDiv to CMC, serial 23448 of May 31, 1951; enclosure 10, statement of Sergeant Morris L. Estess.

[3] Ibid., enclosure 11, statement of Sergeant Paul M. Manor and PFC Charles E. Quiring.

[4] USMC Casualties.

from Kanggye at midnight, but instead of taking the POW's to a hospital the Chinese turned them over to North Korean Police. According to Pettit, the sick died like flies.[1] The Chinese resumed control over the group for about two weeks, but then the POW's were remanded to the custody of Korean police again. Finally in May, 1951, the survivors were turned over to the Chinese at Camp 1, Chongsong.[2]

Meanwhile, those who remained at Kanggye were exposed to the continuing indoctrination program of the Chinese. At the very outset the POW's were informed that the most progressive among them would be taken south to the front lines and released. This announcement was undoubtedly made to foster co-operation, and it succeeded, at least to the extent that many prisoners vied with each other to make speeches and to produce articles suitable for the camp newspaper. Successful authors received cigarettes as a reward for their literary efforts, courtesy of the Chinese People's Volunteers. The paper, "New Life", consisted generally of one or two pages which reproduced the hand-printed articles written by the prisoners. Six issues were produced during January, 1951, and five of the 30 articles printed were written by Marines. By their own admission the Chinese were able to secure contributions of articles from only a small percentage of the prisoners, though any contributions represented a victory

---

[1] Pettit letter.

[2] Ibid.

for the Communists.

The following article is illustrative of the type which was suitable to the Communists and was published in the camp newspaper. Entitled "We Were Paid Killers", this article, written by a Marine PFC in the 4th Squad, 2d Company, appeared in the fifth edition of "New Life" published on January 22, 1951 at Kanggye, and the text read as follows:

> Since I was liberated, I've been given time to just think and analyze this Korean problem. Often I've asked myself "Were we paid Killers?" "Are these Korean people really our enemy?" "Why am I here?" These questions have brought me to the conclusion that the American capitalists have made us nothing short of "paid killers." But we were ignorant of the fact and we followed the capitalists without asking ourselves "Why?" I am sure none of us would kill a fellow American in cold blood. But we have killed these innocent people just because MacArthur and Truman said, "they are our enemy." In reality they are a peace loving people and it is only the capitalists lust for more power and money that had caused bloodshed. And we were the cannon fodder for their willful desires. But now we are enlightened to these facts. I believe none of us will be fooled again.[1]

The young author of "We Were Paid Killers" did not serve the Communists' purpose for long. He became an aggressive reactionary and on several occasions was put in solitary confinement in rat-infested holes. He never fully regained the trust of his fellow captives, however, even though he had become "a red hot reactionary."[2]

---

[1] ComNavFE Report of Chicom Indoctrination.

[2] Major Gerald Fink, U. S. Marine Corps, MS comments.

The articles written at Kanggye by other Marines and by other prisoners of war were of a similar tenor, and President Truman, General MacArthur and Secretary of State Acheson came under heavy attack in several of the articles. Clearly the authors went far beyond doctrinal teachings in the Marine Corps and other services which require that a POW give no more than name, rank, service number, and date of birth.

Peace was the basic theme demanded by the Communists, and it served as a front to hide their true motives. The Soviets had set the stage at the close of World War II when, through fraud, coercion, deception and the use of German collaborators, they compiled large numbers of signatures on various peace petitions which then received wide circulation. A U. S. Senate subcommittee investigating Communist exploitation of American prisoners concluded that the Chinese made extensive use of Soviet methods after adding a few refinements of their own.[1]

Just prior to the outbreak of hostilities in Korea, the Communist World Peace Committee held an international meeting in Stockholm and introduced what has come to be known as the "Stockholm Peace Appeal". In commenting on

---

[1] U. S. Congress, Senate, Permanent Subcommittee on Investigations of the Committee on Government Operations, Hearings on Communist Interrogation, Indoctrination and Exploitation of American Military and Civilian Prisoners, Report No. 2832, 84th Cong., 2d Sess., 1957, p. 2. Cited hereafter as Senate Subcommittee on Investigations POW Hearings. Report No. 2832.

the meeting and the resultant "Appeal", the Swedish Prime Minister, the Honorable Tage Erlander, said on July 16, 1950, "It is with feelings of disgust that we in Sweden witness the brandishing of the name of our capital in international Communist propaganda".[1] The Stockholm Peace Appeal was later circulated throughout many of the POW Camps in North Korea, and Kanggye was the first camp in which this particular petition was circulated. In February, 1951, the first peace committee in the prison camps was organized at Kanggye. A Deputy Director of Cultural Affairs submitted an article to "New Life" congratulating those prisoners who had elected to send a petition to the United Nations Organization pressing for a "true peace".[2] This would indicate that sometime within a month after the arrival of the first group on December 20th some of the prisoners had either agreed to sign or had been coerced into signing a peace appeal.

The Stockholm Peace Appeal served the Chinese Communists in two ways. They scored a propaganda victory whenever any U. N. prisoners of war signed the appeal thus adding weight to their propaganda campaign. Less obvious but of deeper significance was the basic tenet of the Stockholm Peace Appeal to outlaw nuclear war, a type of

---

[1] Great Britain, Keesing's Contemporary Archives, 1950-1952. Vol. VIII, (London: Keesing's Publications Ltd., July 22-29, 1950), p. 10864.

[2] New Life (Kanggye POW Camp, North Korea), January 22, 1951.

war which the Chinese Communists sought diligently to avoid in Korea.[1]

The Chinese demanded that the committee produce a suitable peace appeal indicating that the prisoners had been duped into joining the war in Korea, and that they were being used as cannon-fodder to keep hostilities going so as to swell the coffers of the Wall Street financiers and warmongers. The actual wording was left to the committee. Staff Sergeant Harrison was chosen to draft the document, which he did with the greatest of care. Every effort was made to produce a text that would satisfy the Communists yet at the same time would not provide them with a propaganda victory. In all, five drafts were prepared, but none suited the Chinese. Finally the chief interpreter, Lieutenant Pan, wrote a petition. The committee refused to sign the Chinese version and ordered the other prisoners to follow their lead. When the Chinese threatened and intimidated the committee, the small group agreed to sign if the rest of the prisoners were exempted. The Chinese agreed, and the committee members affixed their signatures, though some members scrawled illegible signatures and others misspelled their own names. Signing of the petition was the last act of the Kanggye peace committee.[2]

---

[1] Allen S. Whiting, China Crosses the Yalu (New York: The MacMillan Co., 1960), pp. 142 and fn 57, p. 98.

[2] British POW Report, p. 11.

Communist efforts to convert the Marines and other prisoners to their own beliefs can be read in their directive prohibiting the use of the term "POW". Instead they used the term "newly liberated friends", and they insisted that the prisoners refer to each other in the same vein. The Chinese stressed the virtues of Communism at every opportunity, in lectures, in discussions, and in casual and informal conversations. They continually exhorted their charges to progress more rapidly in their studies, and the promise of release for the more progressive of the newly liberated friends served as the inducement.

As the indoctrination program continued, many progressive POW's were used to give lectures on the same subjects the Chinese had covered. Group discussion was encouraged, and with the help of progressive POW's the Chinese exerted influence on the "unprogressive" prisoners to quiet their opposition and bring them into line. There were progressives and reactionaries to be found in each major group of POW's - among Marines, commandos, and soldiers.

Throughout the entire indoctrination program the Communists denounced religion as a superstition and a device for controlling people's minds. The Chinese attempted to teach Darwin's theory of evolution, but when they encountered strong resistance to that proposal they dropped the idea. Curiously the POW's were permitted to retain whatever religious articles they had on their person at the time of capture. As a result several bibles, testaments, rosaries and other religious articles were available in camp, and the prisoners were able to hold informal religious discussions and readings by squad groups. The Chinese knew of this practice, but they did not interfere, and at times some of them seemed to indicate respect for the beliefs of the Christians.[1]

Interrogations continued apace with indoctrination. Tactical information had been sought early in the game. The Communists now turned their attention to detailed military questions. In addition to order of battle information, the interrogators queried the Marines about close air support techniques, naval gunfire methods, and amphibious vehicles and craft. They spent even more time delving into the life histories of their prisoners. They sought biographical data, with no detail too small for their purposes. Prisoners were also made to fill out economic questionnaires.[2]

From the very start it became apparent that Chinese interrogation techniques were an integral part of their

---

[1] J. Angus MacDonald, "Religion in POW Camps" (unpublished MS filed with G-3, Historical Branch, HQMC, pp. 6-7.

[2] The technique of requiring POW's to write extensive biographies was employed by the Soviets with captured German prisoners during World War II. Writing biographies helped condition prisoners of war for further cooperation with their captives and at the same time provided considerable information for greater exploitation. The use of biographies by the Soviets was described in a study prepared for the U. S. Army by a German Major General:
Alfred Toppe, The Russian Program of Propagandizing Prisoners of War. MS No. P-018c of Historical Division, European Command PW Project No. 14. Koenigstein: September 1949. Translated by M. Franke, edited by Dr. Frederiksen, p. 12.

indoctrination program. Instead of soliciting truthful answers to their questions, the interrogators were satisfied only with answers that suited their purpose. POW's who were interrogated found themselves arguing with the Chinese over such matters as the amount of income or social status of their parents or families. As the prisoners revised their status and income statistics downward, the Communists seemed more pleased and less prone to argue.

The indoctrination period lasted for about eight weeks. On March 3, 1951, the inmates of Kanggye were assembled and marched from the camp into Kanggye proper. There they were embarked on a train and moved south to Somidong where they arrived on March 5th. Three days later, the 290 prisoners were divided into two groups, one of which included 60 prisoners of whom 24 were Marines. The second group of 230 prisoners included Major McLaughlin, Warrant Officer McCool, and Lieutenants Lloyd and Turner. Lieutenant Messman, the artillery officer who had joined the POW's en route to Kanggye, also accompanied the larger column. The officers were taken to Pyoktong, Korea, where they were confined in the officer's compound of Camp 5 on March 24th.[1] Some of the enlisted prisoners may have been confined elsewhere in Camp 5, but the majority of the enlisted continued the march to Chongsong and Camp 1.

At this time approximately 2,000 United Nations prisoners of war were interned in Camp 5. The camp con-

---

[1] Thrash letter to CMC.

sisted of part of the civilian village which had existed there before the war. Built on a peninsula which jutted out into the Yalu Reservoir, Pyoktong offered little chance for escape. The camp was surrounded on three sides by fast moving water. Egress from the peninsula was under the careful scrutiny of watchful guards. Fences, barricades, barbed wire and searchlights were unnecessary. The prisoners were as effectively hemmed in as if all these deterrents were present.[1]

The Marine officers were placed with approximately 145 other officers. Conditions were extremely severe, and officers and men died in large numbers. A starvation diet and complete absence of anything even remotely resembling medical care contributed to the mounting death toll. The bodies were taken to a hillside graveyard and placed in shallow holes scraped in the frozen dirt. When possible, the men on the burial details whispered short prayers during the interment. Later, when the spring thaw came, hogs routed up the bodies and chewed the remains.[2]

Though he was junior to some Army and Air Force officers, Major McLaughlin was elected by his fellow officer-prisoners to represent them. His role covered all aspects of their camp life, but the Marine's principal job was obtaining food and supervising its preparation and distribution. The Chinese quickly recognized him as

---

[1] Dennis Lankford, *I Defy* (London: Allen Wingate Publishers, Ltd., 1954), p. 32.

[2] Lloyd W. Pate, *Reactionary* (New York: Harper & Bros., 1955) p. 56.

the leader of the entire group of officers, and they concentrated their pressures on him. At first they attempted to subvert his moral and ethical standards by promising better treatment and food for all if he would co-operate in their propaganda ventures. The enemy was attempting to form progressive groups of officers to write propaganda leaflets, appeals for peace, articles condemning the United States and the war, and seditious letters and other literature. When he refused to co-operate, Major McLaughlin was subjected to intimidation, torture and threats of death.

No discussion of Camp 5 at Pyoktong can be complete without at least mentioning Captain Emil J. Kapaun, Chaplains Corps, U. S. Army.[1] The Catholic priest was one of the great heroes of the prison camps. Scarcely a returning prisoner who knew him failed to laud his heroic behavior and selfless interest in his fellow-men.[2] On November 2, 1950, Chaplain Kapaun had voluntarily remained with a group of wounded soldiers from his own unit, the 2d Battalion, 8th Cavalry Regiment, 1st Cavalry (Infantry) Division. After capture he was taken to Pyoktong where he was active in holding secret religious services for all

---

[1] The activities of Father Kapaun are the central theme for the following:
Ray M. Dowe Jr., *The Ordeal of Father Kapaun* (Notre Dame, Indiana: The Ave Maria Press, 1954); and
Father Arthur Tonne, *The Story of Chaplain Kapaun* (Emporia, Kansas: Didde Publishers, 1954).

[2] Father Patrick O'Connor, "Faith Behind Barbed Wire", *Hawaii Catholic Herald*, October 16, 1953.

his fellow-prisoners. He stole food and sneaked into the enlisted compounds to distribute it. Though his ministrations were available to all, Marine Warrant Officer Felix McCool was one of the last to receive the Sacrament of Penance from the priest before the latter died from the effects of malnutrition, gangrene, pneumonia and an embolism.[1]

During the time that most of Kanggye's inmates marched to Chongsong and Pyoktong, the smaller group of 60 undertook a march of an entirely different nature. They were led southward through the rugged mountains of north central Korea by way of Tokchon, Yangkok, and Majon-ni.

Two of the 24 Marines with the group became sick during the long march south. One of these, Private First Class Leon Roebuck, complained of stomach pains on March 10th. Two days later he died and was buried along the route of march.[2] In the second case Private First Class Hans W. Grahl had become ill and had been carried for several days by Corporal Aguirre. Grahl became too sick even to be carried and the Chinese finally left him behind, presumably with Koreans.[3] He was never seen again and is presumed to have died shortly after being left in the wake of the column.

---

[1] *Hawaii Catholic Herald*, October 15, 1953.

[2] Letter from CG, 1st MarDiv to CMC, serial 23448 of May 31, 1951; enclosure 6, statement of Staff Sergeant Charles L. Harrison.

[3] Mathis letter.

On April 5th, after leaving Majon-ni, the prisoners were split into two groups with some Marines in each. It appeared to Staff Sergeant Charles L. Harrison that his group was brought south to a warmer area where they could more easily survive during the chilly spring, and where they could perform working details in rear of the front lines. Sergeant Harrison had considerable experience with Orientals. He had been captured by the Japanese at Wake Island on December 23, 1941, and held prisoner until his release on Hokkaido on September 7, 1945. His previous experience as a prisoner of war taught him how to survive as a POW. He was able to read and speak enough Japanese to gain information and to determine his general location from sign posts. He was helped in this regard by Corporal Saburo "Sam" Shimamura, a U. S. Army interpreter who had been attached to the 1st Marine Division, and by Marine Corporal Andrew Aguirre who learned to speak Mandarin Chinese during a tour of duty in North China after World War II. Between them, they were able to converse with natives and keep informed as to their location.

As a matter of interest, Sergeant Harrison compared the treatment by the Japanese and the Chinese. As he puts it, "The Japs hated our guts and were just plain mean. I admired them for this because they really believed in their cause and were loyal to it." On the other hand, he refers to the false friendship and deceit of his Chinese captors.[1]

---

[1] Harrison letter.

When the other officers, Army and Marine, were marched west to Pyoktong, Lieutenant Frank E. Cold was marched southward with the promise of eventual release. He had been told that his fellow officers were being taken north to a university for further training.[1] Master Sergeant Gust H. Dunis from the Military Police Company was the second ranking Marine in the column. The 56 year old Sergeant Dunis had barely survived the brutal march to Kanggye, and on at least one occasion during that march he sat down in the snow and dared the Chinese to shoot him. En route to the battle line in the spring of 1951 Gust Dunis amused himself and a few Korean natives by removing his false teeth, a feat which earned him the open-mouthed admiration of the natives and an occasional cigarette or piece of yud.[2]

Central direction fell to Staff Sergeant Charles L. Harrison who became the obvious leader and who guided his fellow-Marines on their way to eventual freedom. He was assisted by Corporal Saburo Shimamura and Staff Sergeant James Nash.

When the members of the group were interrogated by Lieutenant Colonel William A. Wood, Operational Intelligence Officer on the staff of Commander, Naval Forces, Far East, Colonel Wood concluded that Harrison had clearly been the

---

[1] Letter from CG, 1st MarDiv to CMC, serial 23448 of May 31, 1951; enclosure 2, statement of First Lieutenant Frank E. Cold.

[2] Martin, p. 109.

most effective leader in the entire group.[1]

By April 13th, the prisoners had arrived in the Chorwon area. They were told they would be released at a safe place somewhere in the Chorwon-Kumhwa area. At that time the United Nations forces were advancing northward.

On April 22nd, the Chinese launched their spring counter-offensive. Four days later they brought some 300 newly captured prisoners into the Chorwon area. This number included four Turks, two British, one U. S. Navy pilot and one U. S. Marine pilot, Captain Paul L. Martelli. Captain Martelli, an F4U fighter pilot from VMF-323, was shot down on April 3, 1951, and during the two and a half years he spent as a prisoner he proved to be a staunch resister to Communist indoctrination and a thorn in the side of the Chinese.[2]

The bulk of the new prisoners were from the U. S. 24th and 25th Divisions. A temporary prisoner of war camp was set up and the newly captured prisoners were joined by the two small groups already in the area. The POW's who by then had five month's experience in CCF hands helped organize camp routine.

The Chinese informed the 58 POW's from Kanggye that half of them would be released and half would be used to help fight for peace within the POW camp, but they deliberately withheld the information as to which individuals

---

[1] Wood interview.

[2] Fink, MS comment.

would be released. The POW's were taunted with vague promises of freedom and, in the words of one of the Chinese interpreters, would be left to "sweat it out." Finally on May 18th, 18 Marines from the original group and Shimamura, the nisei interpreter, were separated from the main group. The remaining 39 members of the original group were marched north again. This group included Technical Sergeants Mathis and Roberts, Corporal Aguirre and PFC Yesko.[1] Upon his release at the end of the war, one of the Army personnel who returned north with this group, Lieutenant George P. Shedd of the 3d Infantry Division, reported that the Chinese told him they were not released because of the tactical situation.[2] Shimamura and the 18 Marines were given safe conduct passes and told they would be taken to the area in which the 1st Marine Division was operating. There they were to be released. For once, they did not have to walk. The group of 19 was taken to Chunchon by truck. They were then taken under guard and marched around in the vicinity of the front lines. On May 24th, when they were fairly close to the battle area, an artillery bombardment registered nearby. The Communist guards fled in confusion seeking cover. Fortunately, they all fled in the same direction. The prisoners ran in the opposite direction and headed for high ground where they successfully eluded the guards. From their vantage point

---

[1] Mathis letter.

[2] *The Washington Post*, August 27, 1953, p. 7.

the escapees watched Communist troops retreating past them during the balance of the day and that night. The next day, May 25th, the Marines fashioned makeshift air panels from wallpaper they stripped from a ruined Korean house. They spelled out "POWS - 19 RESCUE" and their signal attracted the attention of Captain Edward N. Anderson flying an Army observation plane.[1] The pilot radioed their position to an Army reconnaissance unit, and three Army tanks were sent forward to escort the escapees to final safety. They entered friendly lines in the vicinity of Chunchon, the first and only group of prisoners to experience Communist indoctrination and to reach freedom after a prolonged period of internment.

Roughly two months after their return, the 19 men were interviewed by Harold H. Martin, a staff writer for the Saturday Evening Post. In his article describing the experiences of the group, Mr. Martin made a point of the fact that none of the Americans had been converted to Communism but had merely played along with the Communists to gain their own release.[2] Their tactics succeeded.

The lenient policy at Kanggye had been reflected in intensive indoctrination for all and in surprisingly easy treatment for some. After leaving Kanggye, the Marines who the Chinese believed to be progressive were released; the remainder together with the commandos and soldiers from

---

[1] Ibid., May 26, 1951, p. 2.

[2] Martin, The Saturday Evening Post, August 25, 1951, p. 109

Kanggye undertook difficult marches to new camps where the lenient policy was considerably more harsh in its application. The prisoner of war compounds of Pyoktong and Chongsong also proved to be indoctrination centers. Still another camp played a part in the lives of a few of the Marines captured in 1950. The Valley near Kanggye had its own role quite apart from the other places at which Marines were held or processed.

Upon arrival at The Valley, Sergeant Griffith and the Dowling brothers were initially confined in a pig pen which they shared with several other POW's including two Marines, Corporal Robert Arias and PFC George V. Cowen. The latter two had been captured during the heavy fighting in the hills north of Yudam-ni on the 27th and 28th of November. Arias marched from Yudam-ni to The Valley in subzero weather in his stocking feet, a step made necessary when his captors appropriated his shoe pacs for their own use.[1]

Arias and Cowen informed Sergeant Griffith that another Marine had been removed from the separation center and taken southward to make a surrender broadcast. Whether or not the broadcast was made is not known. Sergeant Griffith spoke to the individual only briefly and never saw him again after their brief encounter in The Valley even though later they were confined in the same camp for a short period.[2]

---

[1] Griffith letter.

[2] Ibid.

After a brief incarceration in the pig pen, the Dowling brothers, both still in reasonably good physical condition, were marched away to another camp. Griffith was assigned to a shack with other wounded prisoners. Marine Corporal Harry M. Bringes from 4/11 eventually joined him as an occupant of the shack, having been transferred to this "hospital" from Kanggye. The two Marines struck up a close acquaintance but Bringes refused to eat. Sergeant Griffith forced Bringes to eat, argued with him, babied him, and finally, after almost four months in The Valley, helped bury him in a mass grave. Bringes was one of the few Marines to die from "give-up-itis", the term applied to the apathy that struck countless POW's and claimed a heavy toll of lives.[1]

Whereas only 15 to 20 POW's died at Kanggye, the death rate in The Valley earned that collection center an ominous reputation, at least among its population. There was no organized indoctrination, however, and the POW's were generally left to themselves. Disturbed by the infestation of lice, the filth, the steady attrition among the sick and wounded prisoners, and half starved from an inadequate diet, Sergeant Griffith attempted to escape. He pretended to go to the latrine late one night, and, finding the guard asleep, he limped down the path leading out of the valley. He was undetected and continued walking until dawn when he located a shed next to a Korean hut.

---

[1] Ibid.

Inside the shed he found a complete set of clothing, so he exchanged his threadbare dungarees for the baggy Korean clothes and then hid in a pile of rice bags to rest.[1]

After about four hours sleep, the best he had had in months, Sergeant Griffith arose and walked directly up to the hut where he knocked at the door. Through sign language he made his hunger known and was given a large and most satisfying meal. While he was eating, his host's son was out contacting a military patrol which even then was on Griffith's trail. He had barely finished his meal and a hand-rolled cigarette when a group of Communist soldiers closed in and recaptured him. His shoe pacs were taken from him, and he was made to walk back to The Valley in his threadbare ski socks. The patrol took Griffith to an officer, probably their company commander, who promptly beat the Marine across the face with a stick. Griffith was then made to walk up a nearby hill, and, as he did so, the Chinese officer fired a rifle in his general direction. Griffith was called back by the officer, and then directed to walk up the hill a second time. This time a shot was fired so close to his head the sergeant heard the sharp snap as the bullet narrowly missed him. He was called back a second time and again beaten about the face until his old wounds bled.

Sergeant Griffith was put back into the pig pen which he shared with a soldier who had been caught steal-

---

[1] Ibid.

ing potatoes. Within about a week and a half the soldier became demented and soon died. Griffith endured the pig pen for a month before he was returned to a regular hut. It was there he learned that an Army lieutenant had informed the Chinese of his escape, thus triggering an early search. As for the informer, Sergeant Griffith had this to say:

> I know the Army Lts name and so does a lot of other POWs. However, he died, so there is no need to hurt those he left behind. The story of my escape had been told to some Marine officers who were POWs. They asked me about the Army Lt., at that time he was housed with the Marine officers. They had all the details and had the Lt. reached freedom I am quite sure charges would have been brought against him. The Marine officers always did what they could for us, and to me, whenever I had an opportunity to talk to one of the officers it seemed to give me a big lift. That certain "something" that seems to weld men together prevailed more among the Marine POWs than it did with the other captured UN Troops.[1]

The officer who had informed on Sergeant Griffith was sent to Camp 3 briefly and thence on to the "Bean Camp" located at Suan, about 45 miles south east of Pyongyang. He died while at that camp.[2]

The lenient policy was a mania with the Chinese. It is quite possible that they really believed they were being humane and lenient with the prisoners of war. Anyone who has spent any time in the Orient has undoubtedly seen examples of the callous treatment meted out by many officials to underlings, offenders, criminals or political

---

[1] Ibid.

[2] Perry interview, November 14, 1960. 1stLt Felix Ferranto was one of the officers to whom Griffith related the incident.

prisoners. It would seem that by comparison many of the POW's received less vicious treatment than did some of the local civilian prisoners. But if this is true to any degree, it would also seem that the lenient policy did not filter down to the North Korean military or paramilitary forces. They were brutal and barbaric to a degree difficult to imagine. Although Marines did not often have contact with North Korean forces after October, 1950, one of the encounters serves to illustrate the murderous nature of the enemy.

Having withdrawn from Hungnam in December, 1950, the 1st Marine Division rested and refitted at Masan in South Korea. During the first three months of 1951 the Marines conducted antiguerrilla operations in the mountainous areas surrounding the port city of Pohang-dong.[1] According to official statistics no Marines were captured by the enemy during this period.[2] The vagaries of statistics have obscured the fate of a small group of Marines which did fall into enemy hands.[3]

When hunting guerrillas, units of the 1st Marine

---

[1] 1st MarDiv HistD, January, 1951.

[2] USMC Casualties.

[3] Except as otherwise noted, details of Patrol No. 8 were derived from the following sources:
    1st MarDiv HistD, January, 1951, p. 14; and
    5th Marines, Unit Report, February 1951, Annex B to 1st MarDiv HistD, February, 1951, p. 20; and
    Korean Communications Zone, War Crimes Division, Interim Historical Report, KWC No. 185, pp. 20, 24, 34. Cited hereafter as KComZ War Crimes Report.

Division sent out numerous squad patrols, each generally accompanied by one or more South Korean policemen. The police served as guides and interpreters without whose assistance the Marines would have been unable to differentiate between friendly South Koreans and enemy guerrillas. On January 28, 1951, eleven patrols were sent out by the 5th Marine Regiment. One of these, patrol number eight, was due to be picked up by motor patrol three days later. Patrol eight failed to make the rendezvous.

The men of Company B, 1st Battalion, 5th Marines were particularly surprised when that patrol failed to return. The squad had worked together for some time and at least two of their number, the squad leader and the senior fire team leader, had been in Korea since landing with the 1st Marine Brigade in August the previous year. According to the company commander, these two noncommissioned officers had considerable experience in patrolling, and the squad leader had the reputation of being able to smell the enemy, an appellation reserved for competent and combat-tested Marines.[1] The Company B Marines were generally of the opinion that the squad had either been betrayed by their Korean guide or had been surprised by the enemy dressed in civilian clothing.

The patrol continued on its mission for three days when a Korean woman witnessed its surrender to North Korean

---

[1] Personal interview with LtCol James T. Cronin, USMC, August 30 and September 4, 1960.

guerrillas who had set up an ambush along a trail near her village. Later the woman related the incident to U. S. Army military policemen who were investigating the case.[1]

The Marines were taken to a house in the general vicinity and were kept there as prisoners for a week. The guerrilla commander then directed his lieutenants to prepare to execute the prisoners secretly. Shallow graves were dug in the frozen earth, ready to receive the victims. On February 5, 1951, the day appointed for the executions, the Koreans led the first prisoner forth alone. He was made to strip naked in the chill February winds. Once stripped, his hands were bound behind his back with wire and he was forced to sit down. Completely helpless now, the unfortunate prisoner suddenly found himself serving as a practice dummy for the cruel bayonets of a sadistic enemy. And one by one, the ten Marines died solitary deaths from multiple bayonet slashes in chest and back. Some who resisted or who died too slowly to suit their captors, were slaughtered by crushing butt strokes from the heel or toe of the rifle stock. One of the Marines was interred in a standing position, buried up to his eyebrows. Another had a large rock resting on his chest. The remainder were dropped into shallow graves and hastily covered over. In addition to the ten Marines, ten Republic of Korea soldiers, four National policemen,

---

[1] 5th Marine HistD, March, 1951, p. 25.

and one civilian died in a similar manner. The only difference in treatment meted out by the guerrillas seems to have been more detailed mutilation of the corpses of their Korean victims. Many of the latter had ears and noses cut off and eyes stabbed out.

A patrol from the 2d ROK Division found the bodies on March 7, 1951, while investigating a National Police report. The corpses gave mute testimony of the details of the atrocity. Later, as circumstances would have it, two captured North Korean lieutenants confessed to their participation in the crime. Their confessions were obtained at different times and places, but the factual data was the same. With both the victims and the perpetrators in United Nations custody, the case of the Marine patrol numbers one of the 34 Korean war crime cases referable to higher headquarters for action as a bona fide war crime. And here again, the statisticians came into play. Patrol number eight graced the missing in action lists from February 11th until March 21st, when the names were transferred to the killed in action list.[1] As a consequence, their names are neither listed on the final statistical compilation of Marines who were captured by the enemy and who died in their hands nor are they among the 391 Marines missing and presumed dead. They represent ten of the 3169 ground Marines listed as killed in action.[2]

---

[1] 1st MarDiv, Personnel Daily Summary 82, March 21, 1951; and
1st MarDiv, Casualty Bulletin 45-51, February 11, 1951.

[2] USMC Casualties.

CHAPTER V

A PUNCHBOWL AND A PALACE

Thirty-one Marines were captured by the enemy during 1951. Of that number 11 enlisted Marines were captured in ground combat and 20 officers were downed over enemy territory by ground fire or aircraft accident. In general the aerial and ground combat actions were not directly related to each other. Although the paths of the captured Marines often crossed, the pattern of activity falls into perspective when viewed in the separate elements of ground and air action. For that reason the activities of the 1st Marine Division during 1951 will be set forth first, followed by the individual cases of plane losses and pilot experiences. Where possible, the movement of groups will be highlighted.

The 1st Marine Division was in Eighth Army reserve when 1951 dawned. The Marines performed in an antiguerrilla role until late February when a general advance, Operation Killer, was ordered to deny important positions to the enemy and to destroy as many hostile troops as could be found.[1] In order to use the Marines in the new

---

[1] John Miller, Jr., Owen Carroll, and Margaret E. Tackley, Korea 1951-53 (Washington: Office of The Chief of Military History, Department of the Army, 1958), p. 18.

offensive the 1st Marine Division was committed near Wonju as part of U. S. Ninth Corps. The division's casualties jumped from 62, suffered during antiguerrilla operations in January, to 233 in February as the offensive operations got underway. By March 1st the United Nations offensive had gained positions roughly halfway between the 37th and 38th parallels. A second offensive was launched on March 7th, Operation Ripper, and for the next six weeks small inroads were made on a stubborn enemy.[1]

In April the 1st Marine Division was relieved in the Hongchon area by elements of the U. S. 2d and 7th Divisions. The Marines continued to operate as part of U. S. Ninth Corps; their mission was to advance and secure designated objectives north of the 38th parallel. On April 21st the 1st Marine Division launched its attack on Corps order and encountered moderate to heavy resistance. The 1st Korean Marine Corps Regiment, attached to the 1st Marine Division, seized Hwachon Dam and the Division Reconnaissance Company entered the city of Hwachon. The 5th Marines on the right of the division zone captured the high ground dominating Sinpung-ni while on the left the 7th Marines advanced about 5,000 yards. At 10:15 P.M. that night the Chinese Communists launched their spring offensive with a large-scale attack along the eastern front. The 6th Republic of Korea Division on the left of the Marines began to fall back when the Chinese forced deep penetrations in their posi-

---

[1]Ibid., p. 21.

tions. The enemy rushed into the void left by the ROK's and threatened the exposed flanks of the Marine Division.[1] The night of 22-23 April the Chinese overran the 213th Field Artillery Battalion, a U. S. Army unit which had been supporting the 6th ROK Division and whose positions had been uncovered by the unexpected withdrawal of the South Koreans. The 1st Battalion, 1st Marines, shifted west to protect the division left flank and rear from the new threat. The 4th Battalion, 11th Marines, was directed to provide liaison and forward observer teams to 1/1 and to lay one battery for direct support.[2] During the ensuing action on April 23, Corporal William E. Schultz of Headquarters Battery, 4/11 was captured by the enemy.

The U. S. 2d Division occupying positions to the right of the Marines withdrew and the Chinese quickly rushed troops forward. For several days Marines came under attack from both flanks as well as from the engagement raging across their entire front. In the general withdrawal ordered by the U. S. Ninth Corps commander, the 1st Marine Division fell back to the Soyang River near Chunchon. The 1st Marines covered the withdrawal of the 5th and 7th Regiments and other division units.[3]

---

[1] 1st MarDiv, HistD, April, 1951, pp. 1-3.

[2] 11th Mar, HistD, April, 1951, p. 1. The 4th Battalion, a 155mm Howitzer Battalion, normally provides general supporting fires and does not customarily furnish forward observer teams to infantry units. Instead, missions are unually called for by forward observers of the three 105mm direct support battalions through the appropriate fire direction centers.

[3] 1st MarDiv, HistD, April, 1951, p. 3.

On April 28th and 29th U. S. Ninth Corps divisions again fell back, and formed a general defense north of Hongchon. While the Marine division slogged southward over rain-gutted roads, three captured Marines were taken north by the enemy.

On May 1, 1951, operational control of the 1st Marine Division shifted from U. S. Ninth to U. S. Tenth Corps. For the first three weeks of May the division defended in place and sent strong patrols forward to maintain contact with the enemy. On the 22d, as part of a general United Nations offensive, the Marines attacked northward along the Hongchon-Inje axis scoring gains of about 6,000 meters a day against the enemy's deliberate delaying action.[1] By the end of the month elements of the attached Korean Marines entered Yanggu. Two U. S. Marines had been captured in the ground fighting during May.

Eighth Army had more than restored the positions held the previous month before the Chinese "Fifth Phase Offensive" drove the United Nations forces backward. The new Army positions were established along a relatively narrow transpeninsular line, one which afforded defensible terrain, traversable road systems, and satisfactory lines of communication.[2] During June the United Nations Command continued pressing forward to secure local tactical victories. Termed Operation Piledriver, the June offensive

---

[1] Ibid., pp. 1-2.

[2] Miller, et al., pp. 110-11.

succeeded in attaining its principal terrain objectives. Action for the last part of June was confined to developing defensive lines, patrolling and local skirmishes which, although fierce and bloody, did not materially affect the dispositions of either side.[1] The 1st Marine Division fought a violent battle in the Punchbowl area, a circular depression north of Inje, and suffered heavy casualties. Only the fighting at Inchon in September, 1950, and the Chinese onslaught of November, 1950, had produced greater casualties. The June battle along the southern rim of the Punchbowl cost the Marine Division 183 killed, 2,035 wounded, and 3 missing. The missing are presumed to have been killed during the fighting. No ground personnel were captured by the enemy during the month.

Truce negotiations commenced on July 10, 1951, and all along the front the fighting died down. Action was characterized by artillery fire, air strikes, and naval gunfire bombardment of key coastal areas. Offensive ground operations consisted of limited battalion and regimental attacks to attain favorable terrain, to capture prisoners, and to discourage enemy probes and attacks.[2] With the comparative lull in fighting casualties dropped perceptibly although they did not cease altogether.

An enlisted Marine from the 1st Division was captured

---

[1] Ibid., pp. 111-12.

[2] Ibid., p. 115.

on July 2, 1951, under weird circumstances. PFC Billie J. Lessman of Headquarters Battery, 11th Marines, disappeared. At first there seemed to be no explanation for his absence, no combat action to account for a casualty in his unit, no real reason to explain his disappearance. He simply vanished. Subsequent investigation revealed a drinking party, a one man liquor-procuring detail, a wrong turn -- PFC Lessman was gone.[1]

The 1st Marine Division manned defensive positions throughout the first half of July. Contact with the enemy was maintained by aggressive patrolling. The KMC Regiment located on line between the 1st and 5th Marines attempted to establish a forward patrol base, but their four-day attack encountered extensive mine fields and heavy enemy fire which forced the Korean Marines to resume the defensive. The 1st Marine Division was scheduled to pass to Tenth Corps reserve, and relief of division elements started on July 15th, one day too late for PFC Alfred P. Graham, Jr.

Graham was a member of an H/3/5 patrol which was sent forward of the main line of resistance on July 14th, 1951, and he was captured while returning from the mission. When interviewed after the Korean armistice, Graham related the details of his capture and subsequent imprison-

---

[1] Letter from 1stLt Lester A. Rowden, Jr., 045629, to the Commanding Officer, 11th Marines, August 5, 1951, subject: Report of investigation, case of PFC Billie J. Lessman.

ment.[1] As he told it, both he and another Marine were the rear guard following in trace of the patrol at a distance of about 100 yards when the enemy suddenly opened fire. Graham was knocked out by a concussion grenade, and his companion was killed. The Chinese took PFC Graham prisoner and marched him off to a nearby bunker where he was subjected to a brief interrogation. Shortly thereafter he was marched north a distance of about 25 miles to what he thought was a divisional headquarters. There he was interrogated by a Korean major who claimed to have attended the University of Chicago in 1932. He also encountered another Marine prisoner of war. The latter, although unnamed by Graham during his interview, could only have been PFC Billie Lessman who had wandered into captivity two weeks earlier. The two Marines were forced to stand all night long and were alternately questioned. The following afternoon when the guards seemed slack, the two captives sneaked away and went north hoping to elude their pursuers before eventually turning south. They stopped at a Korean farmhouse and tried to pass themselves off as Russian pilots by drawing a hammer and sickle in the dirt, this in spite of the Marine emblem and letters USMC stencilled on the breast pockets of their combat uniforms.

---

[1] Albert P. Graham Jr., as told to Warren Unna, "Area POW Tells Own Dramatic Story", *The Washington Post*, August 16, 1953, pp. 1 and 11.

After approaching two farmhouses and getting raw potatoes and rice, they visited a third house where they stumbled into seven or eight Koreans and were recaptured. They were beaten with a submachine gun and their hands were bound behind their backs with communication wire. One of Graham's legs was tied to one of Lessman's legs, and the two Marines were marched back to the site of their escape. The Korean major beat them and interrogated them for three days.

Later in the week, their hands still bound behind their backs, the Marines were marched northward for about ten miles and then continued the trip in a truck to a North Korean collection center at Kung Dong about 16 miles south east of Pyongyang. Graham estimated that there were about 120 American and 3,000 South Korean POW's at Kung Dong when he arrived there early in August. After a six-week stay at the collection center, a period during which several POW's died from beriberi, the American POW's began a 31-day march north to a regular camp along the Yalu River.

The first leg of the march took them to Pyongyang. En route the prisoners ate apple cores, cabbage scraps, and whatever else they could find when they made short halts. Some POW's smoked paper, heavy wall paper or whatever else would burn and could be rolled into the shape of a cigarette. At Pyongyang the prisoners were formed into squads and platoons, and they were each given a blanket, a cotton padded overcoat and cheap shoes. A pair of shoes

Graham had been given earlier lasted only three days before falling apart, so he used the wornout pair for wading streams and the new pair for the northward march along Korean roads and trails.

As Graham later indicated, he became ill during the long march. PFC John R. Dunn, a soldier from the 2d Division who had been captured on July 24th, gave his blanket and sugar ration to the sick Marine.[1] Curiously, Dunn was one of the 21 soldiers who later refused repatriation, yet at the time of his association with Graham his conduct appears to have been above reproach. About 120 Americans began the gruelling 31 day march to the Yalu; 80 survived and reached Camp 3 at Changsong on October 16, 1951. Graham's weight had dropped from 155 to about 85 pounds.[2]

Only one Marine was in Camp 3 when Graham and Lessman arrived. He was PFC Robert L. Batdorff who, with two other Marines, had been captured on Fox Hill at Toktong Pass the previous November. The Marines who had been taken to Camp 3 from Kanggye and The Valley had been transferred to nearby Camp 1 in August, 1951.[3]

The relative lull in ground fighting continued until late August when truce negotiations were suspended. General James A. Van Fleet commanding Eighth Army ordered an offensive by Tenth Corps to seize the entire Punchbowl. The

---

[1] Pasley, p. 163.
[2] The Washington Post, August 16, 1953, p. 11.
[3] Griffith letter.

1st Marine Division in concert with the other divisions of Tenth Corps attacked on August 31st. Initial objectives were seized by September 3d and on the 11th the division renewed the attack north to the Soyang River seizing planned objectives on September 18th. Two Marines were captured in the September fighting. They were PFC Delbert L. Marks, Company D, 1st Engineer Battalion, and Corporal Edwin B. Jones from Headquarters, 11th Marines.

After capture the two men were taken west to Kung Dong, probably arriving there shortly after the departure of Graham and Lessman who left with a large group in mid September. Marks and Jones were interned there with four Army enlisted men and one Air Force officer until it was their turn to march north in November.[1]

After the bitter actions at the Punchbowl in September, the 1st Marine Division devoted the following month to defending its gains and improving defenses. Only one ground Marine was captured in October. PFC Billy A. Brown, B/1/1, fell into enemy hands on the 9th. It would appear that he was processed to the rear without much delay because according to the Chinese he was in Camp 5 at Pyoktong in December.[2]

---

[1] Personal notes of Major Gerald Fink made in 1953.

[2] Prisoner of War lists were exchanged by the United Nations Command and the Communist side on December 18, 1951, and Brown was reported in Camp 5 on that list. Major U. S. newspapers printed the complete list of American names on December 19, 1951. In this specific instance, I referred to The Call Bulletin (San Francisco), December 19, 1951, p. 16.

On November 12, 1951, General Matthew B. Ridgway, Commander in Chief, United Nations and Far East Commands, ordered the Eighth Army Commander, General Van Fleet, to cease offensive operations and begin an active defense of the Eighth Army's front.[1] The character of the conflict returned to that of July and early August, minor patrol clashes and small unit struggles for key outpost positions. Only one other ground Marine was captured before the year closed. PFC Lester A. Ribbeck, F/2/1, was taken prisoner on December 29th and eventually reached Ogul, North Korea.

When the battle lines became comparatively stabilized in 1951, the enemy began to develop his antiaircraft defenses to peak efficiency. Marine pilots engaged in close support, observation, interdiction and armed reconnaissance missions began to encounter accurate and intense ground fire. The number of aircraft losses increased and with it the number of Marine aviators who fell into enemy hands.

Having covered the year 1951 from the standpoint of the 1st Marine Division, it is now necessary to retrace activities of 1951 from the standpoint of the 1st Marine Aircraft Wing.

The first Marine aviator to be captured in 1951 has already been introduced briefly; he was Captain Paul L. Martelli who was shot down by enemy small-arms fire on April 3, 1951. He was attacking ground targets when his

---

[1] Miller et al., p. 205.

oil cooler was hit, and 15 minutes later he was forced to parachute from his stricken plane. His wingman reported that he had fallen or broken loose from his parachute and had been killed. As a consequence Captain Martelli was reported killed in action at that time.[1]

The Marine Captain was taken to a temporary collection center the Chinese had established in the Chorwon area. There he met the 18 Marines who were about to be released.[2] Martelli was taken to "Pak's Palace", a notorious interrogation center near Pyongyang. The "Palace" was so named by prisoners of war who titled it after Major Pak, the sadistic North Korean officer who was the chief interrogator. The Secretary of Defense Advisory Committee on POW's concluded that Pak's was the worst camp endured by American POW's in Korea,[3] and Captain Martelli was the first of several Marines who were processed through Pak's Palace.

On May 1st another Marine pilot was captured by the enemy. Captain Mercer Smith took off from K-3 airfield at Pohang-dong. It was 1:15 P.M. and Captain Smith and his wingmate were flying mission number 3320, an armed reconnaissance for Marine Fighter Squadron-311. The two F9F-2B jet fighters approached their objective at 6,000 feet.

---

[1] VMF-323, HistD, April, 1951.

[2] ComNavFE Report of Chicom Indoctrination.

[3] The Secretary of Defense's Advisory Committee on Prisoners of War, POW...The Fight Continues After the Battle. (Washington: U. S. Government Printing Office, 1955), p. 9. Cited hereafter as SecDef Advisory Committee Report POW.

The pilots had observed what appeared to be camouflaged vehicles when suddenly Captain Smith radioed that he had a fire in his cockpit. Smith climbed to 16,000 feet and then ejected from his aircraft. He landed safely and was observed to be alive. As the second pilot flew cover, he saw two enemy soldiers standing over the body of the downed pilot. A rescue helicopter appeared on the scene in response to an emergency call, but the helicopter pilot reported Captain Smith had been killed. From this hasty report Captain Smith, like Captain Martelli, was erroneously reported killed in action.[1]

On May 2, 1951, four Marine aircraft reported to the ground control for a close air support mission. It was 7:15 P.M. and almost dark when the initial attack runs were made. Captain Byron H. Beswick, flying his third mission of the day and his 135th mission of his tour, made a strafing run in an attempt to set fire to a napalm tank which had failed to ignite on impact. His plane was hit by small-arms fire during the run. The plane caught fire, and by the time Beswick was able to bail out burning fuel had been thrown back into the cockpit severely burning his entire face, his hands, one arm and part of his right leg. The wounds were raw and shortly covered by suppurating scabs.

Captain Beswick's wingmates observed him parachute,

---

[1] VMF-311, HistD, May, 1951.

land safely, and run up a hill.¹ Downed pilot procedure was followed, but there was only about an hour and a half before total darkness. The late hour and the intensity of ground fire prevented rescue even though the wingman, First Lieutenant Edwing, remained on station until 7:45 P.M.²

Shortly afterward, the downed Marine was captured and placed with a column made up predominantly of British prisoners from the recently destroyed 1st Battalion, the Gloucestershire Regiment.³ In all, about 300 Gloucestershires had been captured and were being taken north. It was Beswick's good fortune that two British medical officers were with the column. Shortly thereafter the Gloucestershire's doctor, Captain Robert Hickey, and the courageous adjutant, Anthony Farrar-Hockley, together with Beswick and about 40 others were separated from the rest of the column.⁴

The main group proceeded to Chongsong, Camp 1, where they were interned next to a large number of American POW's. A British POW who accompanied the main group and who was later decorated for his heroic behavior while a

---

¹Fiter [sic] Bomber Mission Report 1203, (pencilled) enclosure to VMF-323, HistD, May, 1951.

²VMF-323, HistD, May, 1951, p. 1.

³Eighth U. S. Army in Korea General Order 286, May 8, 1951, cited the 1st Battalion, Gloucestershire Regiment, British Army, for holding a vital hill mass April 23-25, 1951, until overwhelmed by enemy masses. The Gloucesters received the Distinguished Unit Citation.

⁴Anthony Farrar-Hockley, The Edge of the Sword (London: Frederick Muller Ltd., 1954), pp. 116-22.

prisoner of war commented on the terrible condition of the American prisoners of war he found at Chongsong, stating that in those early days the Americans had it worse than the British.[1] It appears that no U. S. Marines had reached Camp 1 at this time although several were at nearby Camp 3.

Captain Beswick, with the smaller group, was led along trails and rough roads, unable to see through the crusted scab which covered his entire face. In spite of his painful burns and temporary blindness, he never cried out or complained. Beswick, a selfless man, even offered to give articles of his clothing to other prisoners to wear.[2]

After a few days, the column made its way to Munha-ri, about a quarter of a mile from the Taedong River. Beswick could see through his scabrous eyelids by this time and he was pronounced sufficiently fit by Doctor Hickey to attempt an escape. The doctor and two other British officers, one heroic young Filipino officer, Lieutenant Thomas Batilio, and the Marine Captain were to make up the escape party, but before they could make good their escape, the Chinese split the group into two segments. One group remained at Munha-ri, and the other, which included Beswick, began to march north again.

---

[1] Francis S. Jones, as told to the author by Lance Corporal Robert F. Mathews, BEM *No Rice for Rebels* (London: Garden City Press, 1956), pp. 36-42.

[2] Letter from Major Anthony Farrar-Hockley, DSO, OBE, MC, September 26, 1960.

It was then June, 1951, and within a few days the wirebound figure of Marine Captain Beswick reappeared at Munha-ri. He and four others had tried to escape while on the march, but they had all been recaptured. In three week's time, most of the escapees were released from the solitary confinement to which they had been committed, but Beswick remained in solitary for an even longer period.[1] Eventually, he reached the officers' camp which was established in October, 1951.

The month of May claimed still another Marine pilot. On the 27th, Captain Arthur Wagner was on an armed reconnaissance strike between Hwachon and Kumhwa. He flew a night fighter, an F4U-5N aircraft, in company with two other Marines from All Weather Fighter Squadron-513. As he made a pass going up valley, northwest towards Kumhwa, one of his napalm tanks caught fire and he was forced to bail out of the flaming aircraft.[2]

Captain Wagner was taken to Pak's Palace where he stayed until mid November. He counselled other prisoners at Pak's and helped chop wood, draw water, and cook. In every way possible, he eased the burden of sick fellow prisoners.[3] The 26 year-old Marine resisted the Communists at every turn.

Captain Jack E. Perry, as briefing officer with

---

[1] Farrar-Hockley, p. 123.

[2] VMF(N)-513, HistD, May, 1951.

[3] Day letter.

Marine Fighter Squadron-311, had to beg combat flights whenever he could. By mid June he had over 80 missions, and he was also acutely aware, at least from an intelligence standpoint, of the deadly accuracy of the Communist antiaircraft fire in Singosan Valley. He had drawn a large red circle around the valley on his briefing map and cautioned all squadron pilots about the 37mm mobile antiaircraft which infested the area between Hwachon and Wonsan.[1] On June 18, 1951, Captain Perry, scheduled another mission for himself, a predawn armed reconnaissance of Singosan Valley. Observing a truck convoy, he put his F9F in a dive to make a run on his target. As he released his first bomb, Captain Perry suddenly felt the impact of an antiaircraft round striking his fuel tank. He ejected and parachuted safely to earth where his wingmates last saw him running for cover.[2] Perry was captured within 30 minutes. His Chinese captors showed him bomb holes from numerous strikes in the area, and they pointed out several wounded soldiers. Then, as he describes it, "They laughed like hell." Although Captain Perry failed to see anything funny, he laughed along with them.[3]

Perry was taken to the Gold Mine, otherwise known as Camp 10, where he spent the next four weeks. Next he went to Pak's Palace, but encountered no particularly cruel or unusual treatment there. During his two week

---

[1] Personal interview with Maj Jack Perry, August 18, 1960.
[2] VMF-311, HistD, June, 1951, pp. 1, 27.
[3] Perry interview.

stay at Pak's he observed what appeared to be Russians but had no direct contact with them. Within two months, some of the Russians were actually conducting interrogations of prisoners. Among the Marines whom Perry met at Pak's were Captains Mercer Smith and Arthur Wagner, both shot down in May.

On July 2, 1951, two additional Marines were captured by the enemy. First Lieutenant Leonard C. Taft, an aviator, was on a photo reconnaissance mission flying an OY-2, a liaison type aircraft which carries a pilot and one passenger. First Lieutenant Robert J. O'Shea, a ground officer rated as an aerial observer, accompanied Taft as his observer.[1] The light plane was unescorted and while over enemy lines it was struck by ground fire and shot down. Both Marines were captured. They were taken to Pak's Palace, and in early September Taft joined Captains Perry and Smith and Lieutenant Bell when they were taken north to the Yalu. Lieutenant O'Shea remained at Pak's for several months.

The following day another Marine aviator was lost to the enemy. Captain James V. Wilkins and First Lieutenant Harold Hintz were members of a four-plane armed reconnaissance flight near Yon-dong when Wilkins' plane was hit by small-arms fire.[2] He parachuted safely but was

---

[1] VMO-6, HistD, July, 1951, p. 2.

[2] VMF-312, HistD, July, 1951, p. 3. The returning pilots reported that Captain Wilkins had been shot down by small-arms fire. However, according to a Hungarian

not seen to move after landing. Standard downed pilot procedures were followed and one of the aircraft flying cover was hit. The pilot was forced to make an emergency landing at a forward area landing strip.[1] Captain Wilkins was captured and taken westward across the peninsula moving only at night until he reached the "Bean Camp", 45 miles southeast of Pyongyang.[2] This area was also known as "The Gold Mine". Captain Wilkins was interviewed by Tibor Meray, correspondant for a Hungarian newspaper, and apparently the interview was printed in Hungarian newspapers as well as having been recounted in Meray's book.[3] The Hungarian referred to Captain Wilkins as an "officer of the Navy Air Force", a common error which persisted throughout most of the war since many of the Communists were unable to differentiate between Navy and Marine pilots.

Two Marine night intruders were lost along the Suan-Yuli road in the early morning hours of July 13th.[4] One pilot reported that he was making a napalm run on an enemy convoy. His napalm tank was seen to explode; presumably the second explosion observed was his aircraft. The pilot

---

reporter, Tibor Meray, who interviewed Wilkins after his capture, antiaircraft fire and not small arms shot him down. See:
  Tibor Meray, *Korean Testimony* (Budapest: Hungarian peace Council and the Institute for Cultural Relations, 1952), pp. 12-13.

[1] VMF-312, HistD, July, 1951, p. 3.

[2] Location based on British POW Report, p. 38.

[3] Meray, pp. 12-13.

[4] VMF(N)-513, HistD, July, 1951, p. 16 and Appendix I.

First Lieutenant W. D. Garmany, was never seen or heard from again. First Lieutenant A. E. Olson, the pilot who was scheduled to relieve him on station, disappeared in the same fashion minutes later, but Olson was taken prisoner only to die in enemy hands.

Most of the Marine aircraft downed in 1951 were hit by antiaircraft or small-arms fire. The Historical Diary of Marine Fighter Squadron-311 for July, 1951, however, bore the cryptic note that one pilot and aircraft were believed to have been shot down by enemy MIG jet aircraft on the 21st.[1] First Lieutenant Richard Bell was flying an F9F-2B jet as part of a 16-plane combat air patrol operating in northwestern Korea near Sinuiju. The area was better known as "MIG Alley." Lieutenant Bell's division of four aircraft had been reduced to three when one pilot aborted due to a pressurization failure in his cockpit. The remaining three planes of the division continued on their mission as did the three other four-plane divisions.

Some enemy MIG's had been observed at 11:15 A.M. near the Manchurian border north of the Yalu River but no contact had been made. The Marines were running low on fuel and they began to return to their base at Pohang-dong, heading on a 160° course at 200 knots and at 31,000 feet. Minutes later 15 MIG-15's attacked from four

---

[1] VMF-311, HistD, July, 1951, Enclosure 1, p. 13.

o'clock high.[1] The enemy passed under the Marine aircraft and subsequent attempts to attack the formation were turned aside when the F9F's turned into the MIG's. The section leader noted that Lieutenant Bell was on his wing when he headed for cloud cover, but thereafter contact was lost.

When Bell failed to return to Pohang-dong he was presumed to have been shot down by the MIG's. Actually Lieutenant Bell engaged the MIG's thereby giving his wingmates the opportunity to break contact without further incident. In so doing he used up his fuel and was unable to return to his own lines safely. The Marine pilot parachuted over enemy territory and was captured. Lieutenant Bell was taken to Pak's Palace, and he made the trip north to a regular POW camp in August with Captains Perry and Smith and Lieutenant Taft.

On July 30, 1951, Lieutenant Harold Hintz was leading one of the three flights which formed a special 12-plane strike. On the approach to the target near Pyongyang his aircraft was apparently hit by ground fire. He began an erratic weave and collided with Lieutenant Colonel H. W. Reed leading one of the other two flights. Only one parachute was observed leaving the aircraft, and both planes

---

[1] The "o'clock" system is normally used to designate direction. The direction of flight (nose of the aircraft) represents 12 o'clock. Thus four o'clock would indicate an attack from the right rear; high would indicate that the enemy attacked from a greater altitude.

spun in.¹ Poor weather and intense antiaircraft fire prevented any further investigation by the remaining members of the strike, so they continued on their mission. Hintz had parachuted safely and he was taken to Pak's Palace. He later recounted that Lieutenant Colonel Reed had also bailed out successfully but was hanged for shooting and killing four of the enemy as they closed in to capture him.²

In August, 1951, Korean intelligence personnel brought word to Modo Island that an American pilot had been dragged through the streets of Wonsan and later hanged. Modo was one of the seven islands in Wonsan Harbor that served as focal points for raiding activity by the 41st Commando which, by then, was no longer attached to the 1st Marine Division. In addition, several Korean intelligence organizations operated from the various islands, and Yodo, the main island, later became the headquarters of the East Coast Island Defense Command. Among those on Modo who heard of the unfortunate pilot's fate was Quartermaster Sergeant James Day of the Royal Marines. QMS Day was shortly to learn firsthand that the pilot who was supposedly hanged was Marine Captain Gerald Fink and the story of his death proved to be grossly exaggerated.

Captain Gerald Fink was flying an F4U Corsair on an

---

¹VMF-312, HistD, July, 1951, p. 21 and Appendix A.

²Fink MS comment.

interdiction mission on August 12, 1951. He was attacking vehicles on a main supply route near Sagaru-ri located southwest of Wonsan and about 18 miles from the east coast. Captain Fink came in low, intent on his target and unmindful of the hail of small-arms fire that rose to meet him. The throttle controls were hit and so severely damaged that the throttle quadrant came off in his hands, and he lost control of his engine. One of the pilots heard someone say, "I'm hit, I'm on fire." It was 10:58 A.M.[1]

When Captain Fink attempted to bail out, the canopy jammed crookedly on its tracks making it impossible for him to get free from the stricken aircraft. Fink punched the canopy with his fist causing it to blow off and at the same time inflicting several cuts to his hands. He finally bailed out at a low altitude and after three swings in his parachute he hit the ground.

North Koreans manning nearby positions opened fire and he was struck in the left knee by a bullet from a submachine gun. The Koreans left their position to rush the Marine, and when he reached for his revolver one soldier struck him in the mouth with the butt of his rifle and knocked out two upper front teeth. Later, the absence of the teeth provided some amusement for his fellow prisoners when he appeared in a Christmas show and sang, "All I Want For Christmas Is My Two Front Teeth." At the moment however, the pain was hardly amusing. The soldiers

---

[1] Statement of Captain J. K. Davis, 038764, U. S. Marine Corps, Appendix A, VMF-312, HistD, August, 1951.

also deliberately broke his arm with a butt stroke. Fink set the arm himself later, and aside from a distinctive lump in his humorous bone his treatment proved highly successful.

The enemy took Captain Fink to a hole in the side of a hill where he was kept for about three days. During that time he was given no food, water, or medical attention. The interrogations to which he was subjected were basic and limited to such questions as:"Who are you? What is your name? Are you an American?"

After removal from the hole, Captain Fink was bound with his elbows crooked over a tree branch across his back and his hands tied tightly in front of him. His three North Korean guards dragged him along through several small villages en route to Wonsan. He was unshaven, unwashed, befouled and ill-smelling. The final humiliation occurred during the day and a half in which he lay outside a shattered building on a street in Wonsan. A virtual procession of Korean women spat on him and then squatted and urinated on him as he lay helpless. His flight suit rapidly took on the aspects of a Korean latrine. If he could pick out a single point in his captivity where his morale was at the lowest ebb, it was in Wonsan. Captain Fink felt that his survival was in the hands of God.[1]

After the ordeal in Wonsan, the Marine was taken on an overland trek towards Pyongyang. En route, he was

---

[1] Fink interview.

temporarily held at a place called "Wu's" near Yangdok. Captain Wu, who had lost his testicles to an unfriendly bullet, bore little affection for United Nations pilots. The Communist demonstrated his attitude during the ten days of Captain Fink's stay by administering repeated beatings with a .45 caliber automatic as he tried to pry information concerning naval organization from his captive. The little information he did elicit could hardly have been of value because the ships Fink named had been sunk at Pearl Harbor or in the Battle of the Atlantic.

After 10 days Captain Fink was moved to Yangdok where he remained for an additional 10 days when torrential rains made roads and bridges impassable. The journey then continued by foot and within two hours after leaving Yangdok Captain Fink was able to convince some of the Modo-based Commandos that the rumors of his death were purely rumor. Quartermaster Sergeant James Day and four of his Royal Marine enlisted men (other ranks) had been captured in Wonsan Harbor. Their small boat had lost power and they drifted helplessly ashore into enemy hands. The small group of Royal Marines was on the way to Pak's when they were joined by the U. S. Marine Captain. QMS Day describes their initial encounter thus:

> On the way we stopped at some wayside hut for the night, and early in the morning I heard some shocking language from outside. This was Jerry Fink, who, although wounded in the knee slightly, and having had a very rough time in the Wonsan area, was insisting very loudly and clearly that he should come in to meet us. I think we mutually decided for the guards, that it was better for

>them if we all were sent the same way together, as we were going in the same direction. After that, we had a very pleasant stroll to Pak's helped on the way by a lift in a truck enginerred by Jerry.[1]

They enjoyed at least one heartwarming experience before reaching Pak's when they spent the night in the hut of a North Korean tailor. Even though he had been subjected to many air attacks by United Nations aircraft, the little tailor showed compassion for the prisoners of war by purchasing some raw peanuts for the group. The peanuts played havoc with their bowels, but the POW's appreciated the kindness and the nourishment. At night, the tailor's mother sat with the prisoners in the hut, held their hands, and sang Christian songs to them in her native tongue. "Nearer My God To Thee" rendered in Korean far behind enemy lines had a strangely soothing effect. Seven years after his release, when reminiscing over some of the strange and terrible and wonderful experiences, Gerald Fink, by then a Major, asked, "How can you hate people like that? You can't call them all bastards."[2] He was, however, to meet several who could qualify for that opprobrious term.

The small group continued on towards the North Korean capital, and as they neared Pyongyang they began passing large numbers of Chinese troops. Their North Korean guards generally stopped them and made them sit

---

[1] Day letter, April 14, 1960.

[2] Fink interview.

along side the road whenever Chinese units were encountered. On one occasion, a Chinese soldier tossed some apples to the United Nations prisoners who ate the fruit, cores and all.

At Pak's, the enemy singled out the Marine to be interrogated first while the Commandos looked on. His interrogator was a mountainous Russian woman so large across her posterior that she required the seating space of two chairs. She wore a filmy blue dress and cheap beads and earrings. To make matters more ludicrous, she wore Korean shoes which Fink later described as Korean boondockers, a Marine term for field shoes.

When the Russian behemoth asked through her interpreter why he had come to Korea, Fink replied, "To kill Communists." He was promptly kicked and beaten with sticks expertly wielded by the North Korean guards. After several minutes of beating, Fink was again interrogated, although as much time was devoted to lecturing him on his inhumanity as was devoted to questioning him about military matters.

The Russian inquisitor accused all Americans of bestiality and of murdering women and children. Fink noticed three blond hairs that were growing from the tip of her bulbous nose. As the interrogation continued, he became fascinated by the hairs. The fascination grew into an obsession, until, unable to restrain himself, he leaned forward and neatly plucked one of the hairs off her nose. The North Korean guards immediately set upon him with punches, kicks, and severe blows with their clubs. The commandos, who were looking on, thought the incident amusing, but they were concerned over possible repercussions.[1] Fink spent the next three days in a vermin infested hole in solitary confinement.

It was at Pak's that Captain Fink first saw a man die from dysentery. One of the Royal Marines with QMS Day's party was unable to withstand the combination of starvation and dysentery. Fink helped QMS Day bury the corpse, and the latter described the act as, "Again ordinary you may say, but you see, most of the POW's at Pak's were in such a weak condition it was an effort to do anything."[2]

The weakened condition of the prisoners was the result of brutal treatment, bare subsistence, sickness, lack of medicine and medical care, hard labor, and the constant threats, beatings, and interrogations. In addition to the Royal Marine who died, an Air Force lieutenant colonel, an Army major and two Army captains died of malnutrition, dysentery and, in at least one case, severe beatings by the enemy.

Daily routine at Pak's consisted of digging bomb shelters, carrying water for the Koreans, chopping wood and carrying it into camp, carrying supplies and rice from Pak's Palace into the local town of Yong Song, digging

---

[1] Day letter, September 29, 1960.

[2] Day letter, April 14, 1960.

trenches, and building mud shacks for the Koreans. The work was accomplished despite the poor condition of prisoners, and the Koreans threatened and beat the POW's with little or no provocation.

Other Marines at Pak's in September, 1951, were Captain Wagner and Lieutenants Ferranto and O'Shea. Lieutenant Ferranto had been alone in Chinese hands from the time of his capture in November, 1950, until he was taken to Chongsong in the spring of 1951. When Captain Perry and three other Marine aviators arrived at Chongsong on August 12, 1951, the Marines informed Ferranto that Captain Wagner was at Pak's Palace and that he could be trusted. The information was vital to Ferranto because he was taken south to Pak's shortly thereafter.[1]

Captains Fink, Amann and Wagner frequently held counsel to determine their courses of action and to coordinate their false stories. In general the interrogators pressed for information of naval organization and strategy, apparently not being able to differentiate between Navy and Marine pilots. Lieutenants Ferranto and O'Shea were given hot baths and clean clothes and then were separated from the other POW's[2] Lieutenant Ferranto later summed up his experience in these terms:

> Of my thirty-four months as prisoner more than two years were spent in solitary confinement or isolated with small groups of fellow reactionaries.

---

[1] Perry interview.

[2] Fink interview.

> To my captors I was a hopeless capitolist [sic],
> an organizer with an "unsincere attitude."1

Captain Fink and the surviving commandos remained at Pak's Death Palace from September 8 until October 18th at which time they were sent 18 miles southwest to Kung Dong. The march column included nine Air Force officers and two enlisted men, eight Army officers, six British officers and three other United Nations personnel. They joined the small group of seven men already at Kung Dong, a group that included Marine Corporal Jones and PFC Marks.[2] There was no forced labor so the routine at Kung Dong was less wearing than at Pak's, but the diet was even more restricted. Dysentery, hepatitis and beriberi were rampant among the prisoners. On October 25th the North Koreans administered what they called a "Russian Five-in-One Inoculation." The shot produced high fevers, delirium and extreme diarrhea. Those who were suffering from septic wounds had their dressings changed only every few weeks, and a small aspirin-like tablet was given to the most serious cases.

United Nations air strikes against the Communists continued unabated. While prisoners of war were being collected at Kung Dong, pilots of several United Nations Air Forces were ranging over North Korea attacking ground targets, cutting roads and rail lines, and engaging enemy

---

[1] Letter from LtCol Felix L. Ferranto, USMC (Retired), February 22, 1961.

[2] Major Gerald Fink, U. S. Marine Corps, personal notes dated 1954.

aircraft in MIG Alley. Marine pilots were primarily engaged in the familiar tasks of armed reconnaissance, interdiction, and close air support of ground forces. Some of these Marines were destined to visit Pak's Palace, Kung Dong, and similar places.

On October 4 Marine Fighter Squadron-323 launched a 12-plane strike to cut a railroad near Sariwon. The F4U's approached their target above the cloud cover at 2:30 P.M. After attacking with 100-pound general-purpose bombs, the flight leaders of each of the four-plane divisions held a radio check, and one pilot failed to answer.[1] He was Captain Emanual R. Amann. No one saw him crash, but the Fifth Air Force Joint Operations Center reported that an Air Force pilot had observed an F4U burning in the Sariwon area.[2] Presumably it was Captain Amann's aircraft.

Marine All-Weather Fighter Squadron-513 provided night armed reconnaissance flights as part of Fifth Air Force's interdiction program. Normally a single night-fighter operated with a Navy PB4Y-2 or an Air Force C-47 flare plane. On October 12, 1951, one of the F4U night-fighters was reported overdue.[3]

The Marine pilot, First Lieutenant Robert J.

---

[1] VMF-323, HistD, October, 1951, p. 1, and Appendix D, pp. 1-2.

[2] Statement of Captain J. P. Desmond, 024862, USMCR, Appendix D, VMF-323, HistD, October, 1951, p. 2.

[3] VMF(N)-513, HistD, October, 1951, p. 1.

124

Gillette, survived a crash-landing, and his later exploits were an inspiration to his fellow POW's.

Two more Marine pilots were lost in October. The plane flown by Second Lieutenant Carl R. Lundquist of VMF-312 was hit by ground fire while on a prebriefed rail strike on October 16th. The aircraft lost oil pressure rapidly, and Lieutenant Lundquist was forced to crash-land. A second plane of his flight was also hit, but the pilot reached the coast and made a water landing. An SA-16 rescue plane was orbitting nearby and the second pilot was rescued.[1] Lundquist however, was taken prisoner, but he was fortunate in one respect; he was the only Marine officer captured in 1951 who was not processed through Pak's Palace before being taken north.

On October 30, 1951, First Lieutenant Herman R. Stanfill was shot down while on a close air support mission. It was late afternoon, and Stanfill led another plane in on their target. It was to be the final run before returning to base. The second pilot following in line astern saw Stanfill's plane burst into flames, and then a parachute blossomed. The Marine's wingmates were joined by eight Air Force F-51's and 4 Marine F4U's. As the planes attacked the ridges surrounding the spot where the parachute landed, antiaircraft fire became intense. A helicopter arrived within 15 minutes, but the downed pilot had disappeared into nearby woods. The rescue attempt

---

[1] VMF-312, HistD, October, 1951, p. 1 and Appendix A.

failed.[1] The lieutenant was captured, and eventually he made the trip which was familiar to so many others: Pak's Palace to Camp 2 at Pi-chong-ni.

Meanwhile, during October and early November, 1951, eight additional prisoners of war arrived at Kung Dong. They included Captain Anthony Farrar-Hockley of the Gloucesters, Major Thomas D. Harrison, USAF, and a Turkish private. Major Harrison had lost a leg when he bailed out of his aircraft over North Korea. Finally on November 12th another column of POW's arrived from Pak's. Marine Captains Amann and Wagner and Lieutenant Hintz were among the eight new arrivals. The following day a POW column of about 45 men left Kung Dong and began a death march that was to cover 225 miles in two weeks. The U. S. Marines with the column were Captains Fink, Amann, and Wagner, Lieutenant Hintz, Corporal Jones and PFC Marks.[2]

On the first day of the march North Korean guards threatened to push a sick Air Force captain over a bombed-out bridge. The captain had obviously been in critical condition even before the march began, but in spite of bitter protests by the prisoners the Communists forced the sick officer to attempt the trip. Only the intervention of Captain Arthur Wagner prevented the guards from carrying out their threat to abandon the Air Force

---

[1] VMF-323, HistD, October, 1951, pp. 15-16.

[2] Except as otherwise noted the details of the march are based on an interview with Major Gerald Fink and use of his personal notes dated 1954.

officer.[1] Wagner's effort was to little avail, however, because the Air Force captain died that night. During the remainder of the march Captain Wagner continued to aid his fellow prisoners, frequently carrying those too exhausted to walk themselves.

On November 18th one of the Marines succumbed to muscular and nervous atrophy, extreme malnutrition, and dysentery. The victim was Lieutenant Harold Hintz who had had a mid air collision with another Marine aircraft over Pyongyang on July 30th. There were, in addition to his serious illnesses, some elements of "give-up-itis" in the Lieutenant's death. At least five more POW's died during the march. Six of the POW's were shoeless and they left a spoor of blood as they walked. The one-legged American flier, Major Harrison, hobbled along in rear of the column using a long pole as a crutch. Somehow he was able to complete the march although he finished the latter phase riding in an ox-cart with sick POW's who included Captain Farrar-Hockley.[2]

On November 22, 1951, the battered column reached the Chongsong River. Temperatures were in the low 30's, and there were chunks of ice in the fast flowing river. The prisoners were forced to strip naked and wade across the river, an undertaking which induced several cases of frostbite and caused the deaths of at least two prisoners.

---

[1] Day letter, April 14, 1960.

[2] Farrar-Hockley, pp. 196-97.

The Marines banded together during the terrible march, and the Royal Marines were drawn close to the U. S. Marines.[1] QMS Day and Captain Fink had several long talks and they became fast friends. Day also helped take care of Captain Anthony Farrar-Hockley who fell seriously ill before the column finished its march.[2] On the last two days of their ordeal, Corporal Jones had to be carried and the other Marines shared the burden.

Of interest was the action of the Turkish POW. In turn for better rations, he was armed with a gun given him by the Koreans, and he stood guard over his fellow prisoners. On another occasion he attacked a French Warrant Officer, Fabien Falise, in a fit of pique.[3] His was one of the rare cases of misconduct by a Turk, and appropriate Turkish authorities were later notified of his behavior. It has been rumored that he was lost overboard en route home after the war.

The Koreans showed utter disregard for the welfare and lives of their prisoners during the death march. What was meant to be the POW food ration was sold on the black market. The guards confiscated wrist watches and the few valuable bits of clothing still retained by the United Nations personnel.

On November 26, 1951, after the excruciating march

---

[1] Day letter, April 14, 1960.

[2] Farrar-Hockley, p. 196.

[3] Fink notes.

which had taken a toll in death and debilitation, the exhausted prisoners reached Chongsong. The officers and enlisted men were separated at this point, and Corporal Jones and PFC Marks were taken to Camp 3 where PFC's Graham, Lessman, and Batdorff were confined. The officers entrucked to Camp 2 at Pi-chong-ni which had opened in October. There they joined a number of the officers who had previously been at Kanggye and later Pyoktong: Major McLaughlin, Lieutenants Lloyd, Reid, Turner, and Messman, and Warrant Officer McCool. In addition, Captain Jesse V. Booker, the first Marine POW of the war, had been brought down with a large group from the Manpo Camp. Other Marine officers captured in 1951 who had preceded this column had also been taken to Camp 2, and these included Captains Perry, Martelli, Smith and Beswick, and Lieutenants Bell and Taft.

Four Marine officers were captured in the last few weeks of 1951. They joined their compatriots in Camp 2 the following year. These four officers included two whose planes were disabled by antiaircraft fire during bombing runs: they were Captain Charles F. Martin of VMA-121, lost on November 19th, and Major Judson C. Richardson of VMF(N)-513, lost on December 14th.[1]

Major Richardson, the executive officer of Marine All-Weather Squadron-513, was flying a night armed recon-

---

[1] VMA-121, HistD, November, 1951, p. 2 and statement of Lt. J. C. Corthay, USNR, Appendix 2, VMF(N)-513, HistD, December, 1951.

naissance in a Corsair F4U-5N. When attacking three or four trucks on the enemy MSR near Singosan valley, he was taken under fire by automatic antiaircraft and his plane was hit several times. Major Richardson jettisoned his bomb load without arming it and prepared to bail out. After loosening his shoulder harness and seat belt he found that he was too low to parachute, so he attempted to land the aircraft in a ditching attitude. The impact threw him about 100 feet from the plane and he suffered a broken right arm and wrenched left shoulder. He was seized by Chinese soldiers while trying to crawl for cover.[1]

For the next two weeks Major Richardson was subjected to frequent interrogation dealing mainly with his political beliefs and family background. The Chinese kept him awake by slapping his face and blowing smoke in his eyes. Two days after Christmas the Marine major was taken to the Mining Camp near Pyongyang.[2]

Four days before Christmas Lieutenant Colonel William G. Thrash was flying a torpedo bomber, a TBM-3R, in conjunction with a major strike launched by VMA-121. Lieutenant Colonel Thrash's passengers were the commanding officer and the assistant operations officer of the 1st 90mm Anti-Aircraft Artillery Battalion, 1st Marine Aircraft

---

[1] Major Judson C. Richardson Jr., letter to the Commandant of the Marine Corps, February 23, 1954, Report on Period of Captivity. Filed in service record of Judson C. Richardson Jr., 011918, Code DF, HQMC, Washington 25, D. C. Hereafter all such reports will be cited as "--name-- Report of Captivity."

[2] Ibid.

Wing, Colonel C. W. May and Second Lieutenant Richard L. Still respectively. The two ground officers were accompanying the attack planes in order to analyze the enemy's antiaircraft defenses which by this time were formidable indeed. The TBM was hit by flak at 11:30 A.M. The large torpedo bomber descended in a lazy 360-degree turn and crashed in the snow.[1] The pilot and Lieutenant Still parachuted and survived; Colonel May was apparently unable to open his canopy and he died in the crash.

Lieutenant Colonel Thrash and Lieutenant Still were brought to the Mining Camp where they joined Major Richardson during the last week of December. Their daily fare consisted of two skimpy meals of rice and bread occasionally supplemented with soup made from cabbage or pork rind. The POW's were required to dig coal in the nearby mine shafts, a labor which taxed their declining strength. The coal was loaded in baskets and passed by hand from the mine shaft to small hand carts in which it was hauled over icy roads to the nearby camp.

Interrogations by Chinese continued. They sought to confirm data already obtained and add to their information of UN aircraft and communications, organizations and equipment, and unit locations. The Marines were coerced and threatened with death. Major Richardson reported that he finally wrote untruthful answers to five

---

[1] 1st 90mm Anti-Aircraft Gun Battalion, 1st Marine Air Wing, HistD, December, 1951, Enclosure 3, p. 2; and Speedletter from the Commanding Officer, 1st 90mm A.A.A. Bn., to the Commandant of the Marine Corps, dated December 31, 1951.

questions concerning the Navy.[1]

The three Marines remained at the Mining Camp from late December, 1951, until February 23d, 1952. On that date Major Richardson was taken to Pak's Palace where he was told his previous lies had been detected. A Korean officer asked what unit was employing bacteriological warfare and threatened that he would never leave Korea unless he answered. The pilot denied that any such warfare was being waged, and the next day he rejoined the other Marines for a journey north to Pyoktong and thence to Camp 2.

December, 1951, was important in still another way. It marked the first exchange of POW lists between the Communist side and the United Nations Command. The list handed to the United Nations representatives contained 11,559 names and the location of 11 camps. The distribution of names was as follows:

    3,198 American
    7,142 South Korean
      919 British
      234 Turk
       40 Filipino
       10 French
        6 Australian
        4 South African
        3 Japanese (probably nisei)

---

[1] Richardson Report of Captivity.

1 Canadian

1 Greek

1 Netherlander

The American representative on the two-man Special Committee stated that with tens of thousands of South Koreans missing a figure of only 7,000 Koreans was wholly unbelievable.[1] In addition he claimed that the names of 1,058 Americans previously mentioned in broadcasts or publications were omitted from the list. The Communist side replied that 570 had died, 153 had escaped, and 3 had been released.[2]

The United Nations Command listed 111,734 North Koreans and 20,740 Chinese. In their turn, the Communists complained of romanized names and the omission of 40,000 names. The latter group consisted of South Koreans who had been pressed into service by the enemy; therefore they were not considered genuine POW's by the UNC.[3]

As for the Marines, 19 officers and 39 enlisted were accounted for. Two Navy hospital corpsmen attached to the 1st Marine Division were also listed. They were Hospitalman Chief E. L. Smith and Hospitalman 3d Class Herman Castle. The name of Associated Press correspondent Frank

---

[1] Keesing's Contemporary Archives, III, January 5-12, 1952, p. 11931.

[2] Great Britain Foreign Office. *Korea. A Summary of Developments in the Armistice Negotiations and the Prisoner of War Camps*. Cmd. 8596. June, 1952, p.7.

[3] Ibid.

Noel also appeared. Mr. Noel had been captured on November 29, 1950 when he was trapped with Major McLaughlin's heterogeneous group en route from Koto-ri to Hagaru. Nine Marines later repatriated who were then in enemy hands were not listed. Major Richardson, Captain Martin, and Lieutenant Stanfill had been shot down late in the year and had not yet arrived at a regular POW camp when the Chinese compiled their list. The names of Lieutenant Ferranto, captured in November, 1950, and Lieutenant O'Shea, the air observer who was shot down in July 1951, were also omitted. These two officers were confined near Pak's Palace at the close of 1951. Since they were in Korean hands rather than with the Chinese, presumably their omission was unintentional. The names of four enlisted Marines captured in April and May, 1951, were also missing.

The Communists' list of POW's gave a picture of their growing camp system. Marines represented only a bare fraction of the total number of prisoners of war, but they were present in most of the regular camps then in existence.

The pattern had been established. Ground personnel were usually processed through one of the North Korean collection camps or interrogation centers near Pyongyang. When a sufficient number was gathered at any one point, the prisoners were moved north by truck or on foot. As a rule, they were taken to Camp 5 at Pyoktong. The entire POW Camp system was controlled from the Pyoktong headquarters. From this point the prisoners were usually sent to another camp after a brief interrogation.

Aviation prisoners were led along much the same path but with one notable exception. In almost every case aviators were brought to Pak's Death Palace regardless of where they were shot down. Otherwise, in 1951, aviators were processed in a manner similar to ground troops.

The Chinese evolved a policy of segregating officers from enlisted personnel and separating noncommissioned officers from lower ranks. Initially, segregation meant placing officers in one squad or hut and enlisted men in another. Early in 1951 officers were put in separate companies and removed to different though nearby areas. By mid-1951 commissioned personnel were moved a short distance beyond the confines of enlisted camps. Noncommissioned officers were also separated from the men. Finally in October, 1951, a special camp had been opened for officers at Pi-chong-ni, about 10 miles east of Pyoktong and four miles south of the Yalu River.

The Chinese assigned more than 300 officers to two companies in Camp 2. Additional officers were assigned to the main camp later, but as a rule they were all captured before January, 1952. The officer-prisoners immediately established their own internal command structure based on seniority. The senior United Nations officer present (SOP) assumed responsibility for command of all POW's. This was a hazardous job. The senior officers of each service or national group were frequently jailed and severely punished on the slightest excuse.

Major John N. McLaughlin was the senior Marine present. Lieutenant Commander Ralph Bagwell, USN, a Navy flyer, was the next senior officer of the naval service and thus on one occasion assumed Major McLaughlin's role when that officer was serving one of his many solitary confinements.[1]

Daily routine was established by the Chinese.[2] Prisoners were routed out at dawn and assembled for roll call and physical training exercise. On occasion they were taken for an early morning walk escorted by armed guards. An hour of reading was required before breakfast. This part of the indoctrination program was held by the POW squad leader or monitor appointed by the Chinese. Breakfast was usually a poor grade of rice sometimes supplemented with dikon (turnip) soup. At about 10:00 A.M. a bell in the school house living quarters signalled time for political study. Study in this sense generally meant a harangue by one of the Chinese political officers. At half past noon, the normal lunch hour, prisoners had a brief respite but no lunch. Hot drinking water was provided and even that was a much anticipated luxury. Political study was required again for two hours in the after-

---

[1] The Navy and Marine Corps are separate and distinct services; yet because both are within the same military department (Department of the Navy) there is a close and, to an outsider, an often confusing relationship.

[2] Details of daily routine are derived from Farrar-Hockley, pp. 210-11; Davies, pp. 60-68; and Fink MS comments.

noon. The evening meal consisted of rice, though on occasion soya beans were added. The Sunday fare differed in that rice and pork soup were provided for breakfast, and pork gravy and bread appeared at the evening meal. One small pig was furnished each week as the pork ration for roughly 350 officers, and each person received one or two small cubes of fat.

In the evening the officers were marched to company headquarters and formed in ranks below the steps leading to the main entrance. They stood there to receive a lecture in Chinese from the company commander. About every five minutes an interpreter would break in and translate the message. The Chinese had the means to assure their prisoners participated in study periods and lectures. Food, water, and medicine can be strong persuaders.

Religious expression in Camp 2 was limited. Captain Samuel J. Davies, Anglican Chaplain of the Gloucesters, was the only one of four UN Chaplains captured who survived the war. Chaplain Davies was confined in the officers' camp from October, 1951, until the end of hostilities. Except for a period of solitary confinement he regularly held Sunday morning services at which the Collect, Epistle and Gospel were recited. On Sunday evenings he visited the POW's assigned to kitchen duty and the makeshift hospital located about 50 yards outside the barbed wire compound. The Anglican priest also held community services on Wednesdays.

The Roman Catholic community held its own services

under the leadership of Army Captain Ralph Nardella. This officer assumed responsibility for Catholic services by reason of one of Father Emil Kapaun's dying wishes. Marine officers took no more and no less interest in religious services than did their fellow prisoners.[1]

As 1951 drew to a close the Camp Commander, a fanatical Communist named Ding, ordered the United Nations prisoners of war to prepare and send a New Years greeting to the Commander of Chinese Forces in Korea, General Peng-Te-huai. The senior UN officer, Lieutenant Colonel Gerald Brown, USAF, was determined that the prisoners would not sign. Major John N. McLaughlin voluntarily organized Marine resistance. In the opinion of one of the senior Air Force officers, McLaughlin knew the risk he took and appreciated that severe punishment was virtually certain.[2] The senior officers of other groups also helped organize resistance, and no greetings were sent. An informer reported the resistance to the Chinese and furnished the names of the "reactionary leaders."

The Chinese bitterly resented the organized effort against them, and the United Nations officers who organized the resistance were soon tried by Chinese court-martial.[3]

---

[1] For a more detailed description of life in Camp 2 at this period see:
Farrar-Hockley, pp. 208-52; and
Davies, pp. 66-86.

[2] Letter from LtCol Thomas D. Harrison, USAF, to Director of Personnel, USAF, forwarded to CMC 25Feb54.

[3] Ibid.

In January, 1952, the six ranking officers were sentenced to solitary confinement ranging from three to six months. These officers were Lieutenant Colonel Gerald Brown, USAF; Lieutenant Colonel James P. Carne, D S O, former commander of the Gloucester Battalion; Major Dennis Harding of the Gloucesters; Lieutenant Colonel Charles F. Fry, USA; Major David F. MacGhee, USAF; and Major John N. McLaughlin, USMC.[1]

This step was the first really organized resistance to the Chinese. Although the principals were subjected to months of solitary confinement, coercion, torture, and very limited rations during the bitterly cold months of early 1952, their joint effort laid the foundation for comparatively effective resistance within Camp 2 during the remainder of the war.

---

[1] The "confessions" and sentencing of the six officers are described in the following:
Ibid.; and
LtCol Thomas D. Harrison, "Why Did Some G.I.'s Turn Communist?" Colliers November 27, 1953, p. 27; and
Farrar-Hockley, pp. 215-18; and
Davies, p. 90. Chaplain Davies was no longer permitted to visit the nearby hospital after the officers refused to sign a holiday greeting.

CHAPTER VI

A TUG OF WAR

As 1952 began, the two opposing ground forces settled down to bunker warfare much like the trench warfare of World War I. Air activity maintained the same pattern that had evolved during the previous year. For the sake of clarity ground and air combat in 1952 will be treated separately. There were important developments within the POW Camps, and these will also be considered.

No decisive actions were fought, and there was no significant change in the battlelines. For the Marines the fighting cost between 200 and 300 casualties each month in the Punchbowl area. Later, after shifting westward, the 1st Marine Division faced steadily increasing aggressiveness as the enemy launched larger and more frequent attacks against outpost positions. Enemy pressure reached its peak in October, a month in which 41 Marines were captured. Thereafter fighting slowed down as both sides prepared for another cruel winter in the bunkers.

Ground troops were mainly concerned with improving defensive positions, strengthening bunkers, increasing the amounts of defensive and protective barbed wire surrounding their fighting holes, and adding to the density of anti-personnel minefields. Offensive combat patrols and defensive ambush patrols were widely employed. Reconnaissance patrols roamed the valleys between the opposing defensive lines in the mountains.

In April, 1952, the Commanding General, 1st Marine Division, directed that living and fighting bunkers be combined and built to withstand a direct hit from a 105mm round. An extensive outpost line of resistance (OPLR) was established. A combat outpost line (COPL) backed up the OPLR and protected the main line of resistance (MLR).[1]

The dangers of outpost duty were illustrated forcibly in mid-April. At 11:30 P.M., April 15th, a green flare was observed opposite the 5th Marines' sector. Shortly thereafter an estimated 400 enemy probed the OPLR. The Chinese quickly overran a five-man outpost and assaulted the main part of outpost number 3. The defenders established a perimeter defense in the southeast corner of the outpost and after more than three hours of close combat and hand to hand fighting the Communists were driven off. They left 25 of their dead behind. An additional 45 Chinese were believed wounded and perhaps another 25 were killed but their bodies were evacuated. Three Chinese were captured. Company E, 2d Battalion, 5th Marines, with reinforcements from Weapons Company, 2/5, suffered six killed and 36 wounded.[2] The five Marines who had been overrun

---

[1] 5th Marines Command Diary, April, 1952, p. 1. Historical Diaries were replaced by Command Diaries during 1952-53 which will be cited hereafter as CmdD's.

[2] Ibid., pp. 15-16.

in their forward outpost were reported missing. They were Privates First Class James L. Hale, John A. Jacobs, Jr., and Louis Romero of E/2/5 and Joe A. Glenn and Robert Kostich of W/2/5. All five were captured by the enemy.[1]

Preparations were being made even then to displace the 1st Marine Division from the Punchbowl area in U. S. Tenth Corps zone of action westward to the coast in U. S. First Corps' zone. The movement was completed by May 1st and the Marines occupied positions astride the historic invasion route to Seoul.[2]

On May 9, 1952, a combat patrol from Company A, 1st Battalion, 5th Marines, was sent out to destroy an enemy outpost. The patrol met heavy resistance and Private First Class Arthur J. Gregory was seriously wounded by an artillery or mortar round. Other patrol members placed him on a stretcher and while attempting to evacuate him they came under attack by the enemy. A Chinese grenade landed on Gregory's stretcher inflicting additional wounds. The remainder of the patrol withdrew believing him to be dead. PFC Gregory was reported killed at action.[3]

Gregory was captured and immobilized for four months with serious wounds in arms, legs and feet, and in the right shoulder. The young Marine was treated at four

---

[1] USMC Casualties.

[2] Miller, et al., p. 208.

[3] Commander Naval Forces Far East, Report of Intelligence Processing "Operation Little Switch-April 1953". Cited hereafter as ComNavFE Report of Little Switch.

medical processing centers en route north, living in a series of caves, bunkers and Korean huts. In describing his diet he wrote:

> For the first month I ate only boiled rice and roasted peanuts. I lost probably fifty pounds during the first month or two. The next place I was at, I was fed noodles much of the time. Still at another place we had a variety of food and much of it I thought was pretty good. I learned to like steamed rice and still do.[1]

In November, 1952, PFC Gregory was taken to the POW hospital at Camp 5, Pyoktong, where he remained until shortly before repatriation. He heard that five or six other Marines were somewhere in Camp 5, but never saw any of them. Later he was joined by a Marine PFC captured in October, 1952, and the two remained together thereafter.[2]

The intensity of ground combat fell off in June. The following month probes and patrol clashes increased and 700 Marines were killed or wounded. In August, 1952, the enemy threw company and battalion strength attacks against Marine outposts. Friendly casualties mounted; 159 Marines were killed and 1293 were wounded. Through June, July and August, however, the 1st Marine Division lost no prisoners to the enemy.

The heavy action of August carried over to September, with an intensive effort by the Chinese to seize Marine positions east of the Sachon River. There, positions afforded excellent observation of the Chinese main defensive line and enabled the Marines to lay accurate destruc-

---

[1] Letter from Arthur J. Gregory, September 1, 1960.

[2] ComNavFE Report of Little Switch.

tive and harassing fires on the enemy.[1]

On September 4th Chinese began a series of limited attacks to seize Bunker Hill, the dominating terrain in the 1st Marines sector, and Combat Outpost Bruce in the 5th Marines sector. Their effort coincided with the relief of the 5th Marines by the 7th Marines. The timing was excellent for their purposes because it exploited the natural confusion which exists during a relief of lines.

Shortly before midnight on the 4th the enemy directed intense mortar and artillery fires against Marine outposts and the main line of resistance. Waves of Chinese soldiers followed so closely behind the advancing fires that they suffered some casualties from their own fire. Forward bunkers on Combat Outpost Bruce were destroyed. A squad attempting to reinforce that outpost was hit by artillery fire and six Marines were wounded. The Chinese assaulted from three sides, but after an hour of close-in fighting they were driven off.[2] Three Marines were captured in the fight. They were Privates First Class James L. Irons, Donald W. Lynch, and Norbert Schnitzler.

Six days later Corporal Robert A. Strachan, G/3/7, was captured in the same general area. Like the Marines captured in April, 1952, those taken in September were

---

[1] 1st MarDiv, CmdD, September, 1952, p. 1.

[2] 5th Marines CmdD, September, 1952, p. 6.

sent north to Camp 3 at Changsong where they had no contact with the men captured earlier in the war.[1]

In October the 7th Marines consolidated positions. They manned about eight platoon combat outposts and 15 ambushes of from two to four men each. Planned patrol activity included three squad combat patrols and six fire team reconnaissance patrols, each 24-hour period.[2]

On October 6th an estimated reinforced battalion of Chinese struck the 7th Marines combat outposts across the regimental front. The major action occurred on an H/3/7 outpost. The enemy attack was preceded by heavy preparatory fires beginning at 6:30 P.M. An hour later the outposts called for "Box Me In" fires. Supporting artillery complied by encircling the outposts with preplanned defensive fires. Communications with the outposts ceased. Friendly reinforcements were driven back to the main line of resistance. At 9:15 P.M. limited radio communications were re-established. Shortly thereafter Chinese voices were heard on one of the nets. Enemy troops entered the trenches at about 9:30 P.M. and forced the outnumbered Marines to withdraw.

After midnight two reinforced squads of H/3/7 fought their way out to restore the combat outpost. By 7:15 A.M. the following morning the COP was retaken and 12 Marines

---

[1] Based upon an analysis of reports made by POW's recovered during Operation Little Switch.

[2] A Marine rifle squad contains three four-man fire teams commanded by a sergeant squad leader.

were rescued.[1] The bitterly contested action cost the Chinese an estimated 200 killed. The 7th Marines suffered 10 killed, 128 wounded and 22 missing of whom 13 were taken prisoner. Two of the POW's, Second Lieutenant Henry L. Conway, Jr., G/3/7, and Corporal Sonny Oehl of the regimental 4.2 inch Mortar Company, were taken to an annex of Camp 2; PFC Ollie Asher of H/3/7 never made it to an organized camp; the remaining 10 Marines eventually reached Camp 3 at Changsong.

Most of the Marines were wounded prior to capture. The seriously wounded were taken to the Camp 5 hospital at Pyoktong for treatment. For example, Private Alberto Pizarro-Baez was wounded in one leg and forced to walk on the damaged limb when taken off the outpost hill. Later two other Marines carried him for about two weeks as they moved to the rear, finally completing the trip to Pyoktong by truck. Upon arrival there part of Pizarro-Baez's leg was amputated in a small aid station. The following month his gangrenous stump was amputated a second time. In spite of having had anesthetic he felt the pain when the Chinese sawed through the bone.[2] When the leg was partially healed he was taken to an area of Camp 3 at Changsong and assigned to a company which included 12 other Marines. According to Pizarro-Baez none of these Marines co-operated with the enemy, and three of them actively

---

[1] 7th Marines, CmdD, October, 1952, pp. 4-5.

[2] Letter from Alberto Pizarro-Baez, August 21, 1960.

resisted. He did not recall their names.[1]

While the Marines captured on the 6th and 7th of October were being taken north, the outposts along the 1st Marine Division front settled into an uneasy quiet. The enemy's interest in two of the 7th Marines outposts, Warsaw and Ronson, was well-known. These outposts straddled a nose of ground leading up to the main battle position called The Hook. Company C, 1st Battalion, 7th Marines, manned The Hook and outposts Ronson and Warsaw on October 26, 1952. In terms of men taken as prisoners of war, this proved the most costly single night in the entire Korean War.

As darkness settled the Communists opened fire with an intense bombardment of mortar and artillery fire on Marine positions. The enemy attacked in regimental strength following their well-established pattern of advancing directly behind their supporting fires. As soon as the bombardment rolled past the trenchworks Chinese soldiers invested the positions.

OP Ronson received heavy incoming fires at 6:10 P.M. and in 28 minutes the position was overrun by the attackers. OP Warsaw came under fire at 6:20 P.M. and the defenders requested "Box Me In" artillery support. Within three quarters of an hour Marines and Chinese were locked in a hand to hand struggle for possession of OP Warsaw. The outcome was uncertain for over three hours, but the Chinese

---

[1] Ibid.

overran the position before midnight.

While the fight raged at the OP's, enemy soldiers slipped around both flanks of OP Ronson and struck at the main line of resistance. At about 7:30 P.M. they succeeded in penetrating the main position of C/1/7. Company A/1/7 was ordered to support C/1/7, to contain the penetration, and to restore the lost ground.

Marine PFC Eddie P. Vidal was manning a Browning Automatic Rifle on the The Hook when the Chinese struck. He described the bunkers and trenches as almost completely destroyed by the day-long fires and the sudden intense preparatory fires.[1] Vidal and two fellow PFC's, Billy J. Vitruls and Vodiska (first name unknown), were on a forward position. When the Chinese attacked, Vidal and Vodiska were in their fighting holes and Vitruls was inside the living bunker. An incoming round burst next to Vidal and threw him high in the air. He described a sensation resembling that of walking on a hot pavement, and when he tried to move he found one foot gone and the other leg mangled and hanging by shreds.[2]

Chinese assault troops closed on the position after Vidal had expended his ammunition and disassembled his automatic rifle. Vodiska had been killed and Vitruls was captured in the living bunker. According to Vidal the

---

[1] Letter from Eddie Peno Vidal, Cpl, USMC (Retired), August 10, 1960, p. 1.

[2] Sworn statement of Cpl Eddie P. Vidal, January 25, 1954, made at Fort Sam Houston, Texas. Filed in Vidal's record of service, Code D.F., HQMC, Washington 25, D. C.

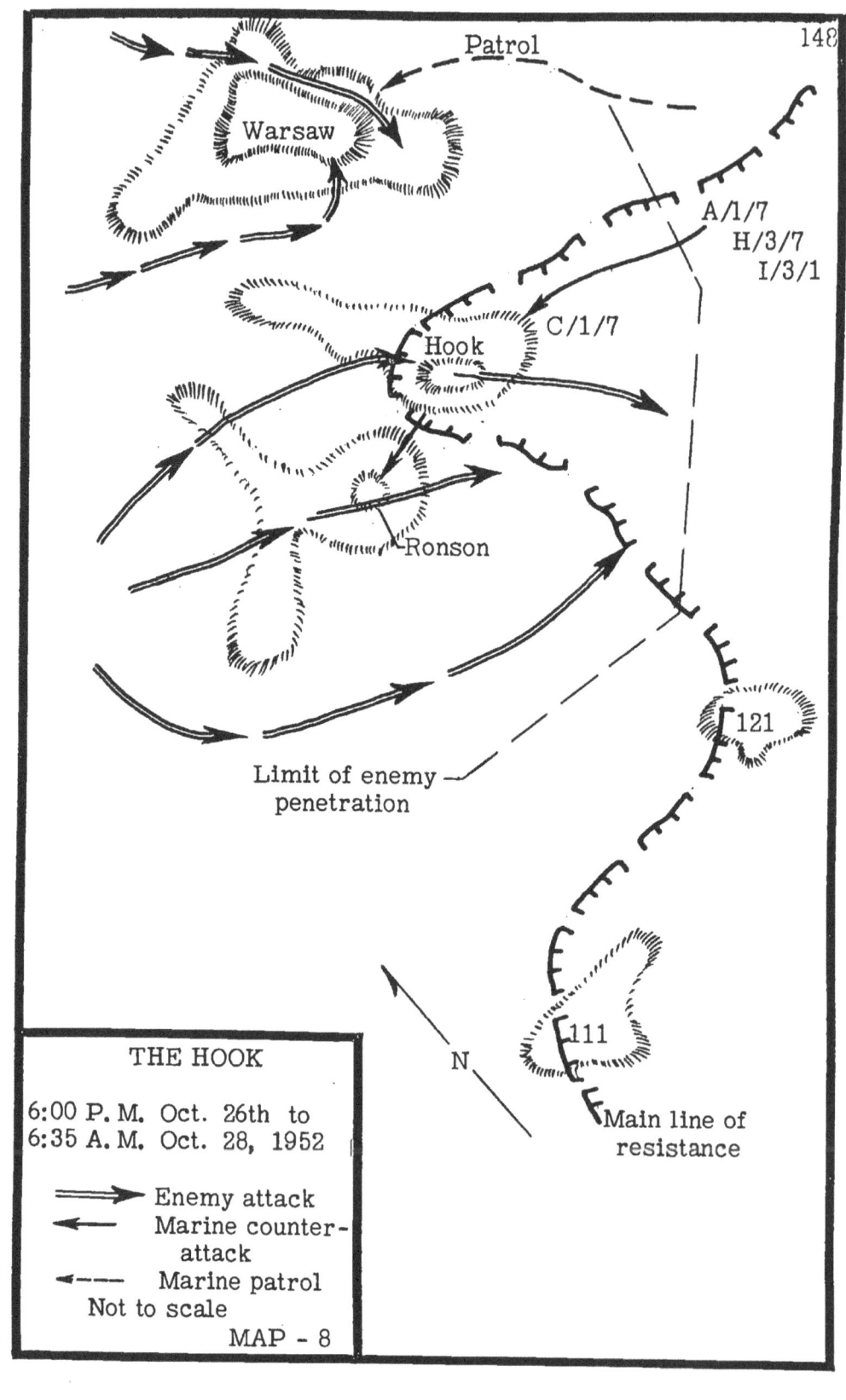

Communist soldiers pointed to their dead and wounded lying around the position and then beat the legless Marine severely with their submachine guns.[1]

Twenty-seven Marines were captured during the night and early morning hours. They were marched, carried, or dragged off the hill and taken into the Chinese lines. All 27 were recovered alive during the prisoner exchanges the following year.[2]

When action at The Hook reached its peak an estimated battalion struck Outpost Vegas 3,000 yards to the west. The enemy took Vegas under a cross-fire shortly after midnight, but the Marine platoon successfully defended its position. Forty minutes later the enemy withdrew. Two nearby outposts, named Carson and Reno, were relatively unbothered the night of the 26th.[3]

Action at The Hook continued throughout the 27th as the 7th Marines, with elements of the 1st Marines attached, struggled to regain their lost outposts. Finally at dawn on the 28th The Hook was restored and Outposts Ronson and Warsaw were reoccupied. In addition to the 27 Marines captured, the Marines suffered 70 killed and 386 wounded. The Chinese lost an estimated 532 killed and 216

---

[1] Vidal letter, p. 5.

[2] USMC Casualties.

[3] 7th Marines, Summary of Action 26 October-1 November, 1952. "Hook, Reno, Ronson". G-3, Historical Branch Archives, HQMC; and
LtCol R. D. Heinl Jr., USMC, memorandum to Director of Marine Corps History, October 28, 1952.

wounded.

The deceptive nature of the Chinese lenient policy can be read in the experience of PFC Eddie P. Vidal after his capture. Two enemy soldiers grabbed him by the wrists and dragged him to their own lines. He was placed in a horseshoe-shaped bunker with another seriously wounded Marine, PFC Ollie Asher, who had been captured in the H/3/7 action on October 7th. Asher's right leg was mangled and gangrenous and he was blind. Vidal wrote that the two were reduced to drinking their own urine when the Chinese refused them water and food. Asher died about November 16, 1952, five weeks after his capture.[1]

PFC Vidal was operated on about November 1st. The Chinese took him to an underground bunker and removed most of his left leg with a hacksaw. No anesthesia was used. His right stump was trimmed at the same time.[2] Throughout the operation Chinese soldiers held the Marine down while the hacksaw rasped through the bone. Private Alberto Pizarro-Baez who had been captured on October 7, 1952, reported a similar experience.[3]

Vidal was kept in a cold, damp bunker after his operation. His clothes had been taken from him, and he had only two sacks to use as blankets. The Communists withheld water for a week and denied him food for 17 days.

---

[1] Vidal letter, p. 6.

[2] Vidal sworn statement, January 25, 1954.

[3] Personal interview with Pvt Alberto Pizarro-Baez, April, 1953.

In describing his experience in the bunker he wrote:

> I don't remember how long I was in this hole. I do remember that some of the days they came to interrogate me and to tell me that I was a war-monger because I had blood in my hands and finger nails [sic] Blood from the Peace Loving People. They kept telling me the Americans had come to Korea to kill inoccent [sic] people.
>
> I told them that if I could have my way, I would do it all over again.[1]

The legless Marine and several fellow prisoners of war were taken north by truck to Pyoktong. There the seriously wounded were assigned to a hospital in a large temple. Other Marines at the hospital were Corporal George E. Noeth, Privates First Class Theodore A. Jeurn, Lione E. Peterson, and David P. Lang, and Private Robert L. L. Dunn.[2] All five had been captured in the same action with Vidal.

The Chinese permitted POW's from the main camp to visit the hospital on Christmas Eve, 1952. Gifts of sweet rolls, candy, and cigarettes and, as a finale, Christmas carols lent an almost festive air to the holiday, the only pleasant day in nearly a year.

In January, 1953, the Marines were transferred to Camp 3 where they were assigned to Company 6. Here Vidal heard of six Marines who had been foiled in an escape attempt when a soldier informed on them. According to the rumor, the six would-be escapees were punished by being tied to poles and having cold water thrown on them

---

[1] Vidal letter, p. 9.

[2] Ibid., p. 12.

in freezing weather. Vidal added:

> After this I didn't hear of any escape, or of any escape committee formed by U. S. Marines. If there was one, I didn't know of it.[1]

A soldier, Manuel D. Martinez, Jr., from Truchas, New Mexico, befriended Vidal in Camp 3. Martinez cared for the Marine, washed his bandages and dried them with the heat of his own body, carried him to the latrine, stole water from the Chinese to use for washing the wounds, and shared his food with the Marine.

Vidal reported that he was frequently placed in the hole for refusing to fill out an autobiography or make a propaganda recording. In recounting his experience in Camp 3, he indicated that he met PFC Vitruls, the member of his fire team who had been captured inside the living bunker. Vitruls was well-respected by his fellow prisoners and on one occasion struck a Chinese guard for pushing him, an act for which he was beaten and consigned to the hole for punishment.[2]

With but two exceptions the Marines captured in The Hook action were assigned to Camp 3. The exceptions were PFC Francis J. Kohus, A/1/7, who became squad leader of a small, isolated group, and PFC Lione Peterson who remained at Pyoktong. After his release from the temple hospital, Peterson joined a newly formed company of Camp 5 with

---

[1] Ibid., p. 14.

[2] Ibid., p. 17.

PFC Arthur Gregory.[1]

In December, 1952, Radio Peking broadcast numerous recordings made by prisoners of war. Among them was a short Christmas greeting from Arthur J. Gregory to his parents. The message gave his name, rank, and service number, a brief hello, and a sentence to the effect that he had been well-treated. This was the first indication that Gregory was alive. He later indicated that the prisoners who made this series of broadcasts were required to write out their message for approval before recording it.[2] Private Pizarro-Baez had recorded a Christmas greeting in Puerto Rican, but there is no record of it having been broadcast.[3]

Several Marines voluntarily made recordings of this nature. In general they viewed it as an opportunity to get word out they were alive through the simple expedient of a holiday greeting. An exhaustive study of U. S. Army POW's revealed the same pattern. Recordings were made by more than one out of five soldiers. Three quarters of the

---

[1] Gregory letter.

[2] Ibid.

[3] The Foreign Broadcast Intercept Service in Tokyo, Japan, monitored English language broadcasts from major capitals in the Far East. Messages broadcast by POW's over Radio Peking were generally received by the FBIS. According to ComNavFE records, which would have been reflected in the Little Switch Report, there was no record of a broadcast by Pizarro-Baez. In his letter to the author, Pizarro-Baez stated that to the best of his knowledge his broadcast was never received by his mother in Puerto Rico.

recordings were made voluntarily and 84% viewed the results solely as holiday greetings.[1]

Ground action slacked off after the violent October fights. In the closing month of 1952 three other Marines were captured. They were Privates First Class Pedro Aviles of the Division Reconnaissance Company, captured on the 8th, and Albert T. Crabtree of the division, captured on the 27th. Corporal Gathern Kennedy of I/3/11 was captured on the last day of the year.

The Communist pattern for handling enlisted prisoners was clear; newly captured Marines were kept apart from those taken before January 1, 1952. Segregation of non-commissioned officers was advanced in August, 1952. The sergeants were removed from Chongsong and taken to the newly established Camp 4 at Wiwon.[2]

The year 1952 also marked a segregation of aviation personnel. Marine pilots and observers captured in that year encountered entirely different circumstances than those experienced by earlier captives. Some received surprisingly easy treatment. Others were handled brutally. Most of them experienced the constant harassment which was an important part of the Communist administration of

---

[1] Julius Segal. *Factors Related to the Collaboration and Resistance Behavior of U. S. Army PW's in Korea.* Technical Report No. 33 for the Department of the Army. Prepared by the Human Resources Research Office, George Washington University (Washington: George Washington University, 1956), pp. iii, 35-36. Cited hereafter as HumRRO 33.

[2] Griffith letter.

their prisoners of war.

On January 1, 1952, Marine Captain Robert W. Gilardi of VMF-312 was shot down by the enemy. His aircraft caught fire and Gilardi was burned on the face, hands, and feet before he was able to free himself from the stricken plane. He parachuted and became tangled in a tree when he landed. Because of serious injuries, the Marine was unable to loosen his parachute harness, and he hung from the tree for almost twenty-four hours in the subzero cold. By the time Communist soldiers cut him down, his hands and feet were frozen. Captain Gilardi died before reaching a regular POW camp.[1]

In February another Marine was captured. First Lieutenant Kenneth W. Henry was assigned to the Marine Detachment aboard the light cruiser USS Manchester. This type of "sea-going" assignment normally involves performing aerial observation (air spot) for the cruiser's guns. Spotting is made possible by the helicopter carried aboard. On the afternoon of February 8, 1952, Lieutenant Henry accompanied Lieutenant Edwin C. Moore, USN, in an attempt to rescue a Navy fighter pilot. The latter had been shot down by antiaircraft fire at about 9:00 A.M. that morning, and he crashed on a mountainside about 25 miles northwest of Wonsan.[2]

The Manchester neared the search area at about

---

[1] VMF-312, HistD, January, 1952, p. 1, and Fink interview.

[2] Letter from Maj Kenneth L. Henry, August 25, 1960.

1:00 P.M. Lieutenants Moore and Henry took off in an HO3S helicopter and headed inland. They arrived over Ensign Marvin Broomhead, the downed aviator, at about 2:00 P.M. Lieutenant Henry was manipulating the winch and sling when the helicopter suddenly crashed. Moore and Henry climbed out of the wreckage and crawled toward Ensign Broomhead. An enemy machine gun could be heard and it appeared to be firing at a combat air patrol overhead.

The two officers from the Manchester found that Broomhead was seriously injured, having broken both ankles in his crash.[1] Lieutenant Henry was unable to walk due to injuries he sustained in the helicopter crash. Henry and Moore dragged the Ensign to a position hidden from the enemy machine gun. They waited to be rescued, but with darkness setting in, the other friendly helicopters in the area were unable to operate in the treacherous mountains. The three Americans were discovered by a Chinese patrol shortly before midnight.

During the two days following, the officers were processed through a series of headquarters. Lieutenant Moore walked while Broomhead was carried on a litter and the Marine rode on horseback. They were asked the reason for their presence in the area as well as technical data related to their aircraft and radios. Lieutenant Moore caught the brunt of the enemy's interrogation effort.

---

[1] ComNavFE Little Switch Report, p. 14, and enclosure E, pp. 1-3.

Several days later the trio arrived at what Lieutenant Henry identified only as an interrogation center about 10 miles east of Pyongyang. Evidently they were to be sent to Pak's Palace, but the Chinese made a mistake and sent the two Navy pilots north. According to Lieutenant Henry the Chinese had intended to keep Moore at Pyongyang. When they learned that the Marine was an aerial observer and not a helicopter pilot, they did not press their interrogation.[1]

Henry caught pneumonia and recalls little of what occurred until he partially recovered in Camp 5 at Pyoktong some weeks later. During his early days at Pyoktong, he was visited by Captain Wilkins and Captain Gillette, both of whom had been shot down the previous year. Two enlisted Marines talked to him there, but he does not recall their names.

In June, 1952, he was taken to a Korean house in Pyoktong village for three months of intensive interrogation. An Army private had previously suggested to him that by pretending to be ignorant he might evade interrogation. Henry used that device by claiming to have had only three years of high school. Under pressure of the interrogation Lieutenant Henry admitted to duties in such fields as motor transport, legal, and sea duty. He successfully concealed the fact that he had attended certain specialist schools and had fairly extensive theoretical

---

[1] Henry letter.

knowledge of atomic, biological and chemical warfare. As he describes it, "They finally got fed up with me and I spent the rest of my 'tour' living in Korean homes along with Lieutenant James Stanley, USAF, and adding roommates periodically to a total of 14 men before we were admitted to Camp 2 annex in a valley 15 miles east of Camp 2 proper after the Armistice was signed."[1]

On March 4, 1952, Marine Captain Roy C. Gray, VMF-311, was on a railcut mission when he was shot down by ground fire. It was nearly dark when he crash landed in a rice paddy near Sibunni. The impact knocked him unconscious, and he was burned about the face, head, hands, and arms. A North Korean soldier dragged him from the cockpit within minutes after the crash.[2]

Captain Gray reported that he was taken to a bunker nearby and that a Korean soldier cut his flight jacket off to apply ointment to the burns. The next day he was marched westward to a Chinese Army Headquarters. A Chinese girl applied vaseline gauze to his burns. He was interrogated briefly by a young soldier who spoke poor English and who referred to a printed form to ask questions. The interrogator did not force the issue when Captain Gray refused to answer and he seemed sympathetic about the severity of the officer's burns.

---

[1] Ibid.

[2] Maj Roy C. Gray Jr., Report of Captivity, December 7, 1953. All details of then Captain Gray's captivity are based upon his report.

Next Gray was taken to a hospital in a small village between Sariwon and Sinmak. Of roughly 500 patients about five were prisoners of war and the rest mainly Chinese wounded. There appeared to Captain Gray to be no difference in the treatment proferred the patients. Medical facilities were primitive and bandages were changed only sparingly with sometimes as much as two weeks between changes. Wounds became badly infected.

A month after his capture Gray and the five other POW's were moved to a second hospital about 10 miles north of Pyongyang. At their new location the POW's lived in a Korean house and were permitted to move about freely in the sunshine. Their wounds were tended regularly and dressings were changed more frequently. There were no interrogators or political officers at the hospital, and the few doctors who spoke English did not interrogate them for military information.

Because the hospital was not part of the regular POW system and communications were generally poor, this small group of prisoners enjoyed a comparatively pleasant existence. In July, 1952, four months after his capture, Captain Gray was questioned by a North Korean major who came from a nearby interrogation center. Gray was recuperating from a recent skin graft at the time and he was able to evade interrogation by complaining of postoperative pain. The Korean major left and did not return.

The POW's secreted food and gave it to the local Korean civilians who sometimes came to visit them. In turn the Americans received some fresh vegetables. In their association with the civilians the POW's hoped to establish contact with friendly underground agents.

During his first year of captivity Captain Gray did not experience any form of indoctrination or Communist schooling. He encountered his first brief required reading before going north to Pyoktong and eventually to a branch of the officers camp.

In May of 1952 four Marine pilots were shot down and captured in a ten-day period. Major Walter R. Harris of VMF-323 was shot down on May 6, 1952. A week later, on May 13th, First Lieutenant Milton H. "Sammy" Baugh's plane was struck in the engine section by antiaircraft fire near Sukchon during a bombing run. His engine quit and Baugh tried to glide out to sea. Although he tried to stretch his glide he was forced to belly-land a quarter of a mile before reaching the shore. After detonating his IFF emergency switch (Identification-Friend or Foe), the Lieutenant attempted to run for the beach. A group of Chinese soldiers took him prisoner within half an hour.[1]

Baugh was taken to an Antiaircraft Headquarters where he was interrogated at length concerning operational tactics. When he refused to answer he was threatened with death, and thereafter he replied to the questions, providing considerable misinformation on speeds, altitudes

---

[1] Capt Milton H. Baugh, Report of Captivity, December 22, 1953.

and dive angles. For the next five days he was exhibited at a series of antiaircraft units, probably to boost morale with tangible evidence of their shooting prowess.

Antiaircraft fire was responsible for downing Captain John P. Flynn Jr. on May 14th. Flynn parachuted from his stricken two engine night-fighter, an F7F-3N Tigercat, at about 11:00 P.M. when a fire in his right engine burned the wing off.[1] He was subjected to intensive interrogation by North Korean and Chinese Communist Air Force personnel. On about June 25th he was taken to an area commonly referred to as Pike's Peak.

First Lieutenant Duke Williams, Jr., was shot down on May 16th. He was searching for a downed pilot when his plane was hit by antiaircraft fire and he was forced to parachute. His wingmates observed him on the ground in a position indicating that he was under fire. About 15 natives dressed in white were observed taking Williams prisoner.[2] He was eventually taken to an interrogation center about five miles east of Pyongyang and put in a room with four Air Force Lieutenants.

About May 29th Lieutenant Baugh, who had spent a week in solitary confinement, joined Williams and the Air Force officers. The group was taken to 14th Army Headquarters located several miles northest of Pyongyang. This

---

[1] Maj John P. Flynn Jr., Report of Captivity, March 8, 1954.

[2] Statement of Capt John N. Snapper, 031895, USMC, of May 16, 1952, TabR to VMF-212, HistD, May, 1952. Note: VMF-212 was changed to VMA-212 in June, 1952.

was the same area referred to as Pike's Peak. Major Harris was already there. Lieutenant Rowland M. Murphy, a ground officer captured on May 7 near Panmunjom, arrived about June 13. He was kept in a makeshift hospital at the interrogation center where he was subjected to lengthy questioning.[1] Captain Flynn arrived at Pike's Peak about June 25th, but he, too, was kept apart from the other Marines.

Baugh and Williams lived in a dugout from June 1st to July 15th. Along with other captured officers they were required to work on the construction of more dugouts. The Chinese conducted frequent interrogations and required their prisoners to attend political lectures which included Communist ideology and vicious charges accusing Americans of warmongering and waging bacteriological warfare.[2]

In the middle of July Major Harris and Lieutenant Murphy joined Lieutenants Baugh and Williams as members of a draft being taken north. The trip took two days by truck. Upon arrival at Pyoktong the prisoners were confined in two rooms of a Korean hut for about ten days. They were then taken eastward to a steeply walled valley near Obul, North Korea.[3]

The Obul camp was known by various names. All of

---

[1] 1stLt Rowland M. Murphy, Report of Captivity, January 5, 1954.

[2] Baugh Report of Captivity.

[3] Ibid., and Murphy Report of Captivity.

these descriptions are correct. Some called it The Annex. Others referred to it as No Name Valley. The British considered it to be Branch 3, Camp 2, at Chang-ni.[1] The POW unit designations were platoons one and two of Company C. But for the sake of clarity we can consider that Obul housed two groups of prisoners in close proximity to each other. The groups had limited contact initially, but in December, 1952, they were joined in a single unit. In addition, more than 100 POW's were confined alone or in groups of two or three scattered throughout the valley. They were all under heavy guard and no contact was permitted between groups. The prisoners were aware of the presence nearby of other POW's, and they went to great lengths to exchange information. Notes were hidden under rocks at common bathing points or latrines. Songs were sung loudly to convey information. Messages were baked in bread by POW's in the Obul kitchen and information was passed in this way to solitary inmates of the sheltered valley.[2]

Major William Wilson, USAF, was the senior United Nations officer with the two platoons at Obul. Major Walter Harris was the senior Marine, and he commanded the 1st Platoon. The senior officers set about secretly organizing the camp on military lines. Lieutenant Murphy was assigned duties as a member of the escape committee

---

[1] British POW Report, p. 37.

[2] Thorin interview, and Baugh Report of Captivity.

and he shared duty as officer of the day.[1]

Lieutenants O'Shea and Ferranto had arrived in mid May, 1952. O'Shea joined a platoon at Obul while Ferranto was placed in solitary confinement in a North Korean house in the valley.[2]

This period of 1952 represented a turning point in the routine of the main officer's camp. The population of Pi-chong-ni was stabilized in one sense. Only a few new prisoners of war were added to the older camp, but many of the 375 officers frequently disappeared into solitary confinement for real or imagined infractions of camp regulations.

In late January, 1952, Major McLaughlin and five other senior officers had been sentenced to long periods of solitary confinement by a sham court on charges of organizing the camp. When Major Judson C. Richardson, Jr., arrived at Pi-chong-ni in March he found that the Marine officers had formed a tightly knit group and consulted among themselves on every major issue. Yet the atmosphere within Camp 2 was strained. Major Richardson later described the situation in these terms:

> On arrival at Camp 2 on 23 March 1952 I found myself among a group of prisoners haunted and plagued with suspicion that there were informers and opportunists among them. The activities of these suspected persons in the compound had so undermined the morale of the prisoners that American officers talked in whispers, feeling

---

[1] Murphy Report of Captivity.

[2] McDaniel interview.

that no one could place any confidence or trust in another. The low state of morale had so effected the discipline that it was impossible to rectify the situation by normal leadership.[1]

The officers in Camp 2 were generally agreed that Marine Lieutenant Colonel Thrash, who joined the group June 1, 1952, was highly instrumental in restoring discipline and harmony within camp. With Lieutenant Colonel Carne of the Gloucesters in solitary confinement, Colonel Thrash was senior to all other United Nations officers in the compound at Pi-chong-ni and he readily accepted the grave responsibility of leadership.

The Marine officer issued orders concerning the behavior of all personnel in camp. His order included the following:

> There would be no fraternizing with Chinese or competing in athletic events with them.
>
> Study of Communist propaganda would not be countenanced. If study was forced on them, POW's were to offer passive resistance and no arguments.
>
> If POW's were taken from camp and offered alcoholic beverages they were not to drink with their captors under any circumstances.
>
> POW's would not perform labor for the Communists unless that labor benefited the prisoners.
>
> If prisoners were subject to trial or punishment they were to involve no one but themselves.
>
> There would be no letters written using any

---

[1] Letter from Maj Judson C. Richardson Jr., to the Commandant of the Marine Corps, September 21, 1953, subject Exemplary conduct; case of Lieutenant Colonel William G. Thrash, 06141, USMC, Report of.

titles or return address which might prove beneficial to the Communists for propaganda value.¹

By September 15th Lieutenant Colonel Thrash's efforts to influence and organize his fellow prisoners of war outraged the Chinese. The Communists removed him from the compound for "Criminal Acts and Hostile Attitude against the Chinese People's Volunteers." Lieutenant Colonel Thrash spent the next eight months in solitary confinement where he was subjected to constant interrogation, harassment, and duress.² He endured long hours of torture and on one occasion was bound, severely beaten and thrown outside half naked in subzero weather.³ The shock of the severe temperature rendered him unconscious and he nearly died. During his eight-month ordeal there were demands for confessions and for pledges that he would co-operate with the lenient Chinese on his return to the compound.⁴

Marines and many officers from other services formed a steady procession between the school house barracks and either the local Korean jails or a series of small holes which were used for confining prisoners on virtually any

---

¹Fink notes.

²U. S. Fighting Man's Code, p. 126., and Letter from LtCol John N. McLaughlin, USMC, to Commandant of the Marine Corps, December 9, 1953 with endorsement from CMC to the Secretary of the Navy on December 21, 1953.

³Farrar-Hockley, p. 263.

⁴Richardson letter to CMC.

pretext.

"The hole" was a familiar term to POW's. It could mean any given hole, but the experience was about the same. Only the duration of confinement differed. One of the most graphic descriptions of confinement in the hole was tape-recorded by Warrant Officer Felix McCool after his return to the United States.[1] The warrant officer was confined in the hole for spitting out a window and accidentally hitting a guard.

McCool described the hole as three feet square and three and a half feet deep. Spikes were driven down through the lid of the hole forcing an occupant to sit in a hunched position. The bottom was a slimy ooze; the result of prisoners having to void themselves in the hole. Lice and fleas abounded.

In his fiftieth hour McCool was taken to headquarters where he proclaimed his innocence. The Chinese demanded a confession of rape and pillage, and when the Marine refused to comply he was escorted back to the hole. By his seventieth hour he heard POW's in a jail across the street yell, "Keep your chin up, Mac." He reflected on his experience aboard a "Hell Ship" and later working in a coal mine while a prisoner of the Japanese in World War II, and he knew that he hated the Chinese Communists far more than he had hated the Japanese. He described the latter as

---

[1] Tape recording by CWO Felix J. McCool, USMC, Enclosure 1 to letter from CWO McCool to CMC dated September 24, 1954. Filed with G-2 Division, HQMC.

brutal but having character which he felt the Communists lacked.

When he was taken out to sign a confession he caught a glimpse of Lieutenant Colonel Thrash in a solitary cell in the nearby jail. Finally he confessed that he cursed the Koreans and hated the Communists. He refused the demand that he inform on his fellow officers. He thought of an old movie, The Informer , with Victor McLaglen, and he said he might have cried a little. He considered suicide and then cast the idea aside resolving to live and tell about the Chinese Communist lenient policy.

After eighty hours in the hole McCool was returned to camp. Army Captain Clarence Anderson, a doctor, gave him soap and clean clothes. Marine Lieutenant "Ding" Bell and three others poured water over him to help wash off the stink. Captain Gerald Fink sat up half the night with him while he talked and talked.[1]

Lieutenant Gillette had considerable experience in the hole. An abortive escape attempt at Pak's Palace after his capture in October, 1951, earned him a period of solitary confinement. Gillette arrived at Pi-chong-ni in the spring of 1952, and his reactionary attitude caused him to be placed in the hole on more than one occasion.[2]

The Marine and a South African Air Force pilot, Lieutenant Chris Lombard, laid plans for an escape. The two

---

[1] Ibid., and Fink interview.

[2] Fink interview.

were confined in a hilltop school overlooking Camp 2. Gillette began training for the escape by reducing his rations and running whenever possible to improve his wind.[1]

When the two lieutenants made their break they were shot at but managed to get clear of camp. During the night Lombard fell down a mountainside and was so badly injured the Chinese recaptured him shortly thereafter. Gillette carried on alone. The obvious escape route lay to the west, the shortest distance to the coast where a boat might be stolen for the journey south. The Marine officer chose to go east, however, across rugged mountains which offered little in the way of crops or other foods. Whereas most escapees were recaptured within hours, or at best within days, Lieutenant Gillette was free for several weeks before the Communists found him half way across Korea. Quartermaster Sergeant James Day described the attempt as the finest and most determined one he knew of.[2]

Gillette was placed in the hole again, but he was not returned to Camp 2. Instead he became one of the many isolated prisoners secreted in No Name Valley. While in the hole he scribbled a novel on toilet paper, and it later served to amuse his fellow POW's.[3]

Other Marines were committed to the hole, too.

---

[1] Ibid.

[2] Day letter. QMS Day was a member with Captain Farrar-Hockley of a party which planned to escape in 1953. The attempt was thwarted before it got underway.

[3] Fink interview.

Captain Mercer R. Smith was sentenced to four days for arguing with a Chinese officer. In July, 1952, Lieutenant Richard Still was seized in an abortive escape attempt and sentenced to three months in the hole. He emerged unbothered and steeled against the Communists. In September Captain Paul Martelli escaped from the compound. He was captured ten days later and put in the same hole for two months. When released from confinement he was visibly disturbed by the experience but recovered rapidly with no traumatic effect.[1]

In October, 1952, Captain Gerald Fink was put in the hole. No formal charges were lodged against him, but his efforts on behalf of religion no doubt paved the way for his stint of solitary in the hole. In July Fink had discussed with other prisoners the need for a religious symbol in camp and he decided to carve a crucifix. His artistic and mechanical talents were well known. The Marine had already made stethescopes for the captive doctors using resonant wood and rubber tubing stolen from Chinese trucks. His greatest achievement had been construction of an artificial leg for Air Force Major Thomas D. Harrison. The leg was so expertly made that Harrison was able to play volley ball on his new limb. Homemade knives fashioned from the metal arch supports of field boots served as the carving blades. Short lengths of barbed wire hammered into wedge-like points made convenient drills.

---

[1] Ibid.

Using these same crude but effective tools, Captain Fink set about to carve the figure of Christ on the cross. He finished the rough corpus in September. At one point a Chinese guard caught him in the act of carving, and he explained that the bearded figure was Abraham Lincoln. Since the Communists considered Lincoln a kindred spirit, in light of Marxian teachings, Fink was permitted to continue his labors.[1]

The final job of smoothing the corpus required different tools than those already available. After making sure no one was watching him, Captain Fink broke a window in the Chinese company commander's house and used the glass shards to complete the final scraping. Barbed wire was fashioned into a crown resembling the crown of thorns that adorned Christ's head. When the 22-inch corpus was placed on the cross which Fink had prepared, the crucifix was unveiled in camp and christened "Christ in Barbed Wire."

The Chinese seemed to fear the crucifix. They made no attempt to seize it or restrict its use, but Captain Fink was destined for punishment. Within a few days he heard the familiar summons to bring his rice bowl and come. Fellow POW's, seeing him walk down the central passageway of the barracks sang "Comrade Fink is in the clink" to the tune of "You'll never get to Heaven."

He was, indeed, in the clink for ten days. His sentence might have been longer. When the guard kicked

---

[1] Ibid.

"CHRIST IN BARBED WIRE"

Carved in Camp 2, Pi-chong-ni
by Captain Gerald Fink, USMC

The 22-inch corpus is mounted
on a four-foot crucifix. The
crucifix was brought back to
freedom by the POW's who were
confined in Camp 2, and it is
now at the Father Kapaun High
School in Wichita, Kansas.

him into the hole part of the dirt wall caved in dirtying his clothes and rice bowl. Enraged, the Marine leaped out of the hole and struck the guard in the face with his bowl cutting him across the nose. A few anxious minutes passed during which the camp authorities milled around investigating the incident. Captain Fink seized the initiative, dramatically pointed to the guard, and shouted vehemently "If I die from dysentery because of a dirty rice bowl, this man killed me!" He spent the prescribed ten days in the hole and returned to the main compound to find himself the senior Marine present.

In October the senior officers in Camp 2 were removed to a newly built camp some distance down the road. Half the officers were formed into a second company and marched away to their new home. The junior officers remained in Company 1 in old Camp 2.

The aviation personnel captured during 1952 had encountered a new subject in their interrogations. Lieutenant Henry was asked about bacteriological warfare in February when he was captured, but the enemy did not force the issue. The pilots shot down in May were questioned about bacteriological warfare, but most of them were not pressed for information. Captain Flynn, however, was under brutal pressure throughout July when the enemy made made an intensive effort to obtain a confession of participation in bacteriological warfare. Others were to meet similar pressure.

The subject of bacteriological warfare was not new in the Korean war, but the year 1952 saw the Chinese give it a new twist and they made significant gains in their propaganda venture. The earlier history of the war should have given some hint of what the Chinese were attempting to do.

After suffering their first major reverses in Korea in September, 1950, the Communists had charged that Americans were waging bacteriological warfare. Their campaign of vilification continued even after they regained the initiative in November and December of 1950. In early 1951, while the United Nations Command battled epidemics of smallpox, typhus and amebic dysentery, these and other strange diseases raged among the civil population and within the prisoner of war camps. The enemy branded medical efforts to curb these diseases as experiments in germ warfare.[1] On May 8, 1951, the Communist Government of the Korean Democratic People's Republic lodged a formal protest with the United Nations, charging that America was waging bacteriological warfare. Their campaign seemed to abate during the remainder of 1951.

Then on January 13, 1952, the Communists shot down a U. S. Air Force B-26 which was then bombing their positions. Some five weeks after the crew parachuted into North Korea from their stricken bomber, the enemy's propa-

---

[1] Charles Stevenson, "The Truth About Germ Warfare in Korea", *The Readers Digest*, April 1953, pp. 17-20.

ganda campaign picked up momentum. First Lieutenants Kenneth L. Enoch, the navigator, and John Quinn, the pilot, were the first American prisoners of the enemy to be exploited successfully for purposes of germ warfare confessions.[1]

The Chinese had obviously planned their propaganda onslaught well. After they successfully extracted false confessions from Enoch and Quinn, they exposed both prisoners to interrogation by a select group of Oriental medical specialists and newspapermen.[2] The two Americans apparently performed according to plan, and a relentless flood of Communist propaganda was loosed on the world.

The effects of the confessions were far reaching. From that time until the end of hostilities captured aviators of all services were subjected to a degree of pressure and coercion previously unknown by prisoners of war. Prior to the turn of the year aviation and ground personnel received relatively the same treatment in Communist hands. After January, 1952, aviators were singled out for a special brand of treatment designed to wring bacteriological warfare confessions from them.

---

[1] People's China (Peking), May 16, 1952, supplement section. This issue contains an article entitled "Statements By Two American Air Force Officers, Kenneth Lloyd Enoch and John Quinn, Admitting Their Participation in Germ Warfare in Korea and Other Documents."

[2] The Chinese People's Committee for World Peace. Report of the Joint Interrogation Group of Korean and Chinese Specialists and Newspaper Correspondants on the Interrogation of War Prisoners Enoch and Quinn (Peking: The Chinese People's Committee for World Peace, 1952), pp. 1-32.

It may be more than sheer coincidence that the new series of germ warfare allegations was initiated on George Washington's birthday, 1952. On that day, Bak Hon Yong, Minister for Foreign Affairs of the Communist Korean Democratic People's Republic, charged the Americans with renewed bacteriological attacks in North Korea. Bak claimed that flies, fleas, ticks, mosquitoes, and spiders had been spread by aircraft to disseminate contagious diseases over frontline and rear area positions. He did not explain how insects could survive in subzero weather. In what was obviously a co-ordinated effort, Chinese Communist Foreign Minister, Chou En-Lai, followed this up with a similar statement on March 8, 1952. He claimed that 68 formations of American military aircraft made 448 sorties over Northeast China scattering large quantities of germ-carrying insects at Fushun, Hsinmin, Antung, Kuantien, Linkiang, and other areas.[1]

Chou En-Lai's efforts were aided and abetted from another quarter. Tibor Meray, correspondant for the Hungarian daily newspaper, Budapest Szabad Nep, reported in March, 1952, from Korea concerning the fantastic fabrication. His interviews with villagers and his obvious sympathy with the Communist cause helped weave the fabric

---

[1] The Chinese People's Committee for World Peace. Exhibition on Bacteriological War Crimes Committed by the Government of the United States of America (Peking: The Chinese People's Committee for World Peace, 1952), pp. 1-52. Cited hereafter as "Peking Exhibit".

of the lie.[1]

Early in May, 1952, the Chinese People's Committee for World Peace opened their War Crimes Exhibit in Peking.[2] Displays included the written and sound-recorded confessions of Lieutenants Enoch and Quinn, a collection of psychological warfare leaflet containers which they labeled bacteria bombs, specimens of germ-laden insects, a clever array of photographs depicting bomb containers and their supposed cargo of insects, and reports of investigations by various committees and investigating bodies which tended to support their allegations.[3] The display was most convincing. Later a similar display was set up in the officers camp at Pi-chong-ni. Enoch and Quinn and two additional air force officers conducted playlets in the various camps depicting how they were supposedly given orders to perform their germ warfare mission.[4]

Then on July 8, 1952, there occurred the first of a chain of events to link the Marine Corps with bacteriological propaganda.[5] Colonel Frank H. Schwable, Chief of

---

[1] Meray, pp. 42-60.

[2] "Peking Exhibit", p. 2.

[3] Ibid., pp. 15-36.

[4] Fink MS comments.

[5] Except as noted this section is derived from the following sources:
Letter dated March 5, 1953 from the Chairman of the delegation of the Union of Soviet Socialist Republics addressed to the President of the General Assembly, United Nations General Assembly, Agenda item 73, Document No. A/C.1/L.28. Cited hereafter as UN Document A/C.1/L.28. This letter transmits documents entitled "Deposition by

Staff of the 1st Marine Aircraft Wing, accompanied by Major Roy H. Bley, Ordnance Officer of the wing, made an authorized administrative flight in an SNB aircraft. Both officers were newly arrived in Korea, and they inadvertently flew over enemy lines. By this time Communist antiaircraft fire had come to be respected by the pilots flying close support and interdiction missions. Many sturdy combat aircraft had fallen victim to the deadly ground fire. The SNB, or Beechcraft, was not a combat aircraft nor was it suitable for overflying enemy lines, and it was blasted out of the sky by Communist antiaircraft fire within sight of the United Nations front lines.

The two Marine officers parachuted from their stricken plane. Major Bley had received several disabling wounds, and when the two landed, Colonel Schwable went to the Major's assistance. Before ten minutes elapsed the Chinese Communist forces in the vicinity closed in and took them prisoner.

---

the Captured United States Colonel, Frank H. Schwable", and "Deposition of the Captured American Prisoner Major Roy H. Bley"; and

Sworn statement of Col Frank H. Schwable, USMC, September 25, 1953, San Francisco, California. Published in United Nations General Assembly, Eighth Session, First Committee, Agenda Item 24, Document No. A/C.1/L.66, of October 26, 1953. Cited hereafter as UN Document A/C.1/L.66; and

Findings of Fact and Recommendations, U. S. Marine Corps Court of Inquiry, case of Col Frank H. Schwable, USMC, April 1954. Cited hereafter as Schwable Court of Inquiry; and

New York Times, February 21, 1954, p. 6E; and April 28, 1954, pp. 1, 16, and 18; and

Washington Post, March 12, 1954, p. 8.

The enemy had little difficulty in compiling Colonel Schwable's biography. He was in uniform with insignia of rank and naval aviator wings, and he had on his person many articles of identification which a pilot on a routine administrative flight might carry. These included his Armed Services Identification Card, a Virginia driver's license, a flight instrument ticket, membership card to officers' messes in Bethesda and Anacostia, Maryland, pictures of his family, and a copy of his flight plan. If these were not enough, the Red cause was helped four days later when the Department of Defense issued a press release giving considerable data concerning the missing aviator. The Chinese knew they had a prize.

Two weeks after his capture, Colonel Schwable was taken to an interrogation center known as "Pick-up Camp." He remained there in solitary confinement until December 8, 1952. About six weeks after his arrival at the camp Colonel Schwable became aware of Chinese intentions to use him for propaganda. Throughout the period of his captivity the Marine Colonel lived in a filthy lean-to under the eaves of a Korean house. He was badgered, accused of being a war criminal, fed a near starvation diet, denied proper latrine privileges, refused medical and dental attention, and subjected to extremes of temperature. Except for a "two week thinking period" he was intensively interrogated throughout his internment. This was the standard Soviet technique, and the Communists' purpose was served. According to a sworn statement made shortly after his release Colonel Schwable felt sure that had he resisted Communist demands for a BW Confession the enemy would have affixed his forged signature to a document to achieve their ends. The Chinese had taken several samples of his signature before their bacteriological program began. The discomfort, almost constant diarrhea, extreme pain from being forced to sit in unnatural positions, fatigue, and naked threats wore him down. After applying all manner of means to break him down mentally, morally and physically, he states that he was confused and convinced that there was no alternative in the matter.

As he commented later, "In making my most difficult decision to seek the only way out, my primary consideration was that I would be of greater value to my country in exposing this hideous means of slanderous propaganda than I would be by sacrificing my life through non-submission or remaining a prisoner of the Chinese Communists for life, a matter over which they left me no doubt."

There followed many drafts of his confession. The Chinese required specific information; reference by name to key commanders in the chain of command, and compatability of places, dates and times with other confessions already obtained. Colonel Schwable was often told to include certain material in his confession if he was finally to clear his problem.

Near the end of December, almost six months after his capture, the Marine Colonel finally submitted a confession satisfactory to his captors. Late in January, 1953, he was given a typewritten statement containing those extracts of his confession which suited the over-all pattern. He was told to copy it in his own handwriting.

Instead of being left alone as orginally promised, yet another requirement was levied on the Colonel. He was made to record his confession. Later he was photographed reading it. Enoch and Quinn and others knew all about that -- they had gone through much the same routine a year earlier.

The pattern was familiar: degradation and humiliation, physical and mental exhaustion, extensive writing of relatively harmless topics to condition the subject for the ultimate step, intimidation and threats, and finally false hopes and promises combined with instilling a sense of war guilt.

Yet throughout his internment, Colonel Schwable was never physically beaten. He was never starved, though his meals were skimpy and barely adequate by American standards. He was given shelter at all times though it was barely sufficient to prevent frost-bite. This was the lenient policy of the Chinese Communist Peoples' Volunteers.

Colonel Schwable was the senior Marine captured. Next to Major General Dean, Commander of the 24th Infantry Division of U. S. Eighth Army, the Marine Colonel was the senior United Nations prisoner taken by the Communists. Although General Dean spent three years in enemy hands, he was the only prisoner held exclusively by the North Koreans. The General sagely evaluated the greatest problem facing a prisoner of war---that of maintaining his judgment--he has no one on whom he can try out his ideas before turning them into decisions.[1] Perhaps that was Colonel Schwable's problem, too.

The confession which finally evolved suited the Communists master plan admirably well. By cleverly combining factual order of battle data and technical sounding terminology in a text obviously prepared by an American, the enemy, through the medium of Colonel Schwable, created a most convincing lie. It was a much more sophisticated version than the efforts of earlier captives and one of the most damaging to emerge from North Korea.

During Colonel Schwable's ordeal Major Bley was subjected to similar treatment, but he reported that he was beaten on numerous occasions in addition to the mental pressures, constant harassment, marginal diet, and deplorable living conditions during the winter. He signed a confession on January 21, 1953, purporting knowledge of germ warfare activities by the 1st Marine Aircraft Wing.[2]

The Marine officers mentioned in Schwable's statement promptly refuted the germ warfare allegations in sworn statements but even this could hardly counteract the damning effects of the false confession.[3]

---

[1] William F. Dean, General Dean's Story, as told to William L. Worden (New York: The Viking Press, 1954), p. 131.

[2] UN Document No. A/C.1/L.28; and Document No. A/C.1/L.66.

[3] UN Document No. A/C.1/L.37.

Captain Samuel J. Davies, chaplain of the Gloucester's who had been captured in April, 1951, referred to Colonel Schwable's confession, which was broadcast over Radio Peking, as the greatest triumph of the Chinese. The chaplain observed that when the Communists first began their bacteriological campaign the officer prisoners in Camp 2 viewed it with sheer unbelief and ribald amusement. This attitude changed to more serious consideration of the problem, and finally, according to Chaplain Davies, the American officers became apologetic in their relations with the British.[1]

To add credence to their fantastic lie, the Communists had staged massive "bug hunts" by local civilians throughout North Korea and China, and in February, 1952, they had embarked on an extensive inoculation program. Even Major General Dean, isolated though he was, had to bare his arm for a monstrous shot designed, or so he was told, to protect him from the insidious bacteria loosed by the American imperialists.[2]

Marine Lieutenant Turner and Army Captain Joseph Manto conspired to make the Chinese appear ridiculous. Turner fashioned a miniature parachute and painted an Air Force insignia on the canopy. Manto tied a dead mouse to the parachute and hung it on a bush where the Chinese would be certain to find it. The Chinese guard who discovered

---

[1] Davies, p. 133.

[2] Dean, pp. 275-77.

the mouse pointed his rifle at it and yelled for help. A comrade responding to his nearly hysterical call gingerly lifted the mouse with a pair of pincers and dropped it into a glass bottle. This evidence was placed in the bacteriological warfare exhibit in the school house. The Chinese were deadly serious and failed to understand that they were the butt of what to the prisoners was a hilarious joke.[1]

Colonel Schwable and Major Bley were not the only Marines to be pressured for germ warfare confessions. Captain Flynn was under intensive interrogation during the same period. On July 18th a well known Marine naval aviation pilot, Master Sergeant John T. Cain, was shot down while flying an OE light observation plane and he, too, was questioned about bacteriological warfare.[2] Sergeant Cain of VMO-6 had just paid for six months education for nine Korean children who lived near his air base before he was shot down and captured.[3] Four planes made a search of the area but they were unable to find the downed pilot.[4]

Once in enemy hands Sergeant Cain was mistaken for a senior officer because of his graying hair and lack of rank insignia. A week after his capture Master Sergeant

---

[1] Fink interview. This incident is also described by: Edward Hunter, Brainwashing: The Story of the Men Who Defied It. (New York: Farrar, Straus and Cudahy, 1956), p. 154.

[2] MSgt John T. Cain, USMC, Report of Captivity.

[3] Naval Aviation News. NavAer No. 00-75R-3. November, 1953, p. 10.

[4] VMO-6, HistD, July, 1952, Appendix G.

Cain experienced his first organized interrogation. He later reported that he made a mistake at that time by lying about inconsequential things. On August 2d he was put in a jeep and driven north, an experience that nearly cost him his life. The driver ran over a cliff killing himself and two guards. Cain was thrown on a small ledge and temporarily paralyzed when the jeep rolled over him. Other Chinese found him later and took him to 14th Army Headquarters at Pike's Peak where he joined Captain Flynn. According to the sergeant the POW's owed much to Flynn who kept them amused.[1]

In mid August, 1952, Captain Flynn, Master Sergeant Cain, and 11 other POW's were taken north to Obul.[2] A month later the enlisted Marine was removed from Obul and taken to an isolated part of Pi-chong-ni for intensive interrogation. The Chinese insisted that he was actually a lieutenant colonel. Cain was confined in a hole five feet square and six feet deep. Water stood two inches deep in the hole and by October 8th it froze. In an effort to prove that the sergeant was a field officer the Chinese paraded several people in front of him. With a light shining in his eyes Master Sergeant Cain was unable to do more than pick out shadowy forms. When the line-up was completed he was informed that other POW's had identified him as Lieutenant Colonel Cain, Commanding Officer of

---

[1] Cain Report of Captivity.

[2] Flynn Report of Captivity.

VMF-121.[1] How the fanciful identification was arrived at remains a mystery but it is highly probable that the Chinese planted the very answers they sought.

Sergeant Cain was made to stand at attention for periods of five to eight hours. When guards were slack, a Korean woman secretly fed him rice in exchange for which he gave her sugar, soap, and tobacco accumulated while writing a fanciful report concerning the Fleet Logistic Wing, an organization about which he knew absolutely nothing.

In mid November his captors informed him they were through sparring with him. The enlisted pilot was taken to a hillside, blindfolded, and placed in front of a firing squad. He heard rifle bolts click. The commander of the firing squad asked if he was ready to tell all. When Sergeant Cain replied that he was not going to talk, the Chinese returned him to solitary confinement. After a political interrogation he was eventually taken back to Obul where he rejoined Captain Flynn and others.[2]

Later when platoons one and two were combined, Master Sergeant Cain proved to be invaluable in counseling and guiding other enlisted personnel. Major Harris, the senior Marine officer in the annex, later reported that Sergeant Cain assumed more than his share of duties and responsi-

---

[1] Cain Report of Captivity.

[2] *Ibid.*

bility and set an example for all to follow.[1]

On September 9, 1952, another pilot from VMO-6 was shot down and captured. Captain Robert B. Lipscomb was at the controls of an OE-1 with Second Lieutenant Roland L. McDaniel from the 11th Marines as his observer. The plane was hit near Taedok San, a mountain located north of The Hook where ground action was then building up for the October climax.[2]

Lipscomb and McDaniel parachuted into enemy lines where they were seized by the enemy. They were still within artillery range of the front on October 7th when the Chinese launched strong assaults against outposts of the 7th Marines. Most of the Marines captured in the outpost battles were brought to the same collection center at which McDaniel and Lipscomb were being held. Second Lieutenant Henry L. Conway Jr., G/3/7, who was captured on October 6th, joined them and the trio remained together thereafter except during occasional periods of solitary confinement.[3]

In November the three officers were taken to a coal mine about midway between Kaesong and Pyongyang. A brutal North Korean major, called Yellow Jacket because of the color jacket he wore, was in charge of POW's at that loca-

---

[1] Letter from Maj Walter R. Harris, USMCR, to CMC, December 9, 1953.

[2] VMO-6, HistD, September 1952, Appendix G.

[3] Personal interview with Capt Roland McDaniel, USMC, July 26 and December 27, 1960.

tion. The Marines were temporarily separated and McDaniel was tied to a Korean who had been accused as a spy. In recounting this experience McDaniel said:

> The one thing I can't stand is to be tied up. I was tied up with a Korean for about ten days. We were in a hole, and a hole means vermin and rats. It means you can't move, and it means defecating and urinating in your pants. I thought I'd do almost anything to get untied. I really had to think about it to keep my sense of balance. I came out with pneumonia and T.B.[1]

At the coal mine Lieutenant McDaniel was approached by a North Korean interrogator on only one occasion. The Marine refused to talk and he recalls the following conversation. "If you won't co-operate this will be the last time I see you." McDaniel answered, "I have nothing to say." Surprisingly he was not pressed for more information nor was he molested further.

Captain Lipscomb, Lieutenants McDaniel and Conway, and three other officers were taken north to Camp 2 Annex in December, 1952. On arrival at Obul they were placed in solitary confinement before eventually joining Company C. McDaniel, a bachelor, told the Chinese he was married and had two children to avoid giving them any factual information to exploit. His captors were surprised when he refused to write letters to his family. Later he refused an opportunity to make a recording of greeting to his family. On a third occasion he was removed from the annex and interrogated concerning which officer was organizing the POW's in a military manner. Again he refused to answer.

---

[1] Ibid.

Work details in the annex had been organized by this time, and all of the POW's who were physically able to participate were busy unloading food from barges on the Yalu River. At other times they dug root cellars, built a field kitchen, and improved the primitive conditions of sanitation in and around camp.

When Lieutenant O'Shea was shot down in July, 1951, he knew that his pregnant wife was expecting the birth of twins. Although McDaniel did not know O'Shea, he had dated O'Shea's sister and had learned from her that the twins had been born. He was able to inform O'Shea of the successful birth when they met in the annex. He could not, however, recall the sex of the twins.[1] This was just another of the frustrations which so often face a POW.

Two events occurred in the closing weeks of 1952 which bear telling. One event was a birthday celebration and the other, which took place at the same time, was an athletic event.

The birth of the Continental Marines on November 10, 1775, has been honored by U. S. Marines since 1921 as their own birthday. The ceremony is prescribed in the Marine Corps Manual and on each November 10th the same ritual is observed at every post and station and every command and detachment throughout the Corps.[2] Most units also hold a party or ball in conjunction with the traditional program.

---
[1] McDaniel MS comment.

[2] Marine Corps Manual, 1949, Vol. 1 (Washington: U. S. Government Printing Office, 1949), para. 24451.

Camp 2 was no exception in 1952.

Preparations for a suitable celebration began long before November 10th. Marine officers stole eggs, sugar, and flour and the kitchen staff made a cake suitably decorated with the Marine Corps Globe and Anchor by Captain Fink. Another group was assigned the bootlegging task of preparing rice wine.[1] When November 10th arrived, the Marines of Company 1 filed into the library of the old schoolhouse. Quartermaster Sergeant James Day, Royal Marine, was among the invited guests. The small group toasted the President of the United States, the Commandant of the Marine Corps, and finally the Marine Corps itself. The National Anthem and Marine Corps hymn were sung loudly and resoundingly despite regulations to the contrary. In evaluating the ceremony and the reaction of non-Marines QMS Day wrote:

> Firstly some were apprehensive in case of trouble with the Chinese, and its always consequent rash of gaol victims. Some thought it a little childish, and not worth the trouble of interrupting the daily routine of the place. And I feel that quite a lot were rather envious that the small band of USMC should be able to get together and do this sort of thing quite seriously, quite sincerely, and with no thought of any consequence.[2]

It was also in November, 1952, that the Chinese staged a "Prisoner of War Command Olympics." When the idea was first broached to the officer prisoners there was considerable discussion as to whether or not they should parti-

---

[1] Fink interview.

[2] Day letter.

cipate.[1] Most of the Marines in Company 1, Camp 2, were opposed to the idea. According to Major Fink, the Marines in the second company and most of the British were also opposed to participation.[2] When the final decision was rendered by the senior United Nations officer, however, Camp 2 was to be represented.

The senior Air Force officer in camp was designated leader of the officers athletic teams. All services including the British were represented. U. S. Marine athletes were Major McLaughlin, Captains Wagner and Perry, and Lieutenants Stanfill, Turner, and Lundquist.

On arrival at Pyoktong, scene of the POW Olympics, the participants were issued athletic uniforms bearing their respective camp designations. The Chinese did not force the prisoners of war to hold "Fight for Peace" parades as they had attempted to do in the past although a review of competitors was held.

A large number of Communist photographers arrived. They took pictures of athletic events, spectators, and meals. The quantity and quality of food were vastly improved for the occasion, and the Chinese were determined to wring every possible advantage from their effort. Photos taken at the Olympics appeared in the propaganda

---

[1] Farrar-Hockley, pp. 246-48.

[2] Fink interview.

THE OLYMPICS AT PYOKTONG-NOVEMBER 1952

Soccer game.

Tug of war-the officer's team from Camp 2.

193

THE OLYMPICS AT PYOKTONG-NOVEMBER 1952

~~Enlisted~~ Basketball game.

Unidentified photograph-probably not
 taken at the November Olympics.
              Pyoktong Photos courtesy of
               Cpl Eddie P. Vidal, USMC (Ret)

brochure entitled "United Nations P.O.W.'s in Korea".[1] Copies of the brochure were distributed at a meeting of the League of Red Cross Societies in Geneva, Switzerland.[2]

A biased though basically accurate description of the event can be found in a book containing a collection of articles written by prisoners of war and later edited by three turncoats. One article in the book, credited to PFC Billy J. Lessman, U. S. Marine Corps, describes the Olympics in the following terms:

> During the athletic meet the spirit of these P.O.W.'s was very high. This includes both contestants and the spectators who cheered for their favorite sportsmen.
>
> The field was decorated by Korean P.O.W.'s who took pride in their work. Flags of every color represented each camp and the contestants were issued sports uniforms of their camp color.
>
> The food at Pyoktong was also an outstanding factor which helped make the meet the big success it was; pork, chicken, fish and goat were on the menu. The bread was prepared stuffed with meat, sugar, or vegetables.[3]

This sort of description coupled with the visual evidence of photographs must be very convincing to the un-

---

[1] Chinese People's Committee for World Peace. *United Nations P.O.W.'s in Korea*. (Peking: Chinese People's Committee for World Peace, 1953). A very clever piece of propaganda. This 92-page pictorial purports to show the lenient treatment of the Chinese Communist Forces in Korea toward their POW's.

[2] U. S. Congress, House, Committee on Un-American Activities. *Investigation of Communist Propaganda Among Prisoners of War in Korea*. 84th Cong., 2d Sess., 1956, p. 5142.

[3] Andrew M. Condron, Richard G. Corden, and Larance V. Sullivan, (eds.), *Thinking Soldiers* (Peking: New World Press, 1955), pp. 161-62.

initiated. The Olympics at Pyoktong did furnish entertainment and relaxation for the POW's who participated in the events and for those confined in Camp 5 who could observe the games. It must be remembered, however, that the affair was one brief event in the long course of the war and the benefit of the good food did not trickle down to other POW's.

When the officers discussed fielding teams for the various contests they recognized the potential propaganda value which might, and did, accrue to the Communists. No other factor loomed larger in their minds to dissuade them from going. But in the end, the possibility for making contact with other camps and exchanging vital information proved the deciding factor.

The one legged Air Force pilot, Major Thomas D. Harrison, described Major McLaughlin's role as follows:

> In November 1952 he attended an athletic meet in Pyoktong. While there, his skill as an athlete helped restore the prestige of the officers torn down by the enemy's propaganda. In addition he defied the guards by circulating among the enlisted men and pointing out lies contained in the enemy propaganda designed to slander this country, its government, and its leaders. At the same time he collected the names of many U. S. prisoners held in isolated places whom it was suspected that the enemy might attempt to hold after the end of the war.[1]

This seeming preoccupation with names was motivated by the fear expressed by Major Harrison; that the Communists

---

[1] Letter from LtCol Thomas D. Harrison, USAF, to Chief of Staff, USAF, March 11, 1954.

might not repatriate certain prisoners of war. The fear was shared by Marine intelligence officers in Japan who were responsible for keeping records of developments in this sensitive area.[1]

---

[1] Personal observation.

CHAPTER VII

STIGMA AND ASTIGMATISM

The closing days of hostilities brought better treatment for some Marines and increased pressure and coercion for others. Their problems did not end with repatriation. There still remained detailed intelligence processing en route home. This chapter will describe the combat actions of 1953 in which prisoners were lost to the enemy and some of the problems faced by Marine POW's during and after repatriation.

During the last seven months of hostilities in Korea 41 Marines were captured by the enemy. They included a pilot and an air observer who were shot down in separate engagements and 39 others who were captured in fierce outpost struggles which highlighted ground combat. In April, 1953, the belligerents held a preliminary exchange of sick and wounded prisoners of war. The final exchange of POW's took place in August and September after the cease-fire.

The first two Marines captured in 1953 were both shot down over enemy territory. Captain Kenneth L. Spence of VMO-6 was flying an OE-1 aircraft on a reconnaissance behind enemy lines on January 18th. First Lieutenant G. Allen was his observer. At about 5:15 P.M. ground observers saw the plane crash and noted that one parachute blossomed. The ground observers were near enough to hear small-arms fire in the vicinity where the parachute was seen to land, but they were unable to render assistance and search planes failed to locate the downed aircraft because of darkness. The following morning wreckage was sighted but no further observations were made.[1]

Captain Spence was captured and eventually he reached Obul, where he was assigned to the Camp 2 Annex.[2]

It was not until March 10th that another Marine was captured. Again it was an OE-1 light observation plane from VMO-6 which was hit by antiaircraft fire behind Chinese lines. The pilot turned towards friendly lines and then parachuted from the disabled aircraft. He was never heard from again. The air observer, Captain Dee E. Ezell, also parachuted. Although he landed safely, he was captured almost immediately.[3]

Captain Ezell later reported that he was threatened with beatings and death for refusing to reveal more than his name, rank, and serial number.[4] On April 13th the Marine air observer was taken to a POW collection point. He was placed with an enlisted Marine POW for a short while, but the two were separated shortly thereafter.

---

[1] VMO-6, HistD, January, 1953, Appendix 6.

[2] McDaniel interview.

[3] Captain Dee E. Ezell, Report of Captivity.

[4] Ibid.

Captain Ezell did not identify the other Marine, but no doubt the latter had been captured in late March during a struggle at one of the outposts of the 5th Marines.[1]

Ezell was placed in solitary confinement and a Chinese officer was assigned to interrogate him. The Marine described his experience in these terms:

> For the next five (5) months I was made to sit in [sic] middle of the floor with my legs pulled up under my chin all day long. I was interrogated every day and finally designated a "War Criminal" because of my refusal to impart military information. During this period I was beaten, kicked, and spat upon. I was constantly subjected to name-calling, threats and accusations.[2]

Captain Ezell reported that he escaped on about May 13th but was recaptured after eight days of freedom when he fell unconscious from lack of food, exposure, and exhaustion. He was returned to the original place of confinement and court-martialed. During the trial he was informed that his sentence would depend upon his cooperation. Captain Ezell was also accused of participating in bacteriological warfare. He was beaten by Chinese soldiers, denied medical care, provided inadequate rations, and isolated from other POW's. Finally on August 1st, four days after the armistice was signed, Captain Ezell was taken to the Yalu River area and, after five days of solitary confinement, he was placed in a regular POW camp awaiting repatriation.[3]

---

[1] USMC Casualties.

[2] Ezell Report of Captivity.

[3] Ibid.

Captain Ezell was the last Marine shot down and captured by the Communists in Korea, but 39 ground Marines were captured before hostilities ceased.

Enemy ground activity was mainly defensive in nature during the first quarter of 1953.[1] In March the Chinese resisted patrols and raids launched by the 5th Marines. It was not until the night of March 26th that the Communists launched an attack of significant proportions.[2]

Protracted rains and the spring thaw made movement difficult. Roads and trails were awash. Shortly before 7:00 P.M., March 26th, the Chinese directed an intense volume of mortar and artillery fire against combat outposts of the 5th Marines. Heavy fires also fell on approaches to the outposts and on the Marines' direct support artillery positions. Enemy long-range machine-gun fire was zeroed-in on the main line of resistance. Wire communications linking various command posts were disrupted by the Communist fire.

At 7:00 P.M. an estimated company of Chinese struck outposts Berlin and East Berlin in what appears to have been a diversionary attack.[3] The main enemy attack, estimated at regimental strength, fell on a trio of outposts in the right of 1/5's sector--Carson, Reno, and

---

[1] 1st MarDiv, CmdD's, January and February, 1953; and 5th Marines, CmdD's, January and February, 1953.

[2] 5th Marines, CmdD, March, 1953, p. 1.

[3] Ibid., p. 4.

Vegas. Two of the outposts, Reno and Vegas, were quickly overrun by the attackers. Marine reinforcements attempting to recapture the OP's were heavily engaged. Company F, 2d Battalion, 7th Marines, came under operational control of the 5th Marines. At 3:00 A.M. on the 27th the friendly counterattack was held up, and the Chinese continued to hold the two key outposts.[1]

At 3:45 A.M. the entire 2d Battalion, 7th Marines, passed to operational control of the 5th Marines. The counterattack was pressed shortly before noon by elements of both the 5th and 7th Marines with air, artillery, and tank support. Enemy resistance was stubborn and effective throughout the day, and not until 1:01 P.M. on the 28th did the Marines restore their outposts. The Chinese were quick to counterattack with an estimated two battalions the evening of March 29th and again in the early morning hours of the 30th, but their attacks failed and they were driven off.[2]

Second Lieutenant Rufus A. Seymour, the machine-gun platoon leader of C/1/5, had been in command of OP Reno when the Chinese struck. He was captured with several of his men in the ensuing action. Lieutenant Seymour later reported that the Chinese kept him on OP Reno for all of the next day and tried to force him to point out the

---

[1] Ibid.
[2] Ibid.

Marine main line of resistance. The night of the 27th he was taken to the rear where he was subjected to frequent interrogations and solitary confinement.[1] In about two weeks the Lieutenant was taken to the mines about 35 miles southeast of Pyongyang. He reported that he spent four weeks in solitary confinement during which time he was threatened with death and subjected to a mock court-martial for lying.[2]

According to Lieutenant Seymour, he then joined a group of about 40 POW's for two weeks before being blindfolded and driven north to Pyoktong. After the usual registration and interrogation at the Prisoner of War Headquarters, Seymour was taken to Obul and No Name Valley where he was confined with five other lieutenants.[3] The small group was not permitted contact with any of the scores of POW's in isolation throughout the valley but interrogations were less frequent than before and only occasionally were the six officers subjected to Communist propaganda.[4]

In addition to Lieutenant Seymour 18 Marines and two Navy hospitalmen were captured in the outpost action

---

[1] Lieutenant Rufus A. Seymour, Report of Captivity, February 4, 1954.

[2] Ibid.

[3] None of the lieutenants were Marines according to a recapitulation of the camp population at this time.

[4] Seymour Report of Captivity.

the night of March 26th. Private First Class Samuel J. Armstrong, among many others, was wounded during the battle and after his capture he was processed through a series of field hospitals. Armstrong reported that he did not reach a regular POW camp.[1]

Corporal Stephen E. Drummond, a communicator from the 11th Marines and probably a member of a forward observer team from a direct support artillery battery, was also captured in the action. He was not reported as having been in a regular camp[2] and his own narrative later indicates that he was kept mainly in aid stations of field hospitals. Drummond recounted that the Chinese overran his position at about 7:00 P.M. and that a grenade was thrown inside the living-bunker he was then occupying with other Marines. Corporal Drummond was wounded in the right leg. He and one or more others sat in the bunker for several hours, and at about midnight the Chinese entered the bunker and discovered them.[3] Drummond related that he was moved to the Chinese MLR with the help of another Marine. Two days later he was operated on in a cave-hospital. The treatment, he reported, was good, particularly

---

[1] ComNavFE Report of Little Switch. However, it is possible that PFC Armstrong was taken to the Mining Camp, Camp 10, but was kept in a separate area with other wounded from the Reno-Vegas action.

[2] ComNavFE Report of Little Switch.

[3] "Bunkeritis" was a term commonly applied to the tendency to remain inside the heavily reinforced bunkers during periods of intense incoming artillery fires.

for the wounded.[1]

Front line loud-speaker broadcasts were commonly made by both sides during this period of hostilities. Marines of the 1st Division frequently enjoyed the music while disregarding the propaganda of one they called "The Dragon Lady." Hospitalman Waddill later reported that after his capture on Reno he was taken to a frontline bunker where he was interrogated by a Chinese woman. She asked him several questions concerning the kind of music Americans liked.[2] Evidently she was associated with the Chinese phychological warfare unit then operating across from the 1st Marine Division.

Most of the Marines and the two sailors were taken to a place called the Mining Camp or Camp 10.[3] The POW's reported that security on the march was sufficient to prevent escapes and that the hills were virtually crawling with Chinese.[4]

Camp 10 consisted of a series of old Japanese barracks in fair condition. The buildings were stucco with gray slate roofs and concrete floors. Prisoners of war were assigned one squad to a room. Although the Chinese

---

[1] *Washington Post*, September 12, 1953, p. 5.

[2] ComNavFE Report of Little Switch, p. E 10.

[3] The British POW Report refers to Kanggye as Camp 10. According to the Marines, however, a Mining Camp near the battle line was referred to as Camp 10 by the Chinese in 1953. Since Kanggye had ceased to be a regular camp in March, 1951, this appears to be logical.

[4] ComNavFE Report of Little Switch.

did not require any segregation other than keeping the wounded apart from the healthy, there was a natural gravitation in groups according to nationality.[1]

Even the Marines captured as late as March, 1953, were forced to conduct group discussions on subjects directed by the Chinese. Some of the POW's were required to give the names and addresses of three people in their home towns. Obviously the Communists were considering ways and means for establishing contacts for possible propaganda targets. It appears that indoctrination attempts were feeble, however, when compared with the regimen of 1951 and 1952. Treatment of American wounded in Camp 10 was reported by returnees as equal to that provided Chinese wounded.[2]

Camp regulations prescribed that food would not be saved. If prisoners were caught violating this regulation the camp's bread ration would be forfeited for an indefinite period. As an added precaution against escape prisoners of war were not allowed on the main road of camp without a guard.[3]

In addition to the Marines and the sailor captured in March, at least three others captured earlier were confined in Camp 10. They were Privates First Class Pedro Aviles, of the Division Reconnaissance Company, and

---

[1] Ibid., p. E 7.

[2] Ibid.

[3] Ibid., p. E 8.

Albert T. Crabtree, of the 1st Marines, both captured in December, 1952, and Hospitalman Thomas A. Scheddel who had been captured while accompanying a Marine patrol on February 7, 1953.[1]

Private First Class Billy J. Morrow, W/1/5, was among those wounded during the fighting on OP Reno and presumably he died en route to Camp 10 or after arrival there. All other Marines known to have been captured on March 26th eventually returned to friendly hands alive.[2]

After the Chinese were driven off OP's Reno and Vegas and their counterattacks were rebuffed, the 7th Marines continued to relieve the 5th Marines on line. The relief in place was completed on April 4th. The 7th Regiment noted a steady decline in enemy aggressiveness when peace talks were resumed at Panmunjom. With the decrease in ground combat there was a corresponding increase in Communist psychological warfare activity. Propaganda leaflets delivered by mortar rounds appeared frequently.[3]

On April 9th at 3:45 A.M. the Chinese sent two companies to attack a combat outpost on hill 47. Enemy artillery fire sealed off the outpost and prevented reinforcements from aiding the beleaguered defenders. Hand to hand fighting continued until 7:00 A.M. when the Chinese were forced to retire leaving 60 of their dead behind.

---

[1] Ibid.

[2] USMC Casualties.

[3] 7th Marines, CmdD, April, 1953, p. 1.

Additional casualties were estimated to be 90 killed and 70 wounded. The Marines lost 14 killed, 74 wounded and 3 missing of whom Privates First Class Willie C. Stewart and Bernard A. Demski were captured. Demski died in enemy hands.[1]

In April, 1953, three months before the end of hostilities, Operation Little Switch, the first exchange of prisoners of war, took place. About 6,000 Communist Chinese and North Koreans were returned in exchange for about 600 Allied personnel.[2] The Allies included 149 Americans,[3] of whom 15 were Marines,[4] three were Navy hospitalmen attached to the 1st Marine Division, and one was a Navy flyer.

American prisoners of war recovered on Operation Little Switch were examined physically immediately after repatriation. After receiving hospital garb, carefully planned meals, and a brief rest, they were flown to Tokyo, Japan. On arrival in Japan the former POW's were given a detailed physical examination at Tokyo Army Hospital prior to being interrogated by intelligence personnel. Recovered Marines and Navy personnel were processed by members of the Intelligence Department of Commander, Naval Forces

---

[1] USMC Casualties.

[2] U. S. Fighting Man's Code, p. 81.

[3] Kinkead, In Every War..., p. 38.

[4] ComNavFE Report of Little Switch. See Appendix I.

Far East augmented by officers from other Marine staffs.[1]

The Marines and sailors repatriated during Operation Little Switch had all been wounded at the time of capture. The Little Switch returnees included fourteen Marines and two hospitalmen who had been captured on combat outposts on the western front in October 1952 and March 1953, only six months and one month respectively before their repatriation; one hospitalman who had been captured less than three months before while on patrol; a Marine, Private First Class Arthur J. Gregory, who had been captured while attacking an enemy OP the previous May and had been erroneously reported killed in action at the time; and, finally, Ensign Marvin Broomhead who had been shot down in February, 1952. He was the only one of the Navy-Marine group who had been to a regular camp in which long term captives were being held and thur was able to report on Camp 2.[2]

The returnees were all suffering from anemia and minor malnutrition despite the comparatively short term of captivity endured by most of them. Three of the Marines had limbs amputated. PFC Eddie P. Vidal had lost both legs, but he was the most cheerful of the entire group.[3] In the interest of learning operational lessons

---

[1] For composition of the Intelligence Processing Teams and a detailed description of the ComNavFE Special Liaison Group, Tokyo, see ComNavFE Report of Little Switch.

[2] ComNavFE Report of Little Switch.

[3] Personal observation.

all of the Marines were asked their opinion of the leadership of their immediate seniors in command at the time of their capture. In every case they reported that leadership had been good to outstanding.[1]

Based on reports from the Little Switch returnees of all services and allies, it was estimated that 103 Marines were alive and still in Communist POW camps.[2] Later events showed that probably 143 were in Communist hands at that time.

The repatriated Marines and sailors were flown to the United States in three groups along with larger numbers of Army and some Air Force personnel. The first group departed Tokyo on April 28th, the second on April 30th, and the final group on May 4th.[3]

No Marines captured before 1952 were repatriated during Operation Little Switch. Those who did return had been kept apart from earlier captives. Some returnees from other services had been captured in 1950 and 1951, however, and a few had experienced death marches and other brutal treatment. Their stories made a brief impact in local newspapers.

One plane carrying returnees slipped into the United

---

[1] ComNavFE Report of Little Switch.

[2] Commander, Naval Forces Far East, Standing Operating Procedure for Intelligence Processing of Recovered Prisoners of War (mimeographed) Change No. 1, July 24, 1953. Cited hereafter as ComNavFE POW SOP.

[3] The author accompanied the first group as an escort and returned to Tokyo to participate in planning for Big Switch.

States without the usual fanfare and then proceeded directly across country to deposit its passengers at Valley Forge Hospital in Pennsylvania. These passengers had been classified security risks by intelligence personnel and claims of brainwashing and cries of "progressive" were bandied about.[1] There were no Marines among the passengers destined for Valley Forge.

With the April exchange completed, staffs of the major components of Far East Command began to prepare for the anticipated Operation Big Switch, the return of all POW's. Meanwhile, in Korea, ground combat began to increase. The Chinese directed vicious attacks against Republic of Korea divisions in the central sector of the front, driving huge gaps in the line and causing withdrawals of several miles.

Numerous attacks were launched against the U. S. 25th Division which had relieved the Marines on the coastal flank in June. The 1st Marine Division remained in First Corps reserve until July 8th when it assumed operational control of the sector and moved back into line.

Enemy activity consisted of extensive patrol and ambush action with frequent attacks and constant probing of Marine positions. In each 24 hour period the 7th Marines had from 300 to 400 men forward of the main line of resistance either on patrol or manning combat outposts.

---

[1] "Snafu at Valley Forge," Newsweek, May 18, 1953; pp. 41, 44-46; and
William Brinkley, "Valley Forge G. I.'s Tell of Their Brainwashing Ordeal," Life, May 25, 1953, pp. 108-24.

The latter ranged from 13-man squads to platoons of about 40 men. Listening posts, generally manned by fire teams of four men, were maintained forward of the MLR during darkness.[1]

On July 7th the 2d Battalion, 7th Marines, relieved two battalions of the Turkish Brigade on line and assumed operational control of the right half of the regimental sector. The two main outposts were Berlin and East Berlin. Before midnight the Chinese attacked both OP's. As usual the attack was supported by a heavy volume of mortar and artillery fire. Close combat was reported in trenches and communications were lost with East Berlin at midnight. Counterattacks were pressed until the positions were restored shortly after noon on the 8th.[2] On the 9th there were numerous calls from the OP's for "Box me in" fires to break up enemy probes.[3] An estimated reinforced company of Chinese attacked Berlin and East Berlin at 1:30 A.M. They were repulsed an hour and a half later after suffering an estimated 180 casualties.[4] Although Marine casualties for this action were heavy and included several missing in action, only two were captured and repatriated later.[5]

---

[1] 7th Marines, CmdD, July, 1953, p. 1.

[2] 2/7, CmdD, July, 1953, pp. 1-4.

[3] Ibid., p. 5.

[4] 7th Marines, CmdD, July, 1953, p. 3.

[5] PFC's Kenneth F. Neville and Harold E. Richards.

A lull settled across the Marine Division front for almost two weeks. Truce negotiations appeared to be reaching a settlement. Loud speaker broadcasts were heard featuring a female voice and warning the Marines that they would be killed if they patrolled.[1] Patrols continued to search out the OP areas and valleys for signs of the enemy and recovery of bodies lost in the see-saw battles. On the 18th a C/1/7 patrol planted a Marine Corps recruiting sign on an enemy position. The 7th Marines maintained reinforced platoons on the two Berlin outposts. Heavy rains turned the ground into muck.[2]

The night of July 19th an estimated reinforced battalion of Chinese struck the Berlin complex. Close-in fighting developed and by 2:00 A.M. on the 20th, three and a half hours after the initial probes, the Chinese were in possession of both OP's. In preparing to relieve the 7th Marines in the right half of the division sector elements of the 1st Marines began to come under operational control of the 7th Marines on July 20th, just in time to become involved in the intense fighting for Berlin and East Berlin. Of the Marines from the 7th Regiment driven off the Berlin outposts six were killed and 118 wounded. Fifty-six Marines were unaccounted for at the time,[3] and of this number, 10 were captured and returned to friendly

---

[1] 1/7, CmdD, July, 1953, p. 5.

[2] Ibid, Appendix VII, p. 5.

[3] 7th Marines, CmdD, July, 1953, p. 4.

control after hostilities.[1] In addition about three men from the 1st Marines were captured.

While the major action raged at the 2/7 outposts other regimental units were engaged on the left flank. Frequent enemy probes had been directed against a squad outpost, Ava, near the boundary between the 5th and 7th Marines. Private First Class Donald K. McCoy of the 5th Marines was captured on the 20th and it seems likely that he was taken on or near OP Ava.

Following the seizure of OP's Berlin and East Berlin the enemy directed his attention against MLR positions. The Marines adopted a wide-front defense with one company in the Berlin complex short of the lost OP's and three companies on each of the two hill masses backing up the forward position. A decision was rendered by the Commanding General of First Corps not to retake Berlin and East Berlin.[2]

Only routine fighting was reported from the 21st to the 23d. As combat operations entered the final four days of the war, heavy action erupted across the front and continued until the morning of July 27th at which time the armistice was signed and hostilities ceased.[3]

When the fighting officially stopped, the Chinese made several attempts to fraternize. Some approached

---

[1] USMC Casualties.
[2] 1st MarDiv, CmdD, July, 1953, pp. 1-2.
[3] Ibid.

friendly listening posts and asked for water. Others hung up gift bags and shouted greetings across the heavily mined area separating the main positions of the recent belligerents.[1] The friendly attitude shown on the front line and in nearby rear areas had not been in evidence in POW camps along the Yalu River.

Marine Private First Class Alfred P. Graham Jr. recounted that he and large numbers of other sick POW's were taken to Camp 5, Pyoktong, in July, 1953, apparently to ready them for repatriation. Graham had incurred tuberculosis and during his captivity had been required to sleep on the floor in a small room with several other POW's. The prisoners were so crowded in their cramped quarters that they were unable to avoid contaminating each other during the nights when they slept huddled together--coughing.[2]

In the Sergeants' Camp at Wiwon the last six months of captivity were marked by a decrease in correspondence. Sergeant Donald M. Griffith stated that camp authorities insisted POW's use the return address: "c/o Chinese Peoples Committee for World Peace and against American Aggression." Most of the prisoners in Camp 4 refused to write letters using that address.[3]

The officers in Camp 2 refused to elect a chairman

---

[1] Ibid.

[2] Graham interview, *Washington Post*, August 16, 1953.

[3] Griffith letter.

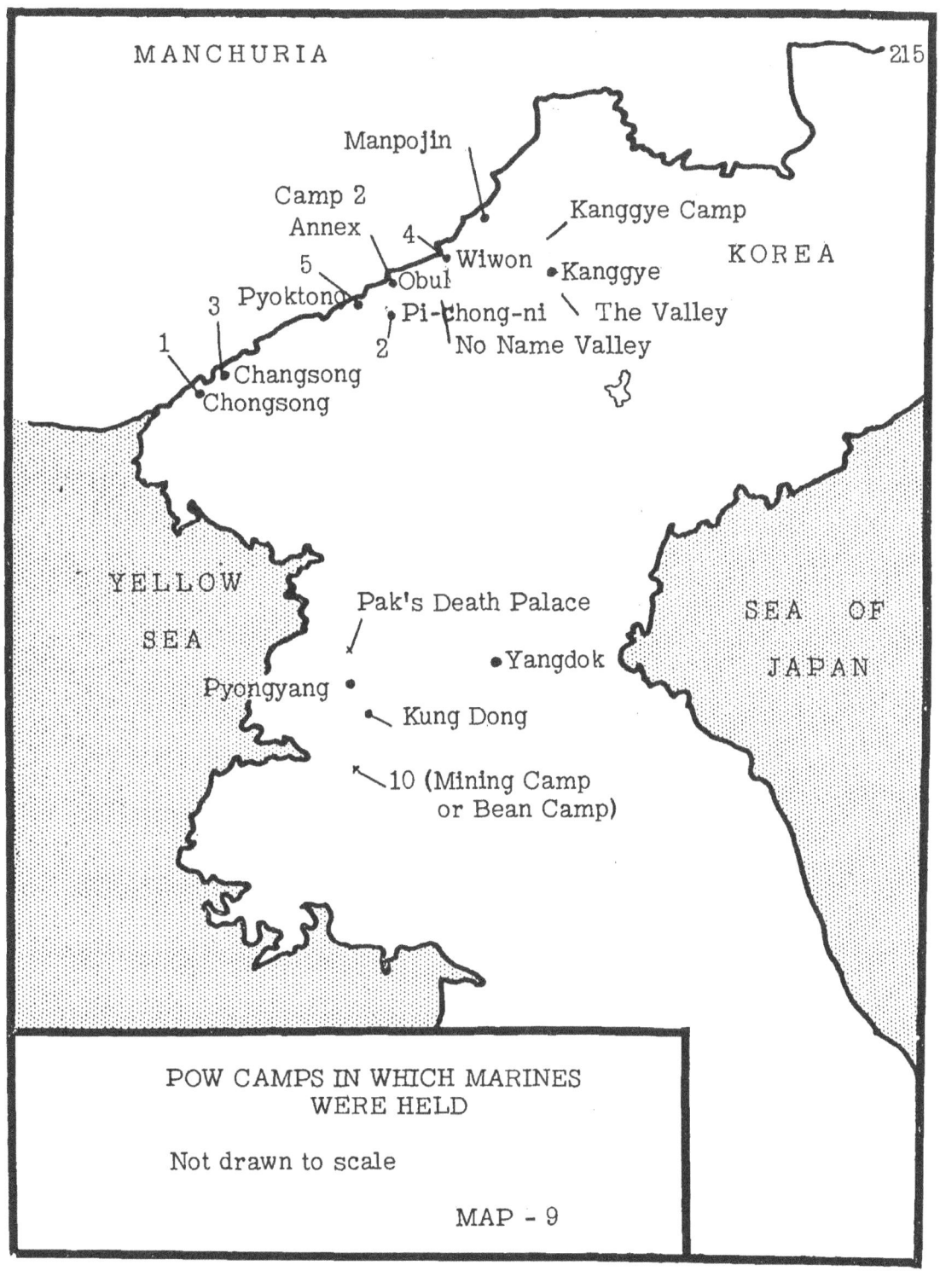

MAP - 9
POW CAMPS IN WHICH MARINES WERE HELD
Not drawn to scale

in March, 1953, because the occupational hazard was too great. The individual elected immediately became a target for Chinese harassment and certain punishment. This problem was solved by electing Major John N. McLaughlin chairman of a sports committee. The Chinese in turn appointed him chairman of the camp, an assignment McLaughlin accepted at the direction of Lieutenant Colonel Alarich L. E. Zacherle, U. S. Army Corps of Engineers, who was then the senior officer present.[1]

Duties as camp chairman made the Marine officer responsible for cooking, police, recreation, and procurement of rations and fuel; in addition to which he was also responsible for the conduct of all POW's in camp. Contrary to Chinese instructions, McLaughlin consulted Lieutenant Colonel Zacherle, the SOP, for policy and procedures. A vigorous athletic and physical conditioning program was organized and it contributed greatly to morale.[2] McLaughlin had assumed similar responsibility at Camp 5 in 1951, and in later months he served on a secret multiservice escape committee and senior officers' organization within Camp 2.[3]

Lieutenant Colonel Zacherle detailed Major McLaughlin

---

[1] McLaughlin Report of Captivity.

[2] Letter from LtCol Alarich L. E. Zacherle, USA, December 21, 1953, to Commandant of the Marine Corps. Cited hereafter as Zacherle letter to CMC.

[3] Letter from LtCol George R. Hansen, USA, n.d., to the Commandant of the Marine Corps, received at HQMC January 25, 1954. Cited hereafter as Hansen letter to CMC.

to represent Camp 2 at a conference in Pyoktong in May, 1953. According to Zacherle, the Major did not desire the job but willingly and cheerfully accepted it when directed to do so.[1] Major McLaughlin seized the opportunity to talk to General Wang Yang Kung, Commanding General of all Prisoner of War Camps, and demanded the Chinese cease persecution and imprisonment in solitary confinement of senior officers. He also pointed out the insufficient diet and Chinese nonconformance with the Geneva Convention. As a result of McLaughlin's efforts Lieutenant Colonels Carne of the Gloucestershires and Thrash of the Marine Corps were released from their solitary cells in a nearby Korean jail and restored to camp.[2]

Anticipating a truce, the senior officers in Camp 2 established a policy to guide behavior of POW's in all camps. Copies of the instructions were issued secretly to most camps except staging areas holding recently captured prisoners. POW's were not to fraternize or perform acts of violence.[3] They were cautioned not to show any great enthusiasm, particularly if Communist cameras were on the scene when a truce was announced.

In May General Wang Yang Kung refused a request of sick officer POW's that padre Davies be permitted to visit them. The general claimed that it was unnecessary for

---

[1] Zacherle letter to CMC.

[2] Thrash letter to CMC.

[3] Farrar-Hockley, p. 264.

the chaplain to go to the patients with prayers because it was well known that sickness could only be cured by medical treatment.[1]

Relations between Marines and the British were generally very good, but on occasion problems arose which needed solving. One such problem concerned singing, "You'll Never Walk Alone." The song was scheduled to be sung at Easter, 1953, when the Chinese agreed to permit the two companies of Camp 2 to hold a joint celebration. The Chinese approved the entire program except this particular song which they believed had political significance. Senior Marines were moved to delete the song for the sake of a celebration and a visit with friends. The British considered it a matter of principle and refused to concede. After discussing the matter the Marines supported their British friends and the show was not held. The British considered it a moral victory; the Chinese were "very much put out."[2]

A second incident of more explosive character arose when the time came for repatriation. As the prisoners were preparing to leave Camp 2 en route to Kaesong and Freedom Village, the Chinese reneged on a promise by confiscating a stone crucifix and candlesticks fashioned by the POW's and which Father Davies had consecrated for use in Anglican worship. Lieutenant Colonel Thrash, again

---

[1] Davies, p. 96.

[2] Farrar-Hockley letter.

the senior American officer, preferred not to risk freedom for the entire group over a trivial matter. Major Denis Harding, the British spokesman, said that not one British officer or warrant officer would leave camp until the religious objects were returned regardless of the American decision. The discussions were held in private. When it came to making a statement to the Chinese, the Americans supported the British and the crucifix and candlesticks accompanied the British to freedom.[1]

Of the Marine officers in Camp 2 we have these reports.

> Most impressive to me was the way they held together, whether they were flyers or ground personnel, although I did receive the impression that the flyers were a kind of "private army" and this I believe is how it should be. I should say that I never knew anything at all to the detriment of any USMC personnel, and that therefore their performance was first class. I attribute this solely to the personal qualities of the officers concerned, and a very close second the spirit of regimemtal pride which was most evident.[2]

> I can say quite happily that the USMC standard of conduct as prisoners of war was of a high order.
> . . . .
> There was no significant difference between USMC ground and air personnel; though there was a very perceptible difference between USMC and a number of other U S personnel in the camps.[3]

Lieutenant Colonel Gerald Brown, a heroic Air Force officer who was SOP in Camps 5 and 2 between tours of

---

[1] Ibid.

[2] Day letter.

[3] Farrar-Hockley letter.

solitary confinement, described Marines thus:

> I was extremely proud of the conduct of U S Marine Corps personnel with whom I came in contact during my period of confinement. Their Espirit [sic] de Corps was perhaps the highest of any branch of the Armed Forces of the United States during this period. I believe that Major McLaughlin did more than any other person in maintaining this espirit with his leadership.[1]

The prisoners of war in Camp 2 Annex were isolated from all contact with the main compound or with other prisoners scattered throughout No Name Valley. By the end of 1952 nine Marine officers and four enlisted Marines had been assigned to one of the two platoons which made up Company C. Major William Wilson, USAF, was the senior POW until his removal to another camp in February, 1953. At that time Marine Major Walter R. Harris assumed responsibilities as SOP.[2]

Major Harris requested permission from the Chinese to organize Spanish classes. When permission was granted the classes afforded a meeting place for issuing orders and policies. Some prisoners were assigned duties to counter Chinese political indoctrination. They were to teach American government and civics. An additional duty was preparing maps of North Korea to be used in escape attempts.[3]

---

[1] Letter from LtCol Gerald Brown, USAF, to CMC, December 14, 1953.

[2] Flynn Report of Captivity.

[3] Letter from the Commandant of the Marine Corps to the Secretary of the Navy dated December 21, 1953, recommending that Major Harris be awarded the Legion of Merit.

Protestant and Catholic services were organized at Camp 2 Annex.[1] One POW later stated that the individual conducting some of the services was shallow and not at all sincere about religion so he did not attend.[2]

In April, 1953, when the weather became more favorable for escapes, the Chinese began construction of a wall of saplings about 15 feet high surrounding the POW quarters. Completion of the wall was marked with an escape by three POW's. The escapees were recaptured within 14 hours, and the guard was doubled around the small compound.[3] Major Harris was taken away to solitary confinement and an Air Force Captain became SOP with Captain Flynn now the senior Marine.[4]

The POW's in the annex planned and prepared for a mass escape to take place in July. They fashioned compasses, knives, and other equipment essential for escape and movement cross-country. When July arrived the noticeable decrease in aerial activity was an indication that hostilities might be drawing to an end.[5]

Captain Flynn was removed from the annex on July 16th, and he reports that he was taken to a small village near Camp 3 and placed in solitary confinement. The captain

---

[1] Ibid.

[2] Thorin interview.

[3] Cain Report of Captivity.

[4] Flynn Report of Captivity.

[5] Cain Report of Captivity.

was charged with committing germ warfare, plotting the murder of the Chinese commander of Company C, seizing weapons and affecting a mass escape attempt, and having a reactionary attitude. Flynn was tried by a Chinese court and sentenced to 20 years imprisonment.[1]

Lieutenant Baugh was removed from the annex at the same time as Flynn but was taken to a part of Camp 2 for interrogation. He reports that he was interrogated extensively for two weeks concerning operational tactics and organization before his return to the annex on August 2d, a week after the armistice was signed. At no time during his interrogation was he informed that hostilities were over.[2]

Announcement of the cease fire was made in Camp 2 in July. The Chinese had cameras ready to photograph the reaction of the POW's, a reaction they probably expected to be joyous. The prisoners had been briefed by the senior officers' organization to show no emotion, and they did not speak when the news was published.

In Camp 2 on the following day Chaplain Davies preached on the theme of the 10 lepers cured of their disease and of whom nine forgot to give thanks.[3] A simi-

---

[1] Letter from the Commandant of the Marine Corps to the Secretary of the Navy dated December 21, 1953, recommending that Captain Flynn be awarded the Navy and Marine Corps Medal. Based upon information extracted from security dossiers.

[2] Baugh Report of Captivity.

[3] Davies, p. 146.

lar religious reaction took place in a remote compound in No Name Valley. When the cease-fire was announced to the small group Captain James V. Wilkins, a Catholic, stepped forward and motioned for the assembled prisoners to remove their hats. He then led them in reciting The Lord's Prayer. When he had finished, the camp commander screamed at him in Chinese, and an interpreter asked why he had stepped from ranks without permission.

The Marine answered, "I am a Christian. We are all Christians. We were offering our thanks to our Lord and Maker for the ending of hostilities." Captain Wilkins was immediately placed in the hole.[1]

Navy Chief Duane Thorin, who inspired the character of the helicopter pilot in James Michener's The Bridges of Toko-Ri, was confined in the annex for several months. He later stated, "The Navy and Marine Corps POW's were generally excellent. The Marines who left something to be desired were more than compensated for by the majority of them."[2]

After announcing the cease-fire, the Communists began bringing together many of the small isolated groups and individuals scattered throughout No Name Valley. One of these groups was headed by Marine Captain Gray who had spent almost a year in a remote Chinese surgical hospital before being brought north to No Name Valley. Captain Gray

---

[1] Lankford, p. 153.

[2] Thorin interview.

had been placed in Branch 3 of Camp 2 on March 10, 1953. His group of seven officers gradually increased to 30. He reported that classes were organized in mathematics, physics, and French. Survival lectures were held as well as conferences on escape and evasion techniques. The officers were divided into escape groups, and they drew straws to determine priorities for escape. Each team presented its plan to a senior body for approval.[1]

On July 1st with the support of other teams the first group went over the fence surrounding their house. Their freedom was short-lived and the guards were doubled. Escape plans were canceled when rumors of peace began to circulate.[2]

Of an estimated 150 POW's in No Name Valley nine were Marine officers. In addition to Captain Gray they included Colonel Schwable, Major Bley, Captains Ezell and Spence, and Lieutenants Gillette, Ferranto, Seymour, and Henry.[3] Colonel Schwable, Major Bley and Lieutenant Seymour were taken south to Kaesong separately. The others joined the annex during August 1953 and made the trip as part of the larger group. On August 17th the POW's in the annex were put aboard trucks and driven to Manpojin. Camp 2 POW's departed Pi-chong-ni on August 19th en route to

---

[1] Gray Report of Captivity.

[2] Ibid.

[3] Based upon a recapitulation of Reports of Captivity; statements of Colonel Schwable and Major Bley in UN Document A/C.1/L/66 of October 26, 1953; Henry letter; Fink interview; and McDaniel interview.

Manpojin. When the two groups were assembled they began the trip south by train.[1]

Captain Flynn was brought to Manpojin in time to accompany the main group to Kaesong. He was kept in a closely guarded car of the train but other Marines saw him.[2] At Kaesong Flynn and 49 other POW's were kept under guard away from the larger groups. Most of Flynn's party were under sentence of a Chinese court. Twenty-three were charged with breaches of camp regulations. Thirteen were former guards at Koje-do, the island camp in which the United Nations Command had held about 130,000 Communist POW's. Captain Flynn and six others were charged with waging germ warfare. Flynn, the senior member of the group, did not know the nature of the charges against the remaining seven.[3] Even as late as the end of August the Marine was threatened with nonrepatriation, and his experience formed the basis for an episode in the novel A Ride to Panmunjom.[4]

On September 3, 1953, Major Bley was called before a military tribunal headed by a North Korean general. He was informed that he was a war criminal but due to the North Korean and Chinese lenient policy he was to be given

---

[1] Ibid.

[2] Cain Report of Captivity.

[3] Flynn Report of Captivity.

[4] Duane Thorin, A Ride To Panmunjom (Chicago: Henry Regnery Co., 1956), pp. 264-67.

a pardon. Bley was then transported south and repatriated.[1] Colonel Schwable reported a similar experience,[2] and two Air Force Colonels reported being forced to make recordings in September 1953 of germ warfare confessions they had previously written.[3]

The United Nations prisoners of war were assembled at Kaesong and held there in several groups. Repatriation began with Operation Big Switch on August 5, 1953, and Marine Private First Class Alfred P. Graham Jr. was the fifth man and the first Marine to debark at Freedom Village. He was with seven other POW's all suffering from severe cases of tuberculosis. Graham was flown to the United States and sent to St. Albans hospital for treatment.[4]

Enlisted POW's were recovered in large numbers during August. Officers generally did not arrive at Kaesong until about August 21st, and after that date they were gradually returned to friendly control. Captain Jesse V. Booker, the first Marine captured by the enemy in Korea, was one of the first Marine officers released. He crossed the line to Freedom Village on August 27, 1953--three years and 20 days after being shot down.[5]

---

[1] Bley statement in UN Document A/C.1/L.66 of October 26, 1953.

[2] Schwable statement in UN Document A/C.1/L.66.

[3] UN Document A/C.1/L.66, pp. 29, 36.

[4] Washington Post, August 16, 1953, p. 1, col.6.

[5] Booker interview.

When Captain Martelli returned he learned that because he had been reported killed in action his wife had remarried.[1] Lieutenant O'Shea discovered that his twins were boys. As might be expected, news good and bad awaited returning POW's of all services and nationalities.

Major Harrison, USAF, was forced to leave his artificial leg behind. Hidden in a hollowed-out compartment in the leg was a written record of deaths, atrocities, and other administrative data. Major Richardson, USMC, had made a copy of the records and secreted them in the hand grip of Harrison's crutches. Another copy of the list was hidden in the walking cane of Infantry Captain Chester Osborne, USA.[2] And Captain Fink's crucifix was brought out of Pi-chong-ni. It now reposes in the Father Kapaun Memorial High School in Wichita, Kansas.[3]

All recovered POW's were questioned by intelligence personnel when they returned to friendly control. Priority was given to accumulating accurate data on living and deceased POW's to assure that none could be held back by the Communists. The recovered personnel were interrogated about atrocities by the enemy and questionable acts by our own men in addition to routine military matters. The collated reports of Operation Little Switch had pinpointed

---

[1] Fink interview.

[2] Fink notes and ms comments.

[3] Tonnes, pp. 239-44; and
Wichita Eagle, November 27, 1955 and May 12, 1957.

some American POW's whose conduct was clearly reprehensible. Others were marked for detailed inquiry either to refute or substantiate charges made against them. Intelligence or security dossiers had been prepared for all POW's and all comments or data concerning a specific individual went into his file. The mass of information included everything from well founded and thoroughly substantiated information, both pro and con, to completely unsupported rumors, hearsay, and even fabrications.[1]

Twenty-one Americans refused repatriation. One author implied that this was the first time in history that American captives chose another form of government to our own.[2] The U. S. Fighting Man's Code suggests that they refused repatriation because they feared vengeance from the men they betrayed or from friends of men who died because of their treason.[3] In either event there were no U. S. Marines among the turncoats.

It should be noted that of approximately 20,000 Chinese POW's 14,343 refused repatriation.[4] After a period of explanations by the Communists, they were shipped to Formosa, the stronghold of Chiang Kai-shek's Republic of China. In addition approximately 38,000

---

[1] Personal observation.

[2] Eugene Kinkead, "The Study of Something New in History," The New Yorker, October 26, 1957, p. 102.

[3] U. S. Fighting Man's Code, p. 42.

[4] Kenneth K. Hansen, Heroes Behind Barbed Wire (Princeton, N. J.: D. Van Nostrand Co. Inc., 1957) p. 298.

Korean civilian internees and 27,000 North Korean soldiers had indicated their refusal to be repatriated to the Communists. They were released on order from Syngman Rhee, the President of South Korea, before the end of hostilities. About 7,000 additional North Koreans refused repatriation and faced the Communist explainers before gaining civilian status on Freedom Day, January 23, 1954.[1] A comparison shows that in addition to the 21 Americans only one British and 335 South Koreans[2] refused to return home opposed to about 87,000 of 173,000 Communists POW's who refused repatriation.

In the United States a series of courts-martial began. The U. S. Army brought to trial 14 of about 47 cases originally approved for court-martial.[3] According to author Kinkead the trials were unpopular with the public.[4] Yet there is little doubt that the unexpected news of Americans refusing to return home coupled with a spate of charges and countercharges between returnees placed a stigma upon POW's in general. The Defense Advisory Committee on Prisoners of War made the following observation when reporting their findings to the Secretary of Defense:

---

[1] Ibid., p. 304.

[2] Ibid., p. 159.

[3] Kinkead, In Every War . . ., p. 73; and U. S. Fighting Man's Code, p. 82.

[4] Kinkead, In Every War . . ., pp. 65-68, 73.

> The prisoner of war situation resulting from
> the Korean War has received a great deal of
> adverse publicity. As is stated in our
> account, much of that adverse publicity was
> due to lack of information and consequent
> misconceptions in regard to the problem.[1]

A total of 7,140 American fighting men of all services were captured by the enemy in Korea. Of this number 2,701 or about 38% died while interned, and 4,418 were recovered.[2] Marine Corps statistics show that 221 Marines were captured, 194 were recovered, and 27 or about 12% died.[3]

Only a handful of the POW's in Korea were able to maintain absolute silence under military interrogation. Nearly all of the American prisoners went beyond the "absolute" name, rank, number, and date of birth restriction.[4] Marines were no exception. Giving false, misleading, or even accurate but unimportant information in response to threats, coercion, and torture was a common occurrence. Captain Fink's list of ships, all sunk during WW I and WW II, was similar to the story of the new B-108 bomber related by an Air Force officer. With proper addition the Chinese might have deduced that a B-108 was

---

[1] Defense Advisory Committee on Prisoners of War letter to the Secretary of Defense, July 29, 1955, cited in POW, p. vi.

[2] Department of Defense Tentative Final Report of US Battle Casualties in the Korean War, P28.1, Program Reports and Statistics, Office of the Secretary of Defense, November 4, 1954.

[3] USMC Casualties. These figures do not include the B/1/5 patrol of 10 men. See chapter IV above. Also see Appendix B.

[4] U. S. Fighting Man's Code, p. 84.

three B-36's.[1] Almost every prisoner of war faced interrogation.[2] In most cases a POW faced threats of death, reduced rations, lack of medical care, solitary confinement, and physical beatings or torture if he failed to respond to questions. Generally each individual had to decide for himself how to react. The decisions which were made appear to have been mainly sound. Only 192 Americans were found chargeable with serious offenses against comrades or the United States.[3] None of these was a Marine. Three hundred seventy-three others, including 49 Marines, were cleared or charges against them were dropped after preliminary investigation.[4]

The Information Section of Headquarters, Marine Corps, issued a paper setting forth the official Marine Corps position concerning prisoners of war. The paper bears no date but judging from the text it was promulgated after January 11th and before the middle of April, 1954. Extracts from two of the twelve paragraphs are particularly pertinent to this thesis:

> When information is developed concerning a returned prisoner of war that raises a question of a violation of the trust placed

---

[1] Fink interview.

[2] HumRRO 33, p. 7. A detailed study of Army POW's disclosed that 97% had been interrogated to some extent and 91% had been made to write biographies. No similar study exists for Marines.

[3] U. S. Fighting Man's Code, pp. 84-5.

[4] POW, p. 81.

> in him, then all pertinent facts must be obtained in order that suspicion may be allayed or confirmed. This is as important to the individual as it is to the Marine Corps and the Nation.
>
> . . . .
> The Secretary of the Navy, upon recommendation of the Commandant of the Marine Corps, has already recognized with awards Marines who appear to have conducted themselves while prisoners of war in the tradition which the Corps has upheld during 178 years of service to its country. On the other hand, the Commandant had felt compelled to convene a Court of Inquiry to investigate the circumstances of a senior officer's conduct while in the hands of the enemy. By these actions, every Marine of high or low rank will know that justice will be impartially rendered.[1]

Lieutenant Colonel Thrash received a gold star in lieu of a second Legion of Merit. McLaughlin, then promoted to Lieutenant Colonel, and Major Harris both received the Legion of Merit. Captain Flynn was awarded the Navy and Marine Corps medal. Master Sergeant Cain was presented a letter of Commendation with ribbon.[2]

Colonel Schwable was the subject of a Court of Inquiry concerning the circumstances surrounding his confession of bacteriological warfare operations. After hearing numerous witnesses and due deliberation the court submitted its findings to the Commandant of the Marine

---

[1] Information Section, Headquarters, U. S. Marine Corps position paper, n.d. Copy in author's personal file. A Court of Inquiry is primarily a fact finding body and its conclusions are advisory. It cannot award punishments although it may recommend trial by court martial.

[2] Copies of citations filed in service records. Records of citations in Code DF, HQMC.
The New York Times, January 12, 1954, p. 3.

Corps. The court was of the opinion "that the Communists have developed, and perfected, a diabolic method of torture which combines degradation, deprivation and mental harassment, and which is aimed at the destruction of the individual's will to resist."[1] In conclusion the court recommended no disciplinary action be taken in the Colonel's case.[2] The court was further of the opinion that Colonel Schwable had resisted this torture to the limit of his ability before giving in.[3]

In forwarding the case to the Secretary of the Navy on April 14, 1954, the Commandant of the Marine Corps made several observations which included the following:

> The involuntary character of the statement as well as its complete falsity have never been questioned. The fact remains however, that it was used as a principal circumstantial buttress in support of one of the most enormous fabrications of modern times....
>
> . . . .
>
> Cognizance of this fact [that he was an instrument in causing damage to his country] must, in my judgment, be taken into account in regard to his future assignment potential with the application of such restrictions of his service to those military activities involving duties of a type making minimum demands for their successful performance upon the elements of unblemished personal example and leadership.[4]

---

[1] Court of Inquiry, case of Colonel Frank H. Schwable, Opinion 4.

[2] Ibid., Recommendation 1.

[3] Ibid., Opinion 8.

[4] Letter from the Commandant of the Marine Corps to the Secretary of the Navy dated April 14, 1954. This letter forwarded the Court of Inquiry, case of Col Schwable.

234

The Secretary of the Navy and the Secretary of Defense concurred with the Commandant's observations.[1]

One Marine was disciplined. Author Eugene Kinkead described his dismissal from the Corps for fraternizing with the enemy as the Corps' sole disciplinary casualty of the war.[2] The name of the dismissed Marine is not reported here for cogent reasons. As an illustration that men are never all good or all bad, however, the following comment describes the sole disciplinary casualty of the Corps:

> I'd say some people were definitely friendly with the Chinese no Marines that I know of even [name ommitted] he was sort of caught in the middle many times and being quiet to [sic] point of clamness at one time and voluble and opinionated at others made enemies![3]

The fear that the Communists might withhold prisoners of war was well-founded. Eleven survivors of a B-29 crew shot down over North Korea on January 12, 1953, were neither reported nor returned during 1953. In early 1954 the crew members still had not been informed that the fighting was over. In August, 1954, more than a year

---

[1] Memorandum from the Secretary of the Navy to the Secretary of Defense dated April 21, 1954; and
 Memorandum from the Secretary of Defense to the Secretary of the Navy dated April 27, 1954.
 The findings of fact, opinions, and recommendations of the Court of Inquiry, case of Colonel Schwable, and the letters and memoranda herein cited were prepared in brochures for release to the press on April 27, 1954.

[2] Kinkead, In Every War..., p. 163.

[3] McCool letter.

after the cease-fire and 19 months after capture, the Communists revealed that they held the 11 airmen. Finally on August 4, 1955, the flyers crossed the Lo Wu bridge at Kowloon and returned to freedom.[1]

A Marine officer was seized by the Communists after the war and held incommunicado for several months. Lieutenant Colonel Herbert Peters was lost in a snow storm while on a routine flight in January, 1954. He landed on a small landing strip he had observed through a fleeting break in the weather. As he taxied to the end of the field he saw that the personnel coming to meet him were wearing Communist uniforms. Before he could turn around and take off, several Communist soldiers leaped on the wings and prevented his departure. In August, 1954, eight months after he inadvertantly landed on the Communist airfield, the Marine pilot was returned to friendly control. No word of his captivity had reached the United Nations Command before his sudden and unannounced return. On the basis of an exhaustive search and scattering reward leaflets throughout the area of the planned flight, it had been assumed that Lieutenant Colonel Peters had been killed and he was so reported.[2] He was the last Marine captured but because the date of his captivity was after the cease-fire he is not numbered among the official POW's.

---

[1] Wallace L. Brown, *Endless Hours: My Two and One Half Years as a Prisoner of the Chinese Communists* (New York: W. W. Norton & Co., 1961), galley proofs.

[2] Interview with LtCol Richard Lauer, USMC, March 10, 1961.

From August 7, 1950, to July 20, 1953, 221 Marines were captured by the enemy. The circumstances of their capture as set forth herein shows that in most cases capture was unavoidable. On the other hand had not Colonel Schwable and Major Bley inadvertantly flown over enemy lines they probably would never have become prisoners of war. Had Private First Class Lessman not wandered off alone he would not have fallen into Communist hands. Had the crew of tank number 22 abandoned their tank when first instructed to do so they might have gone south to Masan instead to north to Kanggye in December, 1950. Perhaps even a few Marines captured in bunkers might have avoided captivity had they been occupying fighting-holes instead of being inside their living-bunkers. Conversely they might have been killed during the artillery bombardments which accompanied the enemy assaults. But in the main, the vast majority of Marines captured had no control over the events which catapulted them into POW camps.

The narratives set forth in this paper lend substance to the claim that Marines as a group comported themselves extremely well. In answer to a question from the audience after his address to the U. S. Army Chaplain School in February, 1957, Army psychiatrist, Major William F. Mayer made this statement:

> . . . The Marines were a statistically significant group from the standpoint of size, something over two hundred; the only thing I can say about them is that more of them survived than we. I think this is a function of discipline and morale and esprit; and the attitude in the

Marine Corps I expressed a little while ago, that if something happens to me, these jokers will take care of me.[1]

The United States Senate investigated Communist handling of American POW's and concluded:

> The United States Marine Corps, the Turkish troops, and the Columbians, as groups, did not succumb to the pressures exerted upon them by the Communists and did not co-operate or collaborate with the enemy. For this they deserve greatest admiration and credit.[2]

A prominent neurologist and consultant to the Secretary of Defense's Advisory Committee on Prisoners of War, Dr. Harold G. Wolff, presented one of the most definitive discussions yet to appear on the POW problem. He concluded that American prisoners of war in Korea had not behaved much differently from other men in other armies and places. Dr. Wolff believes that Americans were made to appear much worse by the enemy's propaganda devices and our own initial ineptitude in countering the Communist propaganda.[3]

Marine POW's in Korea faced a wide variety of problems. The detailed scrutiny of intelligence processing by their own military associates and the investigations of the Congress have shown that as a group the

---

[1] Major William F. Mayer quoted in Headquarters, USA Chaplain School, Fort Slocum, N. Y., Student Handout 2-CD-FD (Dec'57). Copy filed in Chief of Chaplain's office, Pentagon, Washington, D. C.

[2] Senate Subcommittee on Investigations, POW Hearings, Report No. 2832, p. 23.

[3] Dr. Harold G. Wolff, "Every Man Has His Breaking Point -(?)," Military Medicine. February 1960, p. 91.

Marines comported themselves well while prisoners of the enemy. In short, they measured up. To conclude this thesis without a summation of the lessons learned, though that is clearly beyond the original scope of this work, would be incomplete staff work. Therefore a few comments made by the former POW's themselves will serve to express what I have learned:

> Discipline, team work and faith in what you are and in what your government represents, are the factors that this conduct training should be based on.[1]

> ... without USMC training I would never have lived through several tight spots. I am not talking strictly about physical training as I am mental conditioning. It is something that causes you to think, even when you are about to get your gizzard blown out, about what the other guys will think or how it might affect or endanger them.[2]

> I had made up my mind that the loss of both my legs was not going to keep me in my wheel chair and at home for the rest of my liveing [sic] years. No sir not me. A U. S. Marine. I have pride in the Marine Corps and I want the people to know that the Marines are the Greatest of all.[3]

Major Stewart C. Barber, a Marine officer assigned to one of the Joint Intelligence Processing Boards, expressed pride in the six enlisted Marines on his ship and commented that they were most co-operative. All six of these Marines reported that their leadership was good to

---

[1] Griffith letter.

[2] Harrison letter.

[3] Vidal letter, p. 30. Corporal Vidal has had 17 operations on his stumps and is now using his third set of artificial legs. He and his wife have had three daughters born since his return. He is now a successful watchmaker.

excellent. Major Barber concluded, "Our recruit training is superior in achieving the necessary transition from citizen to soldier."[1]

First Sergeant Chester A. Mathis observed, "When the chips are really down, training pays off!!!"[2]

Winston Churchill once described the lot of a prisoner of war. His words can hardly be improved upon:

> It is a melancholy state, you are in the power of the enemy. You owe your life to his humanity, your daily bread to his compassion. You must obey his order, await his pleasure, possess your soul in patience. The days are long; hours crawl by like paralytic centipedes. Moreover the whole atmosphere of prison is odious. Companions quarrel about trifles and get the least possible enjoyment from each others society. You feel a constant humiliation in being fenced in by railings and wire, watched by armed guards and webbed about with a tangle of regulations and restrictions.[3]

Communist treatment and indoctrination of POW's was a new experience to Marines who were captured. They encountered many diverse problems--field grade and company officers, staff NCO's, young and untried privates. Their most important decisions were often made alone, without guidance. Their solutions were not always the best ones, but in the long run most of the Marine POW's came through with flying colors.

---

[1] Letter from Major Stewart C. Barber.

[2] Mathis letter.

[3] Winston S. Churchill, *A Roving Commission* (New York: Charles Scribner's Sons, 1939), quoted in *Reader's Digest*, July 1940.

APPENDIX A

GLOSSARY OF TERMS AND ABBREVIATIONS

AAA	Antiaircraft artillery
BW	Bacteriological warfare
Capt	Captain
CCF	Chinese Communist Forces - an American term
CG	Commanding General
CinCFE	Commander in Chief, Far East. General of the Army Douglas MacArthur was CinCFE at the outbreak of hostilities in Korea. General MacArthur was succeeded by General Matthew B. Ridgway who was succeeded by General Mark W. Clark
CMC	Commandant of the Marine Corps
CmdD	Command Diary
ComNavFE	Commander Naval Forces, Far East. Naval Forces, Far East, constituted the naval component of the Far East Command
CO	Commanding Officer
COP	Combat Outpost
Cpl	Corporal. The lowest ranking noncommissioned officer. In the Marine Corps a corporal is the senior member and leader of a four-man fire team, the smallest tactical unit
CPV	Chinese People's Volunteers. A term used by the Chinese and North Koreans to describe the Chinese Communist Forces in Korea
CWO	Commissioned Warrant Officer
Div	Division
do (or to)	Korean suffix meaning "island" like the Japanese term "jima" or "shima"

encl	Enclosure
Engr Bn	Engineer Battalion
EUSAK	Eighth U. S. Army in Korea
NK	North Korean
MLR	Main Line of Resistance
MTBn	Motor Transport Battalion
OE	Light observation aircraft
OP	Observation post. Sometimes used in referring to an outpost
OPLR	Outpost line of resistance. An imaginary line connecting small security elements established forward of the main line of resistance
OY	Light observation aircraft. A predecessor of the OE
PFC	Private First Class
POW	Prisoner of war; also PW
Progressive	Term used by the Communists and adopted by United Nations troops to denote a POW who co-operated with the Communists and accepted or appeared to accept their teachings
Pvt	Private
QMS	Quartermaster Sergeant. A Royal Marine rank roughly equivalent to an American First Sergeant or Master Sergeant
Reactionary	Term used by the Communists and adopted by United Nations troops to denote a POW who resisted the Communists
Recon	Reconnaissance
ri	Korean suffix meaning village
Rkt	Rocket: Such as a 4.5" Rocket Battery
RM	Royal Marine
ROK	Republic of Korea

SAR	Special Action Report
ser	Serial
ServBn	Service Battalion
Sgt	Sergeant
F4U	Corsair: A World War II vintage propeller-driven fighter-bomber aircraft used for close support of ground troops during the Korean War
F7F	Tigercat: Twin engine, propeller driven aircraft. Used as a night fighter and reconnaissance aircraft in Korea
F9F	Panther: Jet attack aircraft
FMCR	Fleet Marine Corps Reserve. Enlisted status equivalent to officer retired status
FMF	Fleet Marine Force. A term referring to all of the air, ground, and combat service and support units in the Marine Corps. At the beginning of hostilities in Korea the Fleet Marine Forces included two understrength divisions and two understrength aircraft wings. By the end of the war the FMF had expanded to three full-strength divisions and three aircraft wings
FMFLant	Fleet Marine Force, Atlantic
FMFPac	Fleet Marine Force, Pacific
HistD	Historical diary
HQMC	Headquarters, U. S. Marine Corps, Washington 25, D. C.
KCOMZ	Korean Communications Zone. The major U. S. Army command responsible for rear areas in Korea
KMC	Korean Marine Corps
Lt	Lieutenant. (2dLt - Second Lieutenant; 1stLt - First Lieutenant)
LtCol	Lieutenant Colonel
Lt(jg)	Lieutenant (junior grade). A Navy rank corresponding to a 1stLt

MAG	Marine Aircraft Group. The aviation unit comparable to a ground regiment in organization
MarDiv	Marine Division
Marines	Term used to signify a Marine regiment such as the 5th Marines
MAW	Marine Aircraft Wing. The aviation unit comparable to a ground division in organization. Roughly 10,000 Marines in three combat Marine Aircraft Groups and their service and support units
MSgt	Master Sergeant
ni (or ri)	Korean suffix meaning village
SigBn	Signal Battalion
SK	South Korea or South Korean
Squadron	Aviation unit comparable in organization to a ground battalion. In Korea the normal complement of a Marine fighter or attack squadron was 24 aircraft, 50 pilots, and appropriate ground crew personnel and equipment
SOP	Senior officer present. The abbreviation is also used for Standing Operating Procedure
SPBn	Shore Party Battalion. A unit responsible for the combat engineer and logistic support in beach areas during an amphibious operation.
SSgt	Staff Sergeant
TSgt	Technical Sergeant
TBM	Avenger: Gruman torpedo bomber which, in World War II, was the largest and heaviest single engine propeller-driven aircraft
USA	United States Army
USAF	United States Air Force
UNC	United Nations Command
USMC	United States Marine Corps
USMCR	United States Marine Corps Reserve

USN	United States Navy
VMA	Marine Attack Squadron: V - heavier than air; M - Marine; A - attack
VMF	Marine Fighter Squadron
VMF(N)	Marine All-Weather Fighter Squadron. N initially designated a night fighter unit, but during the Korean War the designation was changed to mean an all-weather unit. Later the letters (AW) replaced (N)
VMO	Marine Observation Squadron
4.2"	4.2 inch (mortar company)

APPENDIX B

TABLE OF MARINES CAPTURED BY MONTH

1950

AVIATION

	Jul	Aug	Sep	Oct	Nov	Dec
Captured		<u>1</u>				
Returned		<u>1</u>				
Died						
Presumed Dead						
Total		1				

GROUND

	Jul	Aug	Sep	Oct	Nov	Dec
Captured				1̄	10/48	1̄9̄
Returned					8/38	1̄2̄
Died				1̄	9̄	6̄
Presumed Dead					2/1	1̄
Total				1	58	19

TOTAL

	Jul	Aug	Sep	Oct	Nov	Dec
Captured		<u>1</u>	1̄		10/48	1̄9̄
Returned		<u>1</u>			8/38	1̄2̄
Died				1̄	9̄	6̄
Presumed Dead					2/1	1̄
Total		1	1		58	19

<u>Officers</u>
Enlisted

1951

AVIATION

	Jan	Feb	Mar	Apr	May	Jun	Jul	Aug	Sep	Oct	Nov	Dec
Captured				1	3	1	5	1		4	1	2
Returned				1	3	1	3	1		4	1	2
Died							2					
Presumed Dead												
Total				1	3	1	5	1		4	1	2

GROUND

	Jan	Feb	Mar	Apr	May	Jun	Jul	Aug	Sep	Oct	Nov	Dec
Captured					3/3	2/2	1*/2		2/2	1/1		1*/1
Returned					3/3	2/2	1/2		2/2	1/1		1/1
Died												
Presumed Dead												
Total					3	2	3		2	1		2

TOTAL

	Jan	Feb	Mar	Apr	May	Jun	Jul	Aug	Sep	Oct	Nov	Dec
Captured				1/3	3/2	1	6/2	1	2	4/1	1	3/1
Returned				1/3	3/2	1	4/2	1	2	4/1	1	3/1
Died							2					
Presumed Dead												
Total				4	5	1	8	1	2	5	1	4

* - Ground officer shot down while in aircraft

1952

AVIATION

	Jan	Feb	Mar	Apr	May	Jun	Jul	Aug	Sep	Oct	Nov	Dec
Captured	1		1		4		2/1	1	1			
Returned			1		4		2/1		1			
Died	1											
Presumed Dead								1				
Total	1		1		4		3	1	1			

GROUND

	Jan	Feb	Mar	Apr	May	Jun	Jul	Aug	Sep	Oct	Nov	Dec
Captured		1*/1		-/5	1/2				1*/4	1/40		-/3
Returned		1/1		-/5	1/2				1/4	1/39		-/3
Died										-/1		
Presumed Dead												
Total		2		5	3				5	41		3

TOTAL

	Jan	Feb	Mar	Apr	May	Jun	Jul	Aug	Sep	Oct	Nov	Dec
Captured	1	1/1	1	-/5	5/2		2/1	1	2/4	1/40		-/3
Returned		1/1	1	-/5	5/2		2/1		2/4	1/39		-/3
Died	1									-/1		
Presumed Dead								1				
Total	1	2	1	5	7		3	1	6	41		3

* — Ground officer shot down while in aircraft

1953

AVIATION

	Jan	Feb	Mar	Apr	May	Jun	Jul	Total 1950 to 1953
Captured	1							30/1
Returned	1							26/1
Died								3
Presumed Dead								1
Total	1							31

GROUND

	Jan	Feb	Mar	Apr	May	Jun	Jul	Total 1950 to 1953
Captured			2**/18	2		1/17		19/171
Returned			2/17	1		1/17		17/150
Died				1				18
Presumed Dead			1					2/3
Total			20	2		18		190

TOTAL

	Jan	Feb	Mar	Apr	May	Jun	Jul	Total 1950 to 1953
Captured	1		2/18	2		1/17		49/172
Returned	1		2/17	1		1/17		43/151
Died				1				3/18
Presumed Dead			1					3/3
Total	1		20	2		18		221

** - One of these two officers was a ground officer shot down while flying in an aircraft

APPENDIX C

ALPHABETICAL ROSTER OF OFFICER POW'S
RETURNED TO MILITARY CONTROL

Name	Rank	Service Number	Date of Capture	Unit
Amann, Emanuel R.	Captain	038140	4Oct51	VMF-323
Baugh, Milton H.	1st Lt	010658	13May52	VMF-311
Bell, Richard	1st Lt	045307	21Jul51	VMF-311
Beswick, Byron H.	Captain	029003	2May51	VMF-323
Bley, Roy H.	Major	010450	8Jul52	1st MAW
Booker, Jesse V.	Captain	020617	7Aug50	1st MAW
Clifford, Henry E.	2d Lt	058124	Jul53	7th Mar
Cold, Frank E.	1st Lt	039090	29Nov50	3/7
Conway, Henry L.	2d Lt	054354	6Oct52	G/3/7
Ezell, Dee E.	Captain	029832	10Mar53	1stMarDiv
Ferranto, Felix L.	1st Lt	014978	28Nov50	1stSigBn
Fink, Gerald	Captain	023889	12Aug51	VMF-312
Flynn, John P.	Captain	032419	14May52	VMF(N)-513
Gillette, Robert J.	1st Lt	035468	12Oct51	VMF(N)-513
Gray, Roy C.	Captain	024638	4Mar52	VMF-311
Harris, Walter R.	Major	016518	6May52	VMF-323
Henry, Kenneth W.	1st Lt	043000	8Feb52	Manchester
Lipscombe, Robert B.	Captain	037958	9Sep52	VMO-6
Lloyd, Alan L.	1st Lt	047343	29Nov50	H&S/5

Lundquist, Carl R.	2d Lt	051303	16Oct51	VMF-312
Martelli, Paul L.	Captain	029125	3Apr51	VMF-323
Martin, Charles F.	Captain	032449	19Nov51	VMA-121
McCool, Felix J.	WO	049274	29Nov50	1stServBn
McDaniel, Roland L.	2d Lt	052985	9Sep52	Hq/11
McLaughlin, John N.	Major	08433	30Nov50	X Corps
Messman, Robert C.	1st Lt	039208	27Nov50	K/4/11
Murphy, Rowland M.	2d Lt	052136	7May52	1stMarDiv
O'Shea, Robert J.	1st Lt	048902	2Jul51	Hq/1 Div
Perry, Jack E.	Captain	027307	18Jun51	VMF-311
Reid, Ernest R.	1st Lt	047073	29Nov50	H&S/1
Richardson, Judson C.	Major	011918	14Dec51	VMF(N)-513
Schwable, Frank H.	Colonel	04429	8Jul52	1st MAW
Seymour, Rufus A.	2d Lt	055835	26Mar53	C/1/5
Smith, Mercer R.	Captain	024054	1May51	VMF-311
Spence, Kenneth L.	Captain	031844	18Jan53	VMO-6
Stanfill, Herman F.	1st Lt	047753	30Oct51	VMF-323
Still, Richard L.	2d Lt	050783	21Dec51	90mm AAA Bn
Taft, Leonard C.	2d Lt	047988	2Jul51	VMO-6
Thrash, William G.	Lt. Col	06141	21Dec51	1st MAW
Turner, Herbert B.	1st Lt	039278	29Nov50	1stTkBn
Wagner, Arthur	Captain	032680	27May51	VMF(N)-513
Wilkins, James V.	Captain	021898	3Jul51	VMF-312
Williams, Duke	1st Lt	047570	16May52	VMF-312

APPENDIX D

ALPHABETICAL ROSTER OF ENLISTED POW'S RETURNED TO MILITARY CONTROL

Name	Rank	Service Number	Date of Capture	Unit
Aguirre, Andrew	Cpl	954699	12Dec50	1stTkBn
Antonis, Nick J.	PFC	1056431	12Dec50	1stTkBn
Arias, Robert	Cpl	1106934	27Nov50	E/2/7
Armstrong, Samuel J.	PFC	1183348	26Mar53	5thMar
Atkinson, Edward R.	Cpl	1126839	27Oct52	A/1/7
Aviles, Pedro F.	PFC	1278492	8Dec52	Recon/1Div
Baker, Jerry D.	PFC	1226854	27Oct52	A/1/7
Barnes, Thomas R.	PFC	1188481	27Oct52	A/1/7
Bartholomew, Carl E.	PFC	1335497	20Jul53	1stMar
Bassett, Kenneth J.	PFC	1072425	29Nov50	MP/1Div
Batdorff, Robert L.	PFC	1064002	28Nov50	F/2/7
Blair, William S.	Cpl	630666	24Apr51	7thMar
Blas, Cipriano	Sgt	349552	29Nov50	MP/1Div
Boulduc, Charles A.	PFC	1089611	6Dec50	A/1MtBn
Britt, Joseph P.	PFC	1185707	26Mar53	5thMar
Brittain, Dewey	Sgt	309368	29Nov50	MP/1Div
Brown, Billy A.	PFC	1108329	9Oct51	B/1/1
Bundy, Lionel D.	Cpl	666423	27May52	1stMar

Burke, Stanley A.	PFC	1092495	10Dec50	H&S/1
Byers, Allen	PFC	1190377	26Mar53	H/3/5
Cain, John T.	M/Sgt	497205	18Jul52	VMO-6
Chester, Robert J.	PFC	1316541	19Jul53	7thMar
Coffee, Robert J.	Sgt	659953	29Nov50	1stSigBn
Cowen, George V.	PFC	1046584	28Nov50	D/2/7
Crabtree, Albert T.	PFC	1330622	27Dec52	1stMar
Dague, Joseph M.	PFC	1223883	19Jul53	7thMar
Dennison, Arthur L.	PFC	1263513	27Oct52	H/1/7
Dickerson, Charles W.	Sgt	577914	30Nov50	1stTkBn
Dodson, Emmitt D.	PFC	1286075	27Oct52	A/1/7
Downey, Earl D.	Cpl	654337	29Nov50	MP/1Div
Doyle, Arthur E.	Cpl	1257062	26Mar53	11thMar
Drummond, Stephen E.	Cpl	1257454	26Mar53	11thMar
Dunis, Gust H.	M/Sgt	190383	29Nov50	MP/1Div
Dunn, Robert L. L.	Pvt	1192875	27Oct52	1stMarDiv
Edwards, Arnold R.	PFC	1195452	27Oct52	7thMar
Estess, Morris L.	Sgt	666286	29Nov50	1stSigBn
Flores, Nick A.	PFC	1091431	30Nov50	1stServBn
Foreacre, Louis K.	PFC	1175294	27Oct52	A/1/7
Gabrielle, Fred J.	PFC	1279874	19Jul53	7thMar
Gauthier, Gaston C.	PFC	1165371	27Oct52	C/1/7
Gaynor, Melvin J.	Pvt	1176226	7Oct52	1stSPBn
Glenn, Joe A.	PFC	1221962	16Apr52	W/2/5
Graham, Alfred P.	PFC	1138510	14Jul51	H/3/5
Gregory, Arthur J.	PFC	1180947	9May52	A/1/5
Grey, Vernie L.	PFC	1211153	20Jul53	1stMarDiv

Griffith, Donald M.	Sgt	584417	2Dec50	F/2/5
Grindle, Richard R.	PFC	1092710	11May51	7thMar
Gunderson, Carl J.	PFC	1239397	19Jul53	7thMar
Hale, James L.	PFC	1122176	16Apr52	E/2/5
Hamilton, James F.	Sgt	1121870	19Jul53	7thMar
Harbin, Joseph B.	Cpl	1087610	30Nov50	4.5"Rkt/11
Harbourt, Olaf W. B.	Cpl	1157781	26Mar53	5thMar
Haring, John A.	PFC	1092478	28Nov50	7thMar
Harrison, Charles L.	S/Sgt	274541	29Nov50	MP/1Div
Hart, George F.	PFC	1305304	26Mar53	C/1/5
Hawkins, Clifford R.	Cpl	512295	30Nov50	1stTkBn
Hayton, Ernest E.	Cpl	483542	30Nov50	1stTkBn
Hernandez-Hoyos, Rafael	PFC	1225690	26Mar53	C/1/5
Hilburn, Theron L.	PFC	324007	30Nov50	1stTkBn
Holcomb, Frederick G.	Cpl	1115241	28Nov50	11thMar
Hollinger, Bernard R.	PFC	1239875	26Mar53	1stMarDiv
Irons, James L.	PFC	1272091	5Sep52	1stMarDiv
Insco, Bernard W.	PFC	1114713	24Apr51	11thMar
Jacobs, John A.	PFC	1195842	16Apr52	E/2/5
James, Jesse L.	Sgt	594627	29Nov50	MP/1Div
Jones, Edwin B.	Cpl	661065	19Sep51	Hq/11
Johnson, Richard D.	PFC	1190982	20Jul53	1stMar
Juern, Theodore A.	PFC	1180212	27Oct52	C/1/7
Kennedy, Gathern	Cpl	1228036	31Dec52	I/3/11
Kaylor, Charles M.	PFC	1109493	28Nov50	W/2/7
Kestel, Reginald	Pvt	1226629	27Oct52	1stMarDiv
Kidd, Harold J.	Cpl	1095594	11May51	7thMar

Name	Rank	Service #	Date	Unit
Kirby, John R.	Cpl	1083266	29Nov50	Hq/1Div
Kohus, Francis J.	PFC	1177174	27Oct52	A/1/7
Kostich, Robert	PFC	1214174	16Apr52	W/2/5
Lacy, Jimmie E.	Cpl	1205643	27Mar53	C/1/5
Lang, David P.	PFC	612851	27Oct52	A/1/7
Latora, Phillip N.	PFC	1204275	27Oct52	A/1/7
Lessman, Billie J.	PFC	1152336	2Jul51	Hq/11
Lunsford, Franklin I.	Pvt	1223889	7Oct52	H/3/7
Lynch, Donald W.	PFC	1200468	5Sep52	1stMarDiv
Maffioli, Leonard J.	Cpl	876229	30Nov50	1stTkBn
Manor, Paul M.	Sgt	597958	11Dec50	A/7MtBn
Markevitch, Robert A.	PFC	1150700	26Mar53	5thMar
Marks, Delbert L.	PFC	1172211	7Sep51	C/1EngrBn
Mathis, Chester A.	T/Sgt	271843	29Nov50	MP/1Div
McCoy, Donald K.	PFC	1347761	20Jul53	5thMar
McInerney, James P.	Cpl	1074365	6Dec50	A/1MTBn
Nardolillo, Francis J.	PFC	1160750	27Oct52	A/1/7
Nash, James B.	S/Sgt	293875	29Nov50	MP/1Div
Nation, Carl D.	Pvt	1331590	26Mar53	5thMar
Nelson, Noble I.	PFC	1252507	27Oct52	1stMarDiv
Nevile, Kenneth F.	PFC	1221568	9Jul53	1stMarDiv
Nieman, Warner E.	PFC	1285481	26Mar53	H/3/5
Noeth, George E.	Cpl	1242647	27Oct52	1stMarDiv
Oehl, Sonny	Cpl	1233269	6Oct52	4.2"/7
Osborne, Lloyd E.	PFC	670838	6Dec50	A/1MTBn
Oven, Richard L.	PFC	1193866	26Mar53	5thMar
Pabey, Luis E.	PFC	1259414	27Oct52	C/1/7

Pacifico, Alfred J.	PFC	1305069	19Jul53	7thMar
Padilla, Soloman	PFC	1226900	26Mar53	H/3/5
Pawlowski, Donald J.	Cpl	1168119	27Oct52	1stMarDiv
Peralta, Pedro	PFC	1268214	26Mar53	5th Mar
Peterson, Lione E.	PFC	1231044	27Oct52	A/1/7
Pettit, William R.	T/Sgt	269956	29Nov50	MP/1Div
Phillips, Paul J.	PFC	1087563	11 Dec50	A/7MtBn
Pickett, Wayne A.	Cpl	606930	28Nov50	F/2/7
Pizarro-Baez, Alberto	Pvt	1210521	7Oct52	H/3/7
Pumphrey, Louis A.	Pvt	1260301	7Oct52	H/3/7
Quiring, Charles E.	PFC	1087965	2Dec50	5thMar
Ramos, Augustine	PFC	1245406	7Oct52	H/3/7
Ray, Vernon	PFC	1257309	27Oct52	A/1/7
Ratliff, Roy V.	Cpl	663208	29Nov50	MP/1Div
Razvoza, Richard J.	Sgt	667305	29Nov50	MP/1Div
Ribbeck, Lester A.	PFC	1193721	28Dec51	F/2/1
Richards, Donald R.	Cpl	1295196	26Mar53	H/3/5
Richards, Harold E.	PFC	1305338	9Jul53	7thMar
Ricker, Lance	PFC	1296985	27Oct52	A/1/7
Roberts, Albert J.	T/Sgt	308306	29Nov50	MP/1Div
Robinson, Alvin M.	PFC	1244296	27Oct52	W/1/7
Rose, Donald A.	Sgt	1171076	6Oct52	4.2"/7
Romero, Louis	PFC	1195398	16Apr52	E/2/5
Saxon, Joe A.	Cpl	668057	12Dec50	1stTkBn
Schnitzler, Norbert	PFC	1241142	5Sep52	I/3/5
Schommer, Charles P.	PFC	1241147	19Jul53	7thMar
Schultz, William E.	Cpl	1030979	23Apr51	Hq/4/11

Scott, Mickey K.	PFC	613668	27Nov50	D/2/7
Shanklin, Milas	PFC	1275592	19Jul53	7thMar
Shockley, William N.	PFC	1195637	5Oct52	Hq/1Div
Steege, Leonard E.	PFC	1190684	19Jul53	7thMar
Stewart, Willie, C.	PFC	1324688	9Apr53	7thMar
Stine, James L.	PFC	1325815	20Jul53	7thMar
Strachan, Robert A.	Cpl	1136319	11Sep52	G/3/7
Stumpges, Frederick J.	M/Sgt	274794	29Nov50	Hq/1Div
Trujillo, Pablo B.	PFC	1266204	7Oct52	H/3/7
Tuscano, James E.	PFC	1248932	6Oct52	G/3/7
Vann, George H.	PFC	1031930	27Nov50	K/4/11
Vavruska, Eugene R.	PFC	1293705	7Oct52	H/3/7
Vidal, Eddie P.	PFC	659743	27Oct52	C/1/7
Vitruls, Billy J.	PFC	1202210	27Oct52	C/1/7
Watson, Joseph	PFC	1229887	27Oct52	C/1/7
Wertman, Albert P.	Cpl	1065298	21Feb52	F/2/7
Wessels, Harry P.	Pvt	1271307	19Jul53	7thMar
Wheeler, Theodore R.	Cpl	867966	29Nov50	1stServBn
Wilkins, Edward G.	PFC	1088692	2Dec50	I/3/5
Williams, Calvin W.	Cpl	1072147	29Nov50	Hq/1Div
Williams, Donald C.	Cpl	1098418	29Nov50	1stSigBn
Williams, Michaux L.	PFC	1316575	27Oct52	1stMarDiv
Williford, Troy A.	PFC	669059	28Nov50	F/2/5
Woodard, Preston D.	PFC	1189089	7Oct52	1stMarDiv
Yesko, Daniel D.	PFC	1064801	28Nov50	F/2/7

APPENDIX E

ALPHABETICAL ROSTER OF OFFICER POW'S
WHO DIED OR ARE PRESUMED DEAD

Name	Rank	Service Number	Date of Capture	Unit

CAPTURED AND DIED

Name	Rank	Service Number	Date of Capture	Unit
Gilardi, Robert W.	Captain	021766	1Jan52	VMF-312
Hintz, Harold	1st Lt	038772	30Jul51	VMF-312
Olson, A. E.	1st Lt	048125	13Jul51	VMF(N)-513

CAPTURED AND PRESUMED DEAD

Name	Rank	Service Number	Date of Capture	Unit
Chidester, A. A.	LtCol	05234	29Nov50	Hq/1Div
Eagan, James K.	Major	07760	29Nov50	Hq/1Div
Nelson, F. A.	1st Lt	044100	6Aug52	VMA-212

APPENDIX F

ALPHABETICAL ROSTER OF ENLISTED POW'S WHO DIED OR ARE PRESUMED DEAD

Name	Rank	Service Number	Date of Capture	Unit

CAPTURED AND DIED

Name	Rank	Service Number	Date of Capture	Unit
Asher, Ollie	PFC	1221733	7Oct52	H/3/7
Bringes, Harry M.	Cpl	1112740	1Dec50	Serv/4/11
Darden, Roy	Sgt	507924	29Nov50	MP/1Div
Demski, Bernard A.	PFC	1329771	10Apr53	1stMarDiv
Dowling, Donald F.	PFC	1063264	2Dec50	F/2/5
Dowling, Paul E.	PFC	1063259	2Dec50	F/2/5
Duncan, Donald M.	T/Sgt	337814	10Dec50	H&S/1
Fields, Billy G.	Cpl	1096497	11Dec50	A/7MTBn
Frazure, Richard P.	Sgt	1071737	29Nov50	MP/1Div
Glasgow, James E.	Cpl	1071447	12Dec50	1stTkBn
Gray, William H.	Sgt	387822	29Nov50	H&S/7
Hester, James C.	PFC	653540	26Nov50	H&S/3/7
Ogrodnik, Edwin P.	PFC	1071397	29Nov50	MP/1Div
Reasor, Kyle	PFC	1012299	28Nov50	F/2/5
Roebuck, Leon	PFC	608320	30Nov50	1stServBn
Thomas, George H.	Cpl	277326	29Nov50	H&S/7
Vannosdall, Gilbert A.	Cpl	1068629	20Sep50	1stSigBn
Wegner, R. L.	Cpl	666593	29Nov50	1stSigBn

CAPTURED AND PRESUMED DEAD

Baker, Billy W.	PFC	624946	6Dec50	A/1MTBn
Grahl, Hans W.	PFC	1071285	29Nov50	MP/1Div
Morrow, Billy J.	PFC	1188495	26Mar53	W/1/5

APPENDIX G

ROSTER OF MARINES CAPTURED BY DATE

Date of Capture	Name & Rank	Unit	Remarks
7Aug50	Capt Jesse V. Booker	1st MAW	#
20Sep50	Cpl Gilbert A. Vannosdall	1stSigBn	Died
26Nov50	PFC James C. Hester	H&S 3/7	Died
27Nov50	1stLt Robert C. Messman	K/4/11	#
	PFC George H. Vann	K/4/11	#
	Cpl Robert Arias	E/3/7	#
	PFC Mickey K. Scott	D/2/7	#
28Nov50	1stLt Felix L. Ferranto	1stSigBn	
	Cpl Frederick G. Holcomb	11th Mar	RMC May51
	PFC Charles M. Kaylor	W/2/7	RMC May51
	PFC Kyle Reasor	F/2/5	Died
	PFC Troy A. Williford	F/2/5	#
	PFC Robert L. Batdorff	F/2/7	#
	Cpl Wayne A. Pickett	F/2/7	#
	PFC Daniel D. Yesko	F/2/7	#
	PFC George V. Cowen	D/2/7	#
	PFC John A. Haring	7thMar	RMC May51

\# - Reported on Communist 18 December 1951 list of POW's
P.Dead - Presumed dead
RMC May51 - Returned to Military Control in May 1951
RLS - Returned on Operation Little Switch, April-May 1953.

29Nov50	LtCol A. A. Chidester	Hq/1Div	P. Dead
	Major James K. Eagan	Hq/1Div	P. Dead
	Maj John N. McLaughlin	X Corps	#
	1stLt Frank E. Cold	3/7	RMC May51
	1stLt Alan L. Lloyd	H&S/5	#
	1stLt Ernest R. Reid	H&S/1	#
	1stLt Herbert B. Turner	1stTkBn	#
	WO Felix J. McCool	1stServBn	#
	Cpl Joseph B. Harbin	4.5"RKT/11	#
	Sgt William H. Gray	H&S/7	Died
	Cpl George H. Thomas	H&S/7	Died
	Cpl John R. Kirby	Hq/1Div	#
	MSgt Frederick J. Stumpges	Hq/1Div	#
	Cpl Calvin W. Williams	Hq/1Div	RMC May51
	PFC Nick A. Flores	1stServBn	#
	PFC Leon Roebuck	1stServBn	Died
	Cpl Theodore R. Wheeler	1stServBn	RMC May51
	Sgt Robert J. Coffee	1stSigBn	#
	Sgt Morris L. Estess	1stSigBn	RMC May 51
	Cpl R. L. Wegner	1stSigBn	Died
	Cpl Donald C. Williams	1stSigBn	#
	PFC Kenneth J. Bassett	MP/1Div	#
	Sgt Cipriano Blas	MP/1 Div	#
	Sgt Dewey Brittain	MP/1 Div	#
	Sgt Roy Darden	MP/1 Div	Died
	Cpl Earl D. Downey	MP/1 Div	#
	MSgt Gust H. Dunis	MP/1 Div	RMC May51

Date	Name	Unit	Status
29Nov50 (cont'd)	Sgt Richard P. Frazure	MP/1 Div	Died
	PFC Hans W. Grahl	MP/1 Div	P. Dead
	SSgt Charles L. Harrison	MP/1 Div	RMC May51
	Sgt Jesse L. James	MP/1 Div	#
	TSgt Chester A. Mathis	MP/1 Div	#
	SSgt James B. Nash	MP/1 Div	RMC May51
	PFC Edwin P. Ogrodnik	MP/1 Div	Died
	TSgt William R. Pettit	MP/1 Div	#
	Cpl Roy V. Ratliff	MP/1 Div	#
	Sgt Richard J. Razvoza	MP/1 Div	#
	TSgt Albert J. Roberts	MP/1 Div	#

30Nov50 (Note: Most of the personnel listed as captured on November 29, 1950 were actually captured after midnight that date and thus fell into enemy hands on the 30th. The below named Marines were captured with the same task force as the bulk of those listed above. Differences in date of capture were caused by different reporting units.)

Date	Name	Unit	Status
	Sgt Charles W. Dickerson	1stTkBn	RMC May51
	PFC Theron L. Hilburn	1stTkBn	RMC May51
	Cpl Ernest E. Hayton	1stTkBn	RMC May51
	Cpl Leonard J. Maffioli	1stTkBn	RMC May51
	Cpl Clifford R. Hawkins	G/3/7	RMC May51
1Dec50	Cpl Harry M. Bringes	4/11	Died
2Dec50	PFC Donald F. Dowling	F/2/5	Died
	PFC Paul E. Dowling	F/2/5	Died
	Sgt Donald M. Griffith	F/2/5	#
	PFC Charles E. Quiring	5thMar	RMC May51
	PFC Edward G. Wilkins	I/3/5	#

6Dec50	PFC Billy W. Baker	A/1MTBn	P. Dead
	PFC Charles A. Boulduc	A/1MTBn	#
	Cpl James P. McInerney	A/1MTBn	#
	PFC Lloyd E. Osborne	A/1MTBn	#
10Dec50	PFC Stanley A. Burke	H&S/1	#
	TSgt Donald M. Duncan	H&S/1	Died
11Dec50	Cpl Billy G. Fields	A/7MTBn	Died
	PFC Paul J. Phillips	A/7MTBn	RMC May51
	Sgt Paul M. Manor	A/7MTBn	RMC May51
12Dec50	Cpl Andrew Aguirre	1stTkBn	#
	PFC Nick J. Antonis	1stTkBn	#
	Cpl Joe E. Saxon	1stTkBn	#
	Cpl James E. Glasgow	1stTkBn	Died

1951

3Apr51	Capt Paul L. Martelli	VMF-323	#
23Apr51	Cpl William E. Schultz	Hq/4/11	#
24Apr51	Cpl William S. Blair	7thMar	
	PFC Bernard W. Insco	11thMar	
1May51	Capt Mercer R. Smith	VMF-311	#
2May51	Capt Byron H. Beswick	VMF-323	#
11May51	PFC Richard R. Grindle	7thMar	
	Cpl Harold J. Kidd	7thMar	
27May51	Capt Arthur Wagner	VMF(N)-513	#
18June51	Capt Jack E. Perry	VMF-311	#

2Jul51	1stLt Robert J. O'Shea	Hq/1Div	
	2dLt Leonard C. Taft	VMO-6	
	PFC Billie J. Lessman	Hq/11	#
3Jul51	Capt James V. Wilkins	VMF-312	#
13Jul51	1stLt A. E. Olson	VMF(N)-513	Died
14Jul51	PFC Alfred P. Graham	H/3/5	#
21Jul51	1stLt Richard Bell	VMF-311	#
30Jul51	1stLt Harold Hintz	VMF-312	Died
12Aug51	Capt Gerald Fink	VMF-312	#
7Sept51	PFC Delbert L. Marks	D/1stEngrBn	#
19Sept51	Cpl Edwin B. Jones	Hq/11	#
4Oct51	Capt Emanuel R. Amann	VMF-323	#
9Oct51	PFC Billy A. Brown	B/1/1	#
12Oct51	1stLt Robert J. Gillette	VMF(N)-513	#
16Oct51	2dLt Carl R. Lundquist	VMF-312	#
30Oct51	1stLt Herman F. Stanfill	VMF-323	
19Nov51	Capt Charles F. Martin	VMA-121	
14Dec51	Maj Judson C. Richardson	VMF(N)-513	
21Dec51	2dLt Richard L. Still	1st90mmAABn	
	LtCol William G. Thrash	Hq/1st MAW	
28Dec51	PFC Lester A. Ribbeck	F/2/1	

1952

1Jan52	Capt Robert W. Gilardi	VMF-312	Died

8Feb52	1stLt Kenneth W. Henry	USS Manchester	
21Feb52	Cpl Albert P. Wertman	F/2/7	
4Mar52	Capt Roy C. Gray	VMF-311	
16Apr52	PFC Joe A. Glenn	W/2/5	
	PFC James L. Hale	E/2/5	
	PFC John A. Jacobs	E/2/5	
	PFC Robert Kostich	W/2/5	
	PFC Louis Romero	E/2/5	
9May52	PFC Arthur J. Gregory	A/1/5	RLS
6May52	Maj Walter R. Harris	VMF-323	
7May52	2dLt Rowland M. Murphy	1stMarDiv	
13May52	1stLt Milton H. Baugh	VMF-311	
14May52	Capt John P. Flynn	VMF(N)-513	
16May52	1stLt Duke Williams	VMF-312	
27May52	Cpl Lionel D. Bundy	1stMar	
8Jul52	Maj Roy H. Bley	Hq/1st MAW	
	Col Frank H. Schwable	Hq/1st MAW	
18Jul52	MSgt John T. Cain	VMO-6	
6Aug52	1stLt F. A. Nelson	VMA-212	P. Dead
5Sep52	PFC James L. Irons	1stMarDiv	
	PFC Donald W. Lynch	1stMarDiv	
	PFC Norbert Schnitzler	I/3/5	
9Sep52	Capt Robert B. Lipscombe	VMO-6	
	2dLt Roland L. McDaniel	Hq/11	
11Sep52	Cpl Robert A. Strachan	G/3/7	

5Oct52	PFC William N. Shockley	Hq/1Div	
6Oct52	2dLt Henry L. Conway	G/3/7	
	Cpl Sonny Oehl	4.2"/7	
	Sgt Donald A. Rose	4.2"/7	RLS
	PFC James E. Tuscano	G/3/7	
7Oct52	PFC Ollie Asher	H/3/7	Died
	PFC Melvin J. Gaynor	1stSPBn	
	Pvt Franklin I. Lunsford	H/3/7	
	Pvt Alberto Pizarro-Baez	H/3/7	RLS
	Pvt Louis A. Pumphrey	H/3/7	RLS
	PFC Augustine Ramos	H/3/7	
	PFC Pablo B. Trujillo	H/3/7	
	PFC Eugene R. Vavruska	H/3/7	
	PFC Preston D. Woodard	1stMarDiv	
27Oct52	Cpl Edward R. Atkinson	A/1/7	
	PFC Jerry D. Baker	A/1/7	
	PFC Thomas R. Barnes	A/1/7	RLS
	PFC Arthur L. Dennison	H/1/7	
	PFC Emmitt D. Dodson	A/1/7	
	Pvt Robert L. L. Dunn	1stMarDiv	RLS
	PFC Arnold R. Edwards	7thMar	
	PFC Louis K. Foreacre	A/1/7	
	PFC Gaston C. Gauthier	C/1/7	
	PFC Theodore A. Jeurn	C/1/7	RLS
	Pvt Reginald Kestel	1stMarDiv	
	PFC Francis J. Kohus	A/1/7	
	PFC David P. Lang	A/1/7	RLS

27Oct52 (cont'd)	PFC Philip N. Latora	A/1/7	
	PFC Francis J. Nardolillo	A/1/7	
	PFC Noble I. Nelson	1stMarDiv	
	Cpl George E. Noeth	1stMarDiv	
	PFC Louis E. Pabey	C/1/7	
	Cpl Donald J. Pawlowski	1stMarDiv	
	PFC Lione E. Peterson	A/1/7	RLS
	PFC Vernon Ray	A/1/7	
	PFC Lance Ricker	A/1/7	
	PFC Alvin M. Robinson	W/1/7	
	PFC Eddie P. Vidal	C/1/7	RLS
	PFC Billy J. Vitruls	C/1/7	
	PFC Joseph Watson	C/1/7	
	PFC Michaux L. Williams	1stMarDiv	
8Dec52	PFC Pedro F. Aviles	Recon/1Div	
27Dec52	PFC Albert T. Crabtree	1stMar	
31Dec52	Cpl Gathern Kennedy	I/3/11	

1953

18Jan53	Capt Kenneth L. Spence	VMO-6	
10Mar53	Capt Dee E. Ezell	Hq/1Div	
26Mar53	2dLt Rufus A. Seymour	C/1/5	
	PFC Samuel J. Armstrong	5thMar	RLS
	PFC Joseph P. Britt	5thMar	RLS
	PFC Allen Byers	H/3/5	
	Cpl Arthur E. Doyle	11thMar	
	Cpl Stephen E. Drummond	11thMar	

26Mar53 (cont'd)	Cpl Olaf W. B. Harbourt	5thMar	
	PFC George F. Hart	C/1/5	RLS
	PFC Bernard R. Hollinger	1stMarDiv	
	PFC Robert A. Markevitch	5thMar	
	PFC Billy J. Morrow	W/1/5	P. Dead
	Pvt Carl D. Nation	5thMar	
	PFC Warner E. Nieman	H/3/5	
	PFC Richard L. Oven	5thMar	RLS
	PFC Soloman Padilla	H/3/5	
	PFC Pedro Peralta	5thMar	
	Cpl Donald R. Richards	H/3/5	
27Mar53	Cpl Jimmie E. Lacy	C/1/5	RLS
	PFC Rafael H. Hernandez-Hoyos	C/1/5	
9Apr53	PFC Willie C. Stewart	7thMar	
10Apr53	PFC B. A. Demski	1stMarDiv	Died
9Jul53	PFC Kenneth F. Neville	1stMar	
	PFC Harold E. Richards	7th Mar	
19Jul53	2dLt Henry E. Clifford	1stMarDiv	
	PFC Robert J. Chester	7thMar	
	PFC Joseph M. Dague	7thMar	
	PFC Fred J. Gabrielle	7thMar	
	PFC Carl J. Gunderson	7thMar	
	Sgt James F. Hamilton	7thMar	
	PFC Alfred J. Pacifico	7thMar	
	PFC Charles P. Schommer	7thMar	
	PFC Milas Shanklin	7thMar	
	PFC Leonard E. Steege	7thMar	

19Jul53 (cont'd)	Pvt Harry P. Wessells	7thMar
20Jul53	PFC James L. Stine	7thMar
	PFC Carl E. Bartholomew	1stMar
	PFC Vernie L. Grey	1stMarDiv
	PFC Richard D. Johnson	1stMar
	PFC Donald K. McCoy	5thMar

APPENDIX H

ROSTER OF MARINES RETURNED TO MILITARY CONTROL
MAY 25, 1951

Name & Rank	Unit	Date of Capture
1stLt Frank E. Cold	3/7	29Nov50
Sgt Charles W. Dickerson	1stTkBn	30Nov50
MSgt Gust H. Dunis	MP/1Div	29Nov50
Sgt Morris L. Estess	1stSigBn	29Nov50
PFC John A. Haring	7thMar	28Nov50
SSgt Charles L. Harrison	MP/1Div	29Nov50
Cpl Clifford Hawkins	G/3/7	27Nov50
Cpl Ernest R. Hayton	1stTkBn	30Nov50
PFC Theron Hilburn	1stTkBn	30Nov50
Cpl Frederick Holcomb	11thMar	28Nov50
PFC Charles Kaylor	W/2/7	28Nov50
Cpl Leonard Maffioli	1stTkBn	30Nov50
Sgt Paul Manor	A/7MTBn	11Dec50
SSgt James Nash	MP/1Div	29Nov50
PFC Paul J. Phillips	A/7MTBn	11Dec50
PFC Charles Quiring	5thMar	2Dec50
Cpl Theodore Wheeler	1stServBn	29Nov50
Cpl Calvin Williams	Hq/1Div	29Nov50

APPENDIX I

ROSTER OF MARINES RETURNED TO MILITARY CONTROL DURING OPERATION LITTLE SWITCH - APRIL & MAY, 1953

Name & Rank	Unit	Date of Capture
PFC Samuel J. Armstrong	5thMar	26Mar53
PFC Thomas R. Barnes	A/1/7	26Oct52
PFC Joseph P. Britt	7thMar	27Mar53
Pvt Robert L. L. Dunn	1stMarDiv	27Oct52
PFC Arthur J. Gregory	A/1/5	9May52
PFC George F. Hart	C/1/5	26Mar53
PFC Theodore A. Juern	C/1/7	27Oct52
Cpl Jimmie E. Lacy	C/1/5	27Mar53
PFC David P. Lang	A/1/7	27Oct52
PFC Richard L. Oven	5thMar	26Mar53
PFC Lione E. Peterson	A/1/7	27Oct52
Pvt Alberto Pizarro-Baez	H/3/7	7Oct52
PFC Louis A. Pumphery	H/3/7	7Oct52
Sgt Donald A. Rose	4.2"/7	6Oct52
PFC Eddie P. Vidal	C/1/7	27Oct52

APPENDIX J

MARINE POW'S BY RANK

		Captured	Returned to Military Control	Captured and died	Captured, Presumed Dead
Colonel	Regular	1	1		
	Reserve				
LtCol	Regular	2	1		1
	Reserve				
Major	Regular	4	3		1
	Reserve	1	1		
Captain	Regular	9	9		
	Reserve	8	6	2	
1stLt	Regular	7	7		
	Reserve	9	7	1	1
2dLt	Regular	3	3		
	Reserve	4	4		
WO	Regular	1	1		
	Reserve				
Total	Regular	27	25		2
	Reserve	22	18	3	1
GRAND TOTAL OFFICERS		49	43 (87.7%)	3 (6.1%)	3 (6.1%)

		Captured	Returned to Military Control	Captured and Died	Captured Presumed Dead
MSgt	Regular	3	3		
	Reserve				
TSgt	Regular	4	3	1	
	Reserve				
SSgt	Regular	2	2		
	Reserve				
Sgt	Regular	14	11	3	
	Reserve				
Cpl	Regular	23	18	5	
	Reserve	11	10	1	
	Inducted	5	5		
PFC	Regular	62	54	5	3
	Reserve	17	15	2	
	Inducted	23	22	1	
Pvt	Regular	4	4		
	Reserve				
	Inducted	4	4		
Total	Regular	112	95	14	3
	Reserve	28	25	3	
	Inducted	32	31	1	
GRAND TOTAL ENLISTED		172	151 (87.7%)	18	3
GRAND TOTAL OFFICERS AND ENLISTED		221	194 (87.7%)	21 (9.5%)	6 (2.7%)

SELECTED BIBLIOGRAPHY

Unpublished Official Unit Records

The following are filed in the Unit Files, Historical Branch Archives, G-3 Division, Headquarters, U. S. Marine Corps.

1st Marine Air Wing, Historical Diary, October, 1950.

_____. Special Action Report, October 10, 1950, to December 15, 1950.

1st Marine Division, Historical Diaries, November, 1950, to March, 1952.

_____. Command Diaries, April, 1952, to July, 1953.

_____. Special Action Report on Inchon-Kimpo-Seoul Operation, September 15-October 8, 1950.

_____. Special Action Report, October-December, 1950.

_____. Operation Order 24-50, November 26, 1950.

_____. Casualty Bulletins, September, 1950-May, 1952.

1st Provisional Marine Brigade (Reinforced), Fleet Marine Force, Special Action Report, 2 August to 6 September 1950. A Report of Operations with Eighth U. S. Army in Korea.

1st Motor Transport Battalion, 1st Marine Division. Historical Diary, December, 1950.

7th Motor Transport Battalion, Fleet Marine Force. Special Action Report, Annex VV to 1st Marine Division, Special Action Report, October-December, 1950.

1st Signal Battalion, 1st Marine Division. Special Action Report on Inchon-Kimpo-Seoul Operation. Annex GG to 1st Marine Division Special Action Report, 15 September-8 October, 1950.

_____. Unit Report No. 12, December 3, 1950.

1st 90mm Anti Aircraft Gun Battalion, 1st Marine Air Wing. Historical Diary, December, 1951.

1st Marines, 1st Marine Division. Special Action Report, Annex PP to 1st Marine Division, Special Action Report, October-December, 1950.

5th Marines, 1st Marine Division. Special Action Report, Annex QQ to 1st Marine Division, Special Action Report, October-December, 1950.

_____. Command Diaries, April, 1952, to July, 1953.

_____. Historical Diary, March, 1951.

_____. Unit Report, February, 1951. Annex B to 1st Marine Division, Historical Diary, February, 1951.

7th Marines, 1st Marine Division. Command Diaries, October, 1952, to July, 1953.

_____. Summary of Action, 26 October-1 November, 1952. "Hook, Reno, Ronson."

11th Marines, 1st Marine Division. Special Action Report, Annex SS to 1st Marine Division Special Action Report, October-December, 1950.

_____. Historical Diary, April, 1951.

Battery C, 1st 4.5" Rocket Battalion, Fleet Marine Force. Special Action Report, Appendix 5 to 11th Marines Special Action Report, Annex SS to 1st Marine Division, Special Action Report, October-December, 1950.

2d Battalion, 5th Marines. Special Action Report, Annex B to 5th Marines, Special Action Report, Annex QQ to 1st Marine Division Special Action Report, October-December, 1950.

3d Battalion, 5th Marines. Special Action Report, Annex C to 5th Marines, Special Action Report, Annex QQ to 1st Marine Division, Special Action Report, October-December, 1950.

1st Battalion, 7th Marines, Command Diary, July, 1953.

2d Battalion, 7th Marines, Command Diary, July, 1953.

Marine Aircraft Group-12, 1st Marine Air Wing. Special Action Report, Annex K to 1st Marine Air Wing, Special Action Report, 10 October 1950 to 15 December 1950.

Marine Attack Squadron-121. Historical Diary, November, 1951.

Marine Fighter Squadron-311. Historical Diaries, May, 1951-March, 1952.

_____. Command Diaries, April-May, 1952.

Marine Fighter Squadron-312. Historical Diaries, July, 1951-April, 1952.

_____. Command Diary, May, 1952.

Marine Fighter Squadron-323. Historical Diaries, April, 1951-May, 1952.

Marine All-Weather Fighter Squadron-513. Historical Diaries, May 1951-May, 1952.

Marine Observation Squadron-6, 1st Marine Aircraft Wing. Historical Diaries, July, 1951, to February, 1953.

Unpublished Official Correspondence, Messages, and Memoranda

Commander in Chief, Far East. Message of October 29, 1950.

_____. Situation Reports, daily October-November, 1950.

Commanding Officer, USS Valley Forge. Message of August 7, 1950. Text recorded in Historical Branch Aviation Casualty Card File, case of Captain Jesse V. Booker.

Commanding General, 1st Marine Division. Letter to the Commandant of the Marine Corps, serial number 23448, dated May 31, 1951. This letter forwards statements made by Marines released by the Communists on May 24, 1951. The following enclosures to the basic letter are pertinent to this study:

Enclosure 2. Statement of First Lieutenant Frank E. Cold

Enclosure 6. Statement of Staff Sergeant Charles L. Harrison.

Enclosure 10. Statement of Sergeant Morris L. Estess.

Enclosure 11. Statement of Sergeant Paul M. Manor and Private First Class Charles E. Quiring.

Commanding Officer, 1st 90mm Anti-Aircraft Artillery Battalion. Speedletter to the Commandant of the Marine Corps, December 31, 1951.

Commanding Officer, 1st Tank Battalion. Letter to the Commandant of the Marine Corps, serial 1123, December 27, 1950. This letter forwards statements of Tank Platoon Commanders concerning the loss of four Marines.

    Enclosure 1. Statement of First Lieutenant Jack M. Lerond.

    Enclosure 2. Statement of First Lieutenant Philip H. Ronzone.

Commanding Officer, 1st Marines. Message of October 28, 1950.

Commanding Officer, 7th Marines. Message of November 26, 1950.

Letter from First Lieutenant Lester A. Rowden, Jr., 045629/0407, USMCR to the Commanding Officer, 11th Marines, subject: Report of Investigation, case of Private First Class Billie J. Lessman, 1152336, USMC. August 5, 1951.

Letter from the Commandant of the Marine Corps to the Secretary of the Navy, dated April 14, 1954, transmitting the record of the Court of Inquiry, case of Colonel Frank H. Schwable, USMC.

Memorandum from the Secretary of the Navy to the Secretary of Defense, dated April 21, 1954, transmitting the record of the Court of Inquiry, case of Colonel Frank H. Schwable, USMC.

Memorandum from the Secretary of Defense to the Secretary of the Navy, dated April 27, 1954, concerning the findings and recommendations of the Court of Inquiry, case of Colonel Frank H. Schwable, USMC.

Findings of fact, opinions, and recommendations, Court of Inquiry, case of Colonel Frank H. Schwable, USMC.

Letter from Lieutenant Colonel William G. Thrash, 06141, USMC to the Commandant of the Marine Corps, December 9, 1953; subject, Exemplary Conduct, case of Major John N. McLaughlin, 08433, USMC, Report of and recommendation of award for. Code DLA, HQMC.

Letter from Commandant of the Marine Corps to the Secretary of the Navy, December 21, 1953; subject, Legion of Merit; case of Major Walter R. Harris 016518, USMCR, recommendation for award of (POW). Code DLA, HQMC.

Letter from the Commandant of the Marine Corps to the Secretary of the Navy, December 21, 1953; subject; Navy and Marine Corps Medal; case of Captain John P. Flynn, Jr., 032419 USMC, recommendation for award of. Code DLA, HQMC. Enclosure 3 to this letter is a statement by Major W. R. Harris, 016518, USMCR concerning the outstanding performance of Captain John P. Flynn, Jr. while a POW in Camp 2 Annex at Obul, North Korea.

Letter from Major Walter R. Harris, 106518, USMCR to the Commandant of the Marine Corps, December 9, 1953; subject; Letter of Commendation with Commendation Ribbon; case of Master Sergeant John T. Cain 497205 USMC, recommendation of award of. Code DLA, HQMC.

Letter from Major John N. McLaughlin, 08433, USMC to the Commandant of the Marine Corps, December 9, 1953; subject; Appropriate recognition; case of LtCol William G. Thrash, 06141, USMC, recommendation for. Code DLA, HQMC.

Letter from Major Walter R. Harris, 016518, USMCR, to the Commandant of the Marine Corps, December 17, 1953, filed in the service record of Captain Rowland M. Murphy, 052136, Code DF, HQMC.

Letter from Major Walter R. Harris, 016518, USMR, to the Commandant of the Marine Corps, December 9, 1953, filed in the service record of Master Sergeant John T. Cain, 497205, USMC, Code DF, HQMC.

Memorandum from Lieutenant Colonel R. D. Heinl, Jr., USMC to the Director of Marine Corps History, October 28, 1952.

Sworn statement by Corporal Eddie P. Vidal, January 25, 1954, made at Fort Sam Houston, Texas. Filed in service record of Cpl Vidal, Code DF, HQMC.

Letters from the below named personnel to the Commandant of the Marine Corps; subject – Report on Period of Captivity. These reports are filed in the service records of the originators, Code DF, Headquarters, U. S. Marine Corps, Washington 25, D. C.

Baugh, Milton H., Captain, 010658, USMC.

Cain, John T., Master Sergeant, 497205, USMC.

Ezell, Dee E., Lieutenant Colonel, 029832, USMC.

Fink, Gerald, Major, 023889, USMC.

Flynn, John P. Jr., Major, 032419, USMC.

Gray, Roy C., Lieutenant Colonel, 024638, USMC.

McDaniel, Roland L., Captain, 052985, USMC.

McLaughlin, John N., Colonel, 08433, USMC.

Murphy, Rowland M., Captain, 052136, USMC

Richardson, Judson C. Jr., Lieutenant Colonel, 011918, USMC.

Seymour, Rufus A., Captain, 055835, USMC.

Letters from the below named personnel to the Commandant of the Marine Corps, filed in the service record of Colonel John N. McLaughlin, Code DF, Headquarters, U. S. Marine Corps, Washington, 25, D. C.

Brown, Gerald, Lieutenant Colonel, USAF. December 14, 1953.

Hansen, George R., Lieutenant Colonel, USA, n.d., received at HQMC January 25, 1954.

Harrison, Thomas D., Lieutenant Colonel, USAF. February 25 and March 11, 1954.

Pettit, William R. Master Sergeant, USMC. December 10, 1953.

Zacherle, L. E., Lieutenant Colonel, USA. December 21, 1953.

Interviews

Personal interviews were conducted with the following named persons, and written notes concerning the interviews are in the author's files:

Booker, Jesse V., Major, USMC. July 26, 1960.

Cronin, James T., Lieutenant Colonel, USMC. August 30 and September 4, 1960.

Fink, Gerald, Major, USMC. December 3, 1959 through March 24, 1961

McDaniel, Roland, Captain, USMC. July 25 and December 27, 1960 and March 14, 1961.

Noel, Frank, Correspondent, Associated Press. Tokyo, Japan, May, 1953.

Perry, Jack, Major, USMC. August 18, 1960.

Pierce, Philip N., Lieutenant Colonel, USMC. December 7, 1960.

Pizarro-Baez, Alberto, Private, USMC. Tokyo, Japan, May, 1953.

Thorin, Duane, Lieutenant (j.g.), USN. March 11, 1960.

Wood, William A., Colonel, USMC. April 15, 1960.

The following records of interview are filed in the Interview File, Historical Branch Archives, G-3 Division, Headquarters, U. S. Marine Corps:

First Sergeant Charles C. Dana and Staff Sergeant Richard E. Danford, Company F, 7th Marines. Interviewed by Captain A. Z. Freeman on Kansas Line, Korea, April 7, 1951. Filed as 1st Provisional Historical Platoon Interviews, April 17, 1951, Number 1.

Sergeant Charles W. Dickerson, Staff Sergeant James B. Nash, Technical Sergeant Charles L. Harrison, Sergeant Morris L. Estess, and Corporal Calvin W. Williams. Interview by Historical Division, Headquarters, U. S. Marine Corps, July 25-31, 1951. Filed as Dickerson, C. W., Sgt. interview.

Major Frederick Simpson, USMC, interviewed by Captain Kenneth A. Shutts, USMCR, at the 1st Marine Division Command Post (Forward), Chunchon, Korea, April 11, 1951. Filed as 1st Provisional Historical Platoon Interviews, April 17, 1951.

Personal Letters

Barber, Stewart C., Major, USMC. March 16, 1960.

Day, James, Warrant Officer, Royal Marines (Retired). April 14 and June 17, 1960.

Farrar-Hockley, Anthony, Major. DSO, OBE, MC. British Army. September 26 and October 20, 1960.

Ferranto, Felix, Lieutenant Colonel, USMC (Retired). February 22, 1961.

Flynn, John P., Jr., Major, USMC. March, 1961.

Gregory, Arthur J. September 1, 1960.

Griffith, Donald M., Staff Sergeant, USMC (Retired). November 8 and December 9, 1960.

Harrison, Charles L. Captain, USMC (Retired). July 24, 1960.

Henry, Kenneth W., Major, USMC. August 25, 1960.

Mathis, Chester A., First Sergeant (Fleet Marine Corps Reserve). January 3, 1961.

McCool, Felix J., Commissioned Warrant Officer (Retired). February 3, 1961.

Pettit, William, Master Sergeant (Fleet Marine Corps Reserve). February 3, 1961.

Pizarro-Baez, Alberto, Private First Class, USMC (Retired). August 22, 1960.

Vidal, Eddie P., Corporal, USMC (Retired). August 10, 1960.

Documents

Commander Naval Forces, Far East. <u>Chinese Communist Treatment and Attempted Political Indoctrination of U. S. Marine Prisoners of War</u>. Tokyo: N-2 Department, COMNAVFE, July 11, 1951. Copy filed in Breckenridge Library, Marine Corps Educational Center, Marine Corps Schools, Quantico, Virginia.

_____. <u>Report of Intelligence Processing "Operation Little Switch - April 1953."</u> Yokosuka, Japan: N-2 Department, COMNAVFE, June, 1953. Copy filed in Historical Branch Archives, G-3 Division, Headquarters U. S. Marine Corps.

_____. <u>Standing Operating Procedure for Intelligence Processing and Debriefing of Recovered Navy and Marine Corps Prisoners of War</u>. Change No. 1. Yokosuka, Japan: N-2 Department, COMNAVFE, July 24, 1953. Copy filed in Historical Branch Archives, G-3 Division, Headquarters, U. S. Marine Corps.

Communist China. Department of Cultural Relations With Foreign Countries, Ministry of Culture and Propaganda, DPRK. <u>Depositions of Nineteen Captured U. S. Airmen On Their Participation in Germ Warfare in Korea</u>. Peking: Department of Cultural Relations, 1954.

Communist China. <u>Documents and Materials on the Korean Armistice Negotiations -- With Special Reference to Item 4 of the Agenda Dealing With the Question of Prisoners of War</u>. Vol. II. Peking: The Chinese People's Committee for World Peace, 1952.

Communist China. *Exhibition On Bacteriological War Crimes Committed by the Government of the United States of America.* Peking: The Chinese People's Committee for World Peace, 1952.

Communist China. *Report of the Joint Interrogation Group of Korean and Chinese Specialists and Newspaper Correspondents on the Interrogation of War Prisoners Enoch and Quinn.* Peking: The Chinese People's Committee for World Peace, 1952.

Communist China. *United Nations P.O.W.'s in Korea.* Peking: The Chinese People's Committee for World Peace, 1953.

Great Britain. Foreign Office. *Korea: A Summary of Further Developments in the Military Situation, Armistice Negotiations and Prisoner of War Camps up to January 1958.* Cmd. 8793. March, 1953.

Great Britain. Foreign Office. Korea: *A Summary of Developments in the Armistice Negotiations and the Prisoner of War Camps.* Cmd. 8596. June, 1952.

Great Britain. Foreign Office. *Korea: The Indian Proposal for Resolving the Prisoners of War Problem.* Cmd. 8716. December, 1952.

Great Britain. Ministry of Defense. *Treatment of British Prisoners of War in Korea.* H.M. Stationery Office, 1955.

Korean Communications Zone. *Interim Historical Report.* A Report Prepared by the War Crimes Division, Judge Advocate Section, Korean Communications Zone, Far East Command. Cumulative to June 30, 1953. Korea: KCOMZ, 1953.

Marshall, S. L. A. *CCF in the Attack.* Part II. A Study Based on the Operations of 1st Marine Division in the Koto-ri, Hagaru-ri, Yudam-ni Area, November 20 - December 10, 1950. Prepared by the Operations Research Office, The Johns Hopkins University, Far East Command, 1951.

Secretary of Defense's Advisory Committee on Prisoners of War. *POW.* Washington: U. S. Government Printing Office, 1955.

Segal, Julius. *Factors Related to the Collaboration and Resistance Behavior of U. S. Army PW's in Korea.* HumRRO Technical Report 33 for the Department of the Army. Prepared by the Human Resources Research Office. Washington: George Washington University, 1956.

Toppe, Alfred. (Major General, German Army). German Methods of Interrogating Prisoners of War in World War II. MS P-018a of Historical Division European Command PW Project No. 14. Koenigstein: June 1949. Translated by Theodore Klein, edited by Dr. Frederiksen. Filed in Army Library, Pentagon.

_____. Soviet Procedure for Interrogating Prisoners of War in World War II. MS P-018b of HDEC PW Project No. 14. Koenigstein: July, 1949. Translated by Theodore Klein, edited by Dr. Frederiksen.

_____. The Russian Program of Propagandizing Prisoners of War. MS P-018c of HDEC PW Project No. 14. Koenigstein: September, 1949. Translated by M. Franke, edited by Dr. Frederiksen.

United Nations. General Assembly. Seventh Session, First Committee. Agenda Item 73. A/C.1/L.28, March 12, 1953.

United Nations. General Assembly. Seventh Session, First Committee. Agenda Item 73. A/C.1/L.37. March 27, 1953.

United Nations. General Assembly. Eighth Session. First Committee. Agenda Item 24. A/C.1/L.66. October 26, 1953.

U. S. Congress, House Committee on Appropriations. The Prisoner of War Situation in Korea. 82d Cong., 2d Sess., 1952.

U. S. Congress. House Committee on Foreign Affairs. Return of American Prisoners of War Who Have Not Been Accounted for by the Communists. 85th Cong., 1st Sess. May 27, 1957.

U. S. Congress. House Committee on Un-American Activities. Investigation of Communist Propaganda Among Prisoners of War in Korea. 84th Cong., 2d Sess., 1956.

U. S. Congress. House Committee on Un-American Activities. Communist Psychological Warfare (Brainwashing). Consultation with Edward Hunter. 85th Cong., 2d Sess., 1958.

U. S. Congress. Senate Committee on Armed Services. Discussion With Gen. Matthew B. Ridgway Re Far Eastern Situation, Koje-Do POW Uprising, and NATO Policies. 82d Cong., 2d Sess., May 21, 1952.

U. S. Congress, Senate, Permanent Subcommittee on Investigations of the Committee on Government Operations. Hearings on Communist Interrogation, Indoctrination and Exploitation of American Military and Civilian Prisoners. Report No. 2832, 84th Cong., 2d Sess., 1957.

U. S. Department of the Army. <u>Communist Interrogation, Indoctrination, and Exploitation of Prisoners of War</u>. Department of the Army Pamphlet 30-101, May, 1956.

U. S. Department of Defense. <u>The U. S. Fighting Man's Code</u>. DOD Pam 1-16. Washington: U. S. Government Printing Office, 1959.

U. S. Department of Defense. <u>Tentative Final Report of U. S. Battle Casualties in the Korean War</u>. Office of the Secretary of Defense Progress Reports and Statistics, P28.1. November 4, 1954.

U. S. Department of Defense. <u>Principal Wars in which the United States Participated, U. S. Military Personnel Serving, and Casualties</u>. Office of the Secretary of Defense Progress Reports and Statistics, P28.2. Revised. November 7, 1957.

U. S. Marine Corps, "Korean Casualties, 25 June 1950 - 27 July 1953", Personnel Accounting Section, Code DGB, September 22, 1956. (typewritten). On file in the Casualty Branch, Division of Personnel, HQMC.

Books

Blair, Clay. <u>Beyond Courage</u>. New York: David McKay Co., Inc., 1955.

Brown, Wallace L. <u>Endless Hours: My Two and One Half Years as a Prisoner of the Chinese Communists</u>. New York: W. W. Norton & Co., 1961.

Crosbie, Philip. <u>Three Winters Cold</u>. Dublin: Browne & Nolan, Ltd., 1955.

_____. <u>March Till They Die</u>. Westminster, Maryland, Ireland: The Newman Press, 1956.

_____. <u>Pencilling Prisoner</u>. Melbourne: The Hawthorne Press, 1954.

Condron, Andrew M., Corden, Richard G., and Sullivan, Larance V. (eds.) <u>Thinking Soldiers</u>. Peking: New World Press, 1955.

Miller John Jr., Carroll, Owen, and Tackley, Margaret E. <u>Korea 1951-53</u>. Washington: Office of the Chief of Military History, Department of the Army, 1958.

Davies, Stanley J. <u>In Spite of Dungeons</u>. London: Hodder and Stoughton, 1954.

Dean, William F. *General Dean's Story*. As told to William L. Worden. New York: The Viking Press, 1954.

Deane, Philip Gigantes, Gerassimos *I Was A Captive in Korea*. New York: W. W. Norton & Co., Inc., 1953.

Dowe, Ray M. Jr. *The Ordeal of Father Kapaun*. Notre Dame, Indiana: The Ave Maria Press, 1954.

Farrar-Hockley, Anthony. *The Edge of the Sword*. London: Frederick Muller Ltd., 1954.

Geer, Andrew. *The New Breed*. New York: Harper & Brothers, 1952.

Hansen, Col. Kenneth K. *Heroes Behind Barbed Wire*. Princeton, N. J., D. Van Nostrand Co., Inc., 1957.

Hunter, Edward. *Brainwashing: The Story of the Men Who Defied It*. New York: Farrar, Straus and Cudahy, 1956.

Jones, Francis S. *No Rice for Rebels*. As told to the author by Lance Corporal Robert F. Mathews, B.E.M. London: Garden City Press, 1956.

Kinkead, Eugene. *In Every War But One*. New York: W. W. Norton & Co., 1959.

Kinne, Derek. *The Wooden Boxes*. London: Frederick Muller Ltd., 1955.

Landford, Dennis. *I Defy*. London: Allan Wingate Publishers Ltd., 1954.

Marshall, S. L. A. *The River and the Gauntlet*. New York: William Morrow & Co., 1953.

McCoy, Melvyn H., Cdr. USN, and others. *Prisoners of Japan*. As told to Lieutenant Welbourn Kelley, USNR, New York: Time, Inc., 1944.

Meray, Tibor. *Korean Testimony*. Budapest: Hungarian Peace Council and the Institute for Cultural Relations, 1952.

Meerloo, A. M. *The Rape of the Mind: the Psychology of Thought Control, Menticide, and Brainwashing*. Cleveland: World Publishing Co., 1956.

Millar, Ward M. *Valley of the Shadow*. New York: David McKay Co., Inc., 1955.

Montross, Lynn. *War Through the Ages*. New York: Harper & Bros., 1946.

Montross, Lynn and Canzona, Capt. Nicholas A. U. S. Marine Operations in Korea. Vol. I: The Pusan Perimeter. Washington: U. S. Government Printing Office, 1957.

_____. Vol. II: The Inchon-Seoul Operation. Washington: U. S. Government Printing Office, 1957.

_____. Vol. III: The Chosin Reservoir Campaign. Washington: U. S. Government Printing Office, 1957.

Pasley, Virginia [Schmitz]. 22 Stayed. London: W. H. Allen & Co., Ltd., 1955.

Pate, Lloyd W. Reactionary! As told to B. J. Cutler. New York: Harper & Brothers, 1955.

Red Cross, China. Out of Their Own Mouths. Peking: Red Cross Society of China, 1952.

Sargent, William Walters. Battle for the Mind. Garden City, New York: Doubleday, 1957.

Simmons, Kenneth W. Kriegie. New York: Thomas Nelson & Sons, 1960.

Thorin, Duane. A Ride to Panmunjom. Chicago; Henry Regnery Co., Inc., 1956.

Tonne, Father Arthur. The Story of Chaplain Kapaun: Patriot Priest of the Korean Conflict. Emporia, Kansas: Didde Publishers, 1954.

Voelkel, Harold, Behind Barbed Wire in Korea. Grand Rapids: Zondervan Publishing House, 1953.

White, William Lindsay. The Captives of Korea: An Unofficial White Paper on the Treatment of War Prisoners. New York: Charles Scribner's Sons, 1957.

Whiting, Alan S. China Crossed the Yalu. New York: The Macmillan Co., 1960.

Winnington, Alan and Burchett, Wilfred. Plain Perfidy. Peking: By the authors, 1954.

Articles

Baldwin, Hanson W. "Our Fighting Men Have Gone Soft," The Saturday Evening Post. August 8, 1959.

Brinkley, William. "Valley Forge G. I.'s Tell of Their Brainwashing Ordeal," Life. May 25, 1953.

Francis, Dale. "March Contest Feature." The Catholic Boy. March, 1956.

Harrison, Lieutenant Colonel Thomas D., USAF. "Why Did Some G. I.'s Turn Communist?" Colliers. November 27, 1953.

Heren, Louis. "The Korean Scene," Brassey's Annual: The Armed Forces Yearbook, New York: The Macmillan Co., 1951.

Johnson, Captain James R. "If You Are Captured," Marine Corps Gazette, November, 1952.

Kinkead, Eugene. "The Study of Something New in History," The New Yorker, October 26, 1957.

Martin, Harold H. "They Tried to Make Our Marines Love Stalin," The Saturday Evening Post, August 25, 1951.

Mayer, William E., Major, USA, MC. "Why Did Many G. I. Captives Cave In?" Interview in U. S. News and World Report, February 24, 1956.

McCarthy, Captain Robert C. "Fox Hill," Marine Corps Gazette, March, 1953.

Montross, Lynn. "Ridgerunners of Toktong Pass," Marine Corps Gazette, May, 1953.

Murray, J. C. "The Prisoner Issue," Marine Corps Gazette, August and September, 1955.

"POW Collaboration Charges Exploded," Army-Navy-Air Force Register and Defense Times, April 16, 1960.

O'Connor, Father Patrick. "Faith Behind Barbed Wire," Hawaii Catholic Herald, October 16, 1953.

Scouller, Captain R. E. "Prisoners of War," The Army Quarterly, London:Vol. LXVI, April and July, 1953.

"Snafu at Valley Forge," Newsweek, May 18, 1953.

Stevenson, Charles. "The Truth About Germ Warfare in Korea," The Reader's Digest, April, 1953.

Thorin, Duane. "Code of Conduct Training," Naval Training Bulletin, Spring, 1958.

_____. "Solitary Comfort," U. S. A., New York: U.S.A. Publishing Co., July 3, 1959.

Wolff, Harold G., M.D. "Every Man Has His Breaking Point - (?)" Military Medicine, February, 1960.

Newspapers

Chicago Daily Tribune. July 30, 1960.

Hawaii Catholic Herald (Honolulu), October 15 and 16, 1953.

Herald Tribune (New York), May 1, 1951.

Keesing's Contemporary Archives: 1950-1952. Vol. VIII. London: Keesing's Publications Ltd., 1950.

New Life (Kanggye POW Camp, North Korea), January, 1951.

New York Times. 1950-1955.

People's China (Peking), May 16, 1952.

The Call Bulletin (San Francisco), December 19, 1951.

The Evening Star (Washington), January 21, 1960.

The Minneapolis Star. May 25 and 26, 1951.

San Diego Union. July 7, 1951.

Washington Post. 1950-1953.

Wichita Eagle. November 27, 1955.

Other Sources

British Army. Training Film, Prisoner. 907 MT4(e). Unclassified, copy held by Central Intelligence Agency, Washington, D. C.

Chief of Chaplains, Department of Defense. Biographical file, case of Captain Emil J. Kapaun, USA.

Fink, Gerald, Major, USMC. Personal notes.

Headquarters, U. S. Marine Corps. Public Information News Release 81, September, 1950.

_____. Division of Information Position Paper, n.d., made public in April, 1954. Copy held by the author.

MacDonald, J. Angus, Major, USMC. "Religion in POW Camps." Unpublished MS. Copy filed in Historical Branch, G-3 Division, HQMC.

Mayer, William E., Major, USA, MC. "Communist Indoctrination-Its Significance to Americans," Speech before the Freedom Forum, Searcy, Arkansas, April 15, 1957.

McCool, Felix J., CWO, USMC. Tape recording. Enclosure 1 to letter to the Commandant of the Marine Corps, September 24, 1954. Filed with G-2 Division, HQMC.

Naval Aviation News, Nav Aer No. OO-75R-3, November, 1953.

U. S. Army Chaplain School, Fort Slocum, New York. Student Handout 2-CD-FD (December, 1957). Copy filed in Chief of Chaplains Office, Department of Defense.

Thornton, John W. "POW Story," Unpublished MS. Copy filed in Historical Branch, G-3 Division, HQMC.

www.ingramcontent.com/pod-product-compliance
Lightning Source LLC
Chambersburg PA
CBHW081831170426
43199CB00017B/2699